TEACHER EDUCATION REFORM

CURRENT RESEARCH

edited by
Ivan Reid,
Hilary Constable and Roy Griffiths

P·C·P
Paul Chapman
Publishing Ltd

185396268 6.

Paul Chapman Publishing Ltd
144 Liverpool Road
London
N1 1LA

British Library Cataloguing in Publication Data

Teacher Education Reform: Current Research
I. Reid, Ivan
370.71

ISBN 1-85396-268-6

Typeset by Dorwyn Ltd, Rowlands Castle, Hants
Printed and bound by Athenaeum Press Ltd, Gateshead, Tyne & Wear.

A B C D E F G H   9 8 7 6 5 4

Contents

PART III   MENTORING AND SUPPORTING STUDENT-TEACHERS

PART IV   STUDENTS LEARNING TO TEACH

PART V HEADTEACHERS' AND OTHERS' VIEWS OF THE CHANGES

PART VI CONCLUSION

PART ONE

Introduction

CHAPTER 1

The Reform
Change or Transformation
of Initial Teacher Training?

IVAN REID
Loughborough University

This book has a straightforward aim. It is to review the current and ongoing changes in the preparation of people for the teaching profession in England and Wales in the light of evidence from empirical research. In one sense it attempts to redress something of the balance in a situation much characterized by rhetoric, dogma and myth. At the same time it provides a view of the way in which those charged with preparing students for the teaching profession are coping with implementing the changes and the challenges, problems and limitations which have arisen and are arising.

There can be no doubt that the series of Conservative governments from 1979 have produced the most radical changes in the UK education system to date. In many ways these have mirrored a range of political changes which have severely affected most aspects of social and economic life in UK society. In general these changes can be seen to be what is termed as 'the reform agenda'. This agenda was not applied immediately to education, but rather gained momentum through the first decade of the Thatcher era, culminating in the Education Reform Act 1988, an Act at least as significant as that of 1944.

While changes, both radical and dramatic, have undoubtedly been achieved and set in place, many, if not most, would question whether they amount to reforms in the literal sense of the word, which is '. . . to improve an existing institution, law, practice, etc. by alteration or correction of abuses; to give up or cause to give up a reprehensible habit or immoral way of life' (Hands, 1986). While the contributors to this book would disassociate themselves from any implication that there was abuse, reprehensible habit or immorality in teacher education, the term reform is used here for two reasons. First, because of its currency. Secondly, and mainly, as is outlined below, it is clear that the government and particularly its advisers were and are inspired by beliefs stemming from its literal meaning.

Although it is clear that the 'reform' of teacher training is contextualized within and is part of the reform of schooling and education in general, this is not the place to describe this setting (see, for example, Coulby and Bash, 1991; Chitty, 1992). Interestingly enough, teacher training was not a first priority in the reform agenda for education – legislation on it being before Parliament at the time of writing (Education Bill 1994). Whether this was because of a supposed failure of the efforts to cause change through the offices of Council for the Accreditation and Funding of Teacher Education CATE and DES/DFE directives, the relatively slow development of policy in the field, or difficulty in finding parliamentary time, is unclear.

In effect, the evolution of the professional preparation of teachers has given way to revolution. The unpredictability of the present situation has destabilized teacher education in the UK and this may well affect teacher supply as well as quality.

A DEBATE FOR ALL SEASONS

The education and training of teachers has a long history of debate. The professionalizing of teaching has always been difficult. There appear to be two fundamental elements underlying this difficulty. First, familiarity based on the protracted experience of all citizens of schools and teachers leads to a situation in which almost everyone believes they are an expert in education, capable not only of questioning the professional but also of having superior ideas. Secondly, the status of teaching is related to the status of children in society and hence, by association, teachers are given lower status than professionals working with adults. Related to these are the proprietary attitudes towards children on the part of parents and towards education on the part of politicians. In sum, teaching and schooling are seen as far too serious matters to be left in the hands of the professionals, as is the case of, for example, medicine, the law, etc.

Allied to this is the ongoing concern of falling standards in the achievement of pupils, typically in reality a changing rather than a lowering of standards. Each and every generation appears convinced that its successors are lacking and thus jeopardizing the future well-being of society – usually both economically and morally. Myths and misunderstandings will abound in such circumstances. One important and current example is the apparently profound belief that the most important element in classrooms is the teacher and the most important factor in achievement is the teaching. While these are not without importance it is vital to appreciate that the central classroom activity happens to be learning, which is done by pupils; hence, neither they nor the quantity and quality of learning resources must be overlooked.

Within this context, the 'logic' of the so-called reform of teacher training, which is flawed at each stage, appears to progress as follows. The falling standards of pupils are the result of the low quality of teachers in schools. The cause of poor teachers and teaching lies with the teacher trainers in the universities. The solution is therefore to move more, or even all, teacher training out of universities and to put it into the hands of teachers in schools who have been identified to be wanting as teachers themselves. While this logic may pass some readers by, it may be that the policy advisers and makers were even further misled. For example, it may have been thought that, given the apparent level of control gained over the schools' curriculum, similar control was in the offing for teacher training. However, the search for logic within what is clearly an ideologically based strategy is probably futile. The costs and logistics involved in the provision of school-based teacher training (noted by HMI; DES, 1991), let alone the maintenance of its quality, are very obviously considerably greater than in a system based on higher education institutions (HEIs).

Given the imposition of the National Curriculum on all schools other than the independent sector, it is most surprising that such a curriculum has not been imposed on teacher training. In many ways such an imposition might be much more beneficial than the present increasingly elaborate system. In much the same way, a national figure for the transfer of funding from university to schools for their part in teacher training would have saved endless problems for both sides of teacher training partnerships. The present situation may well result in the collapse of some teacher training programmes and put most under severe strain. The simple fact is that on whatever basis the costings are done, there is simply not the money in the system to meet the costs of courses or to pay university and school staff appropriately. As Wiliam (Chapter 9) demonstrates, even before Circular 9/92 universities were subsidizing teacher training, as indeed were schools.

The imposition of the market-place on professional training and the transfer of limited funding from HEIs has resulted in fairly widespread economic reconsideration. Many schools and HEIs are questioning whether their involvement in teacher training is a cost they can afford to bear. Some have withdrawn, and more are likely to, and in any case the situation has seriously disturbed the nature and relationships within the enterprise in a manner unlikely to improve the quality of courses.

In the 1950s most teachers were trained in two-year certificate courses in teacher training colleges, the rest by a one-year (30-week) PGCE. The responsibility for these courses and their awards lay with Area Training Organizations (ATOs), based on a number of universities, which exercised independent and rigorous oversight of college courses and made awards to successful students. Since then there has been a number of major changes in the preparation of entrants to the teaching profession. First was the extension to three years of training for non-graduates in 1963 and the introduction of three- and four-year BEd degree courses in the mid to late 1960s, leading in the early 1970s to an all-graduate entry to the profession. The importance of these changes can be summarized by the change in title of the non-university institutions involved from training colleges to colleges of education. This reflected a fairly profound change in the conceptualization of the teacher from classroom craftsperson, who needed to learn a trade, to the teacher as an educated person, equipped with knowledge and ability to apply this and his or her intelligence to the profession of teaching pupils. Hence the associated curriculum changes were of much greater depth in both teaching subject(s) and in those spheres of knowledge of direct application to teaching, the role of the teacher and the functioning of schools. From the mid-1980s the effect of government policy has been to swing back towards and beyond the 1950s' model. The past three-and-a-half decades can then be characterized as a series of hoops, swings and roundabouts in teacher education (Reid, 1986).

There has been, and may always be, a debate over the best way to train and/or educate teachers. Insufficient fundamental research has been done on either what constitutes an effective teacher or on how they might be produced. While this situation characterizes many other professions, teaching stands out as the prime example in which, during the 1980s and 1990s, the government has progressively taken the initiative. The writing has been on the wall. For example, in the mid-1980s Reid (1986) concluded a review of the first CATE criteria with, 'The enterprise [teacher education] needs to stop responding to other people's agendas and knee jerking into the future . . . what the teacher education profession should really be about is drawing up its own agenda and then actively seeking its discussion and implementation'. For a variety of reasons this opportunity has not been seized. Despite the considerable efforts of the Universities Council for the Education of Teachers (UCET) at a variety of levels, the initiative has continued to slip away from the teacher training profession, perhaps aided by contributions from within its ranks (such as Hargreaves, 1990) and the development of school-based schemes, notably those of Oxford and Sussex (Furlong *et al.*, 1988; Benton, 1990; Wilkin, 1992a).

Of course it is possible to argue that school-based teacher training is placing the preparation of teachers into the hands of the teaching profession — providing, that is, one fails to recognize the reality that teacher educators are themselves part of that profession. However, the reception by schools has not been in general terms very enthusiastic. There is a range of factors involved, and many schoolteachers see the prime task of schools and their vocation as teaching pupils. They see their schools as neither equipped nor funded for the purpose of training teachers, nor themselves as qualified or empowered other than to play a significant yet defined role. As Barber (1993) of the NUT remarked, 'Given the direction of government policy, it is not impossible to imagine policy-makers in 2010 looking back and wondering how, at the very moment in history when the professionalising of teaching was most needed, it was deprofessionalised.'

WHAT WAS WRONG WITH TEACHER EDUCATION AND TRAINING?

The short answer to this question, even from official sources, is not much. For example, it is clear that the HMI report, *The New Teacher in School* (DES,

1982), informed both the white paper on teacher quality (1983) and Circular 3/84, which set out the first CATE criteria. Among these were some on subject studies and method. What the HMI reported was that a quarter of primary and one in ten secondary teachers were seen when observed to exhibit some insecurity about the subject they were teaching – though it is not clear whether their insecurity was related to academic knowledge or its classroom delivery. In any case since there is no comparative information – for example, what proportion of newly qualified doctors, engineers or lawyers are similarly placed – it is difficult to judge the findings' importance. In the same document HMI identified personal qualities and factors other than initial qualification and experience as factors in teacher effectiveness.

The considerable reservations of HMI on the induction of newly qualified teachers in schools raises further issues: first, about how well resourced and prepared schools (on their own) can be for professional training; and secondly, the variation of professional training between schools is not only marked but also presents very considerable problems in terms of quality control – much greater than that in respect to HEIs.

In a DES (1988) document it was stated that 95 per cent of new teachers were adequately equipped for the job they are required to do, while 90 per cent of beginning teachers felt they were well, reasonably or moderately satisfied with their courses. HMI (DES, 1991) reported that the '. . . initial training of primary and secondary teachers is satisfactory or better in most institutions' (85 per cent of those inspected). If not cause for congratulation hardly one for serious concern, despite again the lack of comparative data. In the same year in a speech the then Secretary of State for Education, Kenneth Clarke, claimed that the '. . . training of teachers is now more rigorous than ever before' (*Guardian*, 23 October 1991).

It is also necessary to recognize that significant changes had been successfully implemented to meet the perceived short-comings of teacher preparation in the years following the setting up of CATE in 1984. This body was under fairly direct control of the Secretary of State, who chose its members – only a minority of whom were professional educators. Certainly there was a clear break with the autonomy of universities in the enterprise. The tightening of central control was achieved through the process of formal accreditation by CATE (Barton, Pollard and Whitty, 1992).

The period since the issue of Circular 9/92 has produced a large number of new PGCE secondary courses based on developed partnerships between universities and schools. These have been achieved despite the considerable other and additional demands and constraints on both partners and in the face of the competition over resources induced by the need to arrange the transfers locally. While it is perhaps too early to evaluate these properly, there are clear indications that some aspects of these courses are seen by some to be improvements to the preparation of teachers. What is clear is that the continued change and debate is unlikely to enable constructive refinements to be introduced easily. Of similar concern is that no national evaluation is underway in order to assess the success or otherwise of new courses and to address for the future the nature and content of teacher training. In a rational society it would be expected that a change of such significance in the preparation of teachers would be premissed on the best possible evidence and that its progress would be constantly monitored using accepted social scientific methodology. This book bears witness to the fact that the teacher training profession is attempting to maintain that level of rationality in the face of the severe challenges to their enterprise and careers. It is to be hoped that their work, and that not included here, will be recognized for what it is, a sound contribution to good practice and evaluation in the field.

SO WHY THE CONCERN AND ACTION?

It is difficult to escape from seeing the 'reform' other than in terms of part of a Conservative political agenda, inspired and supported, if not led, by a group of non-elected and non-professional educators. Such groups, variously titled Centre for Policy Studies, Hillgate Group and Institute of Economic Affairs, produced a series of what in rational terms can only be viewed as outrageous and completely uninformed statements which received considerable press attention (for details of their activities, see Knight, 1990; Lunt, McKenzie and Powell, 1993; Gilroy, 1992; 1994; Demaine, forthcoming). The published work of these groups is gratuitously dismissive of teacher education and training. Hillgate (1986) identified the PGCE as 'largely worthless' and suggested that schools should be able to employ '. . . teachers without formal teaching qualifications'. Warnock (1987) stated that the PGCE year was 'largely wasted', since the course was 'too academic'. Lawlor (1990) claimed that teacher training in HEIs could be done away with since skills could be picked up from being in a classroom – though her only knowledge of the field was from prospectuses. Similarly, O'Hear (1988), a professor of philosophy in a university without involvement in teacher training, summarily dismissed teacher education and, by implication, ran a 'reds under beds' scare. Subsequently he was appointed a member of CATE. The teacher education profession, not surprisingly given their backgrounds, did not find much voice to counter these attacks. Indeed, they found it almost imossible to believe that such unfounded criticism would be listened to, let alone acted upon, by anyone. Some were encouraged in this belief by DES officials' reactions. Among these was Clive Saville, who attended the 1991 UCET conference and who was removed from his responsibility for teacher training shortly afterwards.

It is not possible to demonstrate directly, but it does appear that it is this ideology and its attendant rhetoric which continues to fire the relentless central direction of teacher training. Despite, or perhaps because of, the changes effected and underway, the Education Bill 1994, unless amended, heralds an era that will see the separation, both in terms of funding, and potentially, in siting, of teacher education from higher education. In effect, the deprofessionalization of teaching and the end of the recently won, all-graduate entry status of teaching. There are several aspects to this. For example, solely school-based initial teacher training, whether for graduates and/or others, may lead to qualified teacher status granted by the DFE, but not to the award of a PGCE as at present. The proposed three-year, six-subject BEd for primary school-teachers looks very much like a return to the three-year certificate course.

In sum,

> What is missing from neo-conservative discourse is the image of the teacher as a transformative intellectual who defines schooling as fundamentally an ethical and empowering enterprise dedicated to the fostering of democracy, to the exercise of a greater social justice and to the building of a more equitable social order.
>
> (GIROUX *and* MCLAREN, *1986*)

THE COMPARATIVE CONTEXT

Apart from the social and historical contexts of the 'reform', there are two more worthy of note: what is happening in other societies and in other, similar, professions. Concern over teacher education and training appears widespread internationally, and it could well be that poor economic performance may be the main political motivation. As has been pointed out, such concerns may be generic to the enterprise. What is unique in England and Wales at present is the direct involvement of the government and its agencies, together with ignoring informed opinion from the teacher education profession. It is also true that UK society is relatively isolated in its move towards increasing school-centred experience at the expense of academic and professional study at university. While this is under consideration in other countries, for example, Australia, their approach is much more cautious and it sustains an agenda that includes social justice issues, which feature in both policy and programmes (Knight, McWilliam and Bartlett, 1995). In many societies the desire to improve the quality and professionalism of teachers is being pursued by upgrading their academic qualifications. For example, Singapore has recently moved to an all-graduate teacher training system and BEd degrees are now available for the first time at the Arab Teacher Training College in Israel.

Within the European Union, Britain stands alone (again) in moves towards more or wholly school-based teacher training. Two examples, of the largest states, must suffice. France is moving back from a largely school-based system of training to one centred on newly created teacher training institutions of university status. All entrants to the two-year training courses will be graduates (Heaford, 1993; Holyoake, 1993). In Germany, four-year teacher training is divided into two equal phases. The first phase, in universities, is heavily academic in the traditional contributory disciplines. Davies (1994) comments that teachers there are encouraged to become sophisticated thinkers, 'educated as professionals not technicians', and goes on to quote a *Seminarleiter* (schoolteacher/mentor): '. . . our traditions come from Hegel and Kant: the Germans are theory friendly.' The unification of Germany has extended this system from what was the West to the East.

It is more than interesting that other person-orientated professions' training in the UK is moving in the opposite direction. For example, in nursing, the changes implemented have led to the separation of academic study from clinical experience, with more time given to such study and many nurse training colleges amalgamating with HEIs. The parallels drawn by some between the training of doctors in teaching hospitals and the 'reform' of teacher training completely overlooks the previous, extensive professional education and training received by student doctors in university. In the legal profession the norm now is a university-based postgraduate, professional course, prior to entering a firm. In both, considerable 'on-the-job' training is preceded by postgraduate professional training in an HEI.

THE INQUIRIES THAT FOLLOW

For teacher educators and trainers the last decade has been one of turmoil and change. A succession of edicts, barely based on consultation let alone professional consideration, have emanated from the government via agencies, which have directly affected their work. Alongside these have been significant changes in higher education with growing demands and constraints, together with the introduction of a rapidly revised National Curriculum and its assessment in schools. The transfer of teacher training funding from universities to schools, together with the cuts to student funding in general and government policy, have already led to some shrinkage of posts and opportunity. Many now view their careers as blighted. It would not be surprising to find morale at a very low ebb.

In such circumstances it might be expected that research and innovation would be among the first casualties. This book is a witness to the fact that the profession of teacher educators is alive, well and researching and monitoring its current situation. The response to invitations to contribute was almost overwhelming – sufficient for about two-and-a-half volumes! The selections included here are those which, in the opinion of the editors, provided a range of empirical investigations and evaluations of current practice, change and implications. Pretty severe editing, much by the contributors themselves, has been undertaken in order to maximize the number of contributions and to achieve an empirically based input, as opposed to an ideological or opinionated one.

In many ways this book contains examples of the type of work which in a rational world would precede the consideration of change in any area of the significance of the preparation of people for the teaching profession. As it is, it is to be expected that the contents will inform both good practice and raise questions and reservations concerning the implementation of the 'reform'. At the same time the book should provide encouragement for those who subscribe to the desirability of informed reflective practice based on evidence. It is hoped that it might help herald an era in which further change in the preparation of teachers is premissed on fact and evaluated practice rather than on unsubstantiated belief.

CHAPTER 2

Issues and Themes Raised by the Evidence

ROY GRIFFITHS
University of Manchester

This book reflects both the impressive amount and wide range of empirical research being undertaken in the context of recent and current changes in initial teacher education (ITE) in England and Wales. Overall, the work seems to be motivated by two aims:

1 To monitor the nature of the changes and to identify the benefits and losses which result.
2 To identify, by empirical means, the most effective means of implementing the changes.

Studies addressing these issues have been organized into parts according to four themes:

1 Towards effective partnership practice (Part II).
2 Monitoring and supporting student-teachers (Part III).
3 Students learning to teach (Part IV).
4 Headteachers' and others' views of the changes (Part V).

TOWARDS EFFECTIVE PARTNERSHIP PRACTICE

As the school-based component of ITE has increased, one key change has been the development of partnership between higher education institutions (HEI) and schools. From the very start, evaluation of the nature and effectiveness of partnership schemes has been carried out. The chapters in Part II provide a sample of this work, most studies being based on individual HEI programmes and reporting users' and other participants' evaluations of these schemes.

The Oxford Internship Scheme represents one of the early moves towards more school-based ITE, planned and operated on a joint basis by an HEI, an LEA and secondary schools. Rothwell, Nardi and McIntyre (Chapter 3) report a review of this scheme after six years' operation. On the basis of questionnaire data, they identify the most and least valuable mentor and tutor role activities as perceived by those involved.

The work reported by Foskett, Ratcliffe and Brunner (Chapter 4) addresses the role of communication processes in the success of partnerships. In their evaluation of the Southampton partnership, they concentrate on three features: administrative communication, interpersonal relationships between tutors and mentors, and shared understanding between the partners.

The chapter by Busher and King (Chapter 5) focuses on the further professional studies element of the Loughborough programme, which is an integrated component delivered both in the university and in placement schools. Student-teacher and school co-ordinator views of the management of this element, collected by open-ended questionnaires, are analysed in terms of institutional collaboration and integration of students' understanding.

Wright and Moore (Chapter 6) describe a largely questionnaire-based evaluation of the Hull PGCE partnership. Here particular attention is paid to data on the consistency in provision across the group of partnership schools and the achievement of coherence and progression between elements within the programme.

Galvin (Chapter 7) reports national research into the licensed teacher scheme and discusses those implications of relevance to partnership-based ITE and wider changes in the preparation of teachers. His specific concerns are with the scale of the impact of the scheme, the costs of provision and the quality of the training provided.

It is possible that the non-monetary benefits to schools of belonging to an ITE partnership scheme are underestimated. Haylock's study (Chapter 8) of the reasons given by primary headteachers and teachers for taking students on teaching practice provides some interview-generated data related to the perceived benefits to children, teachers and schools.

The financial background is addressed by Wiliam (Chapter 9), who summarizes the current funding arrangements for ITE and outlines a financial model which estimates the amount of teaching time made available for ITE tuition. One of the examples of the application of this model provided by Wiliam relates to the impact on PGCE courses and making payments to schools.

MONITORING AND SUPPORTING STUDENT-TEACHERS

In developing the detail of partnership schemes, considerable emphasis has been placed on the nature of support provided for student-teachers in school, and particular attention has been given to the role of the mentor. This theme is reflected in the research included throughout this volume. For example, the study by Rothwell, Nardi and McIntyre (Chapter 3) reports views on the value of 18 mentor activities and compares these with ratings of support provided by tutors. Part III contains a sample of further recent studies in this area. They tutors. Part III contains a sample of further recent studies in this area. They point to the fact that support for students is changing and vary in their tendency to see this either as an opportunity for significant development or as a reason to be concerned about decline in quality.

Campbell and Horbury (Chapter 10) report a small-scale study based on interviews with science mentors in the context of the Articled Teacher Scheme. Their views on the role of the mentor, their judgement of their own effectiveness as mentors, and their perceptions of the factors which influence this effectiveness are described.

Aspinwall, Garrett and Owen-Jackson's chapter (Chapter 11) identifies the key elements of the monitoring process which emerged from their evaluation of the introduction of mentoring into the Sheffield Hallam PGCE programme.

Subject specific aspects of mentoring have received little attention to date, so Drake and Dart's interim report (Chapter 12) of their work is welcome. They describe the outcomes of a preliminary analysis of the differences between mathematics mentors and English mentors in their identification of the qualities of a good teacher.

The develoment of the concept of positive mentoring is reported by Brooks, Fitch and Robinson (Chapter 13). Here student-teachers are seen as novice-experts able to diversify their existing skills. They describe the use of problem-solving methods in the facilitation of this process.

According to Constable and Norton (Chapter 14), little is known about the conversations student-teachers have in school about their work. Their study examines the frequency of such encounters, their content and those with whom the interactions take place. An interesting subtheme relates to a comparison of experience reported by those on a partnership course with those on a previous programme.

Collison and Edwards (Chapter 15) examine infant schoolteachers' and student-teachers' perceptions of teachers' contribution to the students' professional learning. The data are obtained through questionnaires, interviews, observation and analysis of conversations. In the interpretation of their results they use a conceptual model of teacher support which involves the role activities of carer, guide, challenger and co-enquirer.

Hawkey (Chapter 16) reports a small-scale study of the nature of peer support, in which one peer observes a second teaching, then the two discuss the lesson. Her focus is on analysis of the communication styles used by the observers and of the criteria used for lesson evaluation.

STUDENTS LEARNING TO TEACH

The nature of support likely to be most effective in helping student-teachers during their early professional development will be partly determined by how student-teachers think and the processes involved in learning how to teach. Prior to the changes resulting from Circular 9/92 (DFE, 1992d), the design of many ITE courses had been influenced by research in these areas. Several of the studies included in Part IV illustrate these efforts and some express concern as to whether competency-based programmes can be as successful in this domain.

The thesis put forward by Bramald, Hardman, Leat and McManus (Chapter 17) is that 'bad' lessons can play an important part in stimulating reflective thinking. Dissonant and perhaps threatening experiences have the potential to create significant changes. They report a study of secondary PGCE students, using a questionnaire, interviews and ecological analysis, which explores these ideas.

Harris's study (Chapter 18) is one of the few providing comparative data from PGCE courses before and after the Circular 9/92 changes. Based on interviews with student-teachers, evidence is reported relating to the quality and range of school-based experience under the different programmes.

Further evidence of the impact of a university-based PGCE on student-teachers' thinking about effective learning activities is provided in the investigation by Kyriacou and Lin (Chapter 19). They report a study using interviews and observation of foreign language student-teachers.

Sands and Bishop (Chapter 20) provide an analysis of the student withdrawals from the Nottingham secondary PGCE course over the period 1988–94. This analysis covers the subject specialisms and previous qualifications of the students, together with the time of year at which withdrawals took place and the reasons given for discontinuing the course.

Fursland's contribution (Chapter 21) identifies some of the costs and benefits of a school-based programme. Of particular interest is the evaluation of the professional perspectives component, in which students explore educational issues by means of action research in the schools. Data were collected largely through interviews with school staff and student-teachers.

Newly qualified teachers are an important source of information about the strengths and weaknesses of the preparation they received during their ITE programme. Newton (Chapter 22) reports on a long-term investigation of Newcastle primary PGCE-trained teachers at the end of their first year of teaching.

HEADTEACHERS' AND OTHERS' VIEWS OF THE CHANGES

The common theme in the chapters contained in Part V is that of the views of interested parties on the changes in ITE. The focus is on the changes to primary ITE, especially valuable given that these are occurring after those in the secondary programmes. The emphasis is also on the views of headteachers, which is appropriate given that they are the major decision-makers regarding entry into partnership.

Hannan (Chapter 23) reports the reactions of Devon headteachers, parents, students and tutors to items taken from the document, *The Initial Training of Primary School Teachers: New Criteria for Course Approval* (DFE, 1993a).

The national survey reported by Carrington and Tymms (Chapter 24) is of special interest, as it reports the views of headteachers on the teacher education changes within the context of their views on changes in primary education generally.

Alfrey and Parsons' chapter (Chapter 25) presents the results of three surveys, one of which focuses on headteachers' views on the government's proposals for the reform of primary teacher preparation. Also included is evidence from headteachers and newly qualified teachers on their level of satisfaction with the HEI-based ITE courses.

CONCLUSION

The research reported in this volume adds to our knowledge base of empirical evidence regarding the processes and effectiveness of ITE. As such, it will inform the development of practice in areas such as partnership management and mentoring. It will also, it is hoped, be taken into account when the future develoment of ITE is being considered.

PART TWO

Towards Effective Partnership Practice

CHAPTER 3

The Perceived Values of the Role Activities of Mentors and Curricular, Professional and General Tutors

S. ROTHWELL, E. NARDI and D. MCINTYRE

University of Oxford

INTRODUCTION

The Oxford Internship Scheme was planned during 1985 to 1987 as a response to endemic problems in initial teacher education (ITE). In particular, it sought to give a much more significant place to the distinctive expertise of experienced practising teachers, and also to operationalize a new conception of the relation between theory and practice in the education of beginning teachers. It was uninfluenced by more recently fashionable concerns with 'reflective practice' in professional education (Schon, 1983; 1987; Zeichner and Liston, 1987); and, being motivated entirely by professional concerns and arguments, it predated government pressures for more school-based patterns of teacher education.

The scheme was initiated, and has since been operated, jointly by Oxford University Department of Educational Studies (OUDES), Oxfordshire Local Education Authority and Oxfordshire secondary schools. The detailed plans were worked out in 1986–7 jointly by 12 senior Oxfordshire teachers seconded for a year to the university department and by the staff of the department. Accounts of the scheme's rationale, its development and its early operation are given in Benton (1990a). The theoretical and research-based thinking behind the scheme is outlined in McIntyre (1988), and its earlier roots can be seen in Judge (1980) and McIntyre (1980).

It is not possible here to describe the internship scheme in any detail. Very briefly, however, in order to make sense of what follows, the scheme involves student-teachers – called interns – each being attached for most of their one-year PGCE course to one school. From October until January they spend two days per week in the school and the rest of their time in the university, and from late January until May they spend virtually all their time in the school. There are typically eight to ten interns in each school, normally in subject pairs. The four key staff roles in the scheme are as follows:

MENTORS   Subject teachers who each guide and co-ordinate two interns' school-based learning in relation to classroom teaching.

CURRICULUM TUTORS   University tutors who are responsible for interns' university-based learning in subject groups in relation to classroom teaching, and who co-ordinate their own and mentors' work in integrated curriculum programmes.

PROFESSIONAL TUTORS   Usually senior teachers in schools who each co-ordinate their own school's ITE work and take direct responsibility for interns' school-based learning in relation to whole-school matters.

GENERAL TUTORS   University tutors (who are in most cases also curriculum tutors) each attached to one school where they work with the professional tutor in taking overall responsibility for the intern group attached to that school and for that group's learning, both in the university and in the school, in relation to whole-school matters.

Until 1992, and to a limited extent during the 1992–3 year, the internship scheme was financially supported by Oxfordshire LEA from its INSET budget. Each school was allocated 0.1 of a teacher's salary for each pair of interns attached to the school. Even as pressures increased on its INSET budget, the LEA maintained that the professional development advantages provided for school staff by the scheme made this expenditure well worth while (cf. McIntyre and Hagger, 1992). Eventually, however, the LEA delegated its full INSET budget to schools on a formula basis, and so was unable to continue its financial support for the scheme. Since this coincided with the introduction of the Government's 9/92 regulations, Oxford University found itself in the same situation as others in having to find from its own resources the funds necessary to support school-based ITE. And since this inevitably had repercussions for the staffing of the Educational Studies Department, it became necessary to review the working of the internship scheme.

By 1993 the internship scheme had already run with very little structural change for six years, and so there was in any case good reason to review in a fairly fundamental way the operation of the scheme. For the same reason, the university department, with the support of the joint Internship Partnership Committee, decided that this review should be based partly on an empirical investigation of the views of the various groups of participants in the scheme. Such an investigation had to be conducted quickly, however, and with limited resources. The two senior authors of this chapter, who as DPhil. students in the department knew the internship scheme quite well but had no vested interests in it, were invited to conduct a questionnaire survey of participant views of the activities undertaken by internship staff. They accepted this task, and in their conduct of it they liaised with a staff group led by the third author.

CONDUCT OF THE INVESTIGATION

The question to be investigated was: What do people involved in the internship scheme consider to be its most and its least valuable aspects, with regard to effective ITE? More specifically, what value do those involved in the scheme attach to the various activities of mentors, curriculum tutors, professional tutors and general tutors?

The questionnaire needed to be quick to complete, to encourage a high response rate and to derive maximum information with minimum demand on everyone's time. Furthermore, it was assumed that the common and expected activities of people in the four roles could be identified in advance with some confidence. The questionnaire format therefore comprised lists of activities for mentors, curriculum tutors, professional tutors and general tutors which were potential components of their work in the internship scheme. Respondents were requested to rate on a five-point scale the value of each activity as part of the role in question, 18 activities being finally listed for each role. In addition, respondents were asked to indicate which five of the 18 activities could be omitted from the role with least damaging consequences to effective ITE. Respondents were also invited to suggest any additional activities which should be included in the roles.

The list of activities was generated through discussion between the researchers (one of whom is an ex-intern) and the liaison group, and was then referred to a number of mentors, professional tutors and departmental tutors, whose comments and suggestions were used to generate the final version of the questionnaire. Respondents were encouraged to use the blank back page of the questionnaire to add their own comments on internship and on its revision.

Questionnaires were distributed early in December 1993, for return by the first week in January. They were sent to the 181 ex-interns who had completed the course in July 1993; they were asked to complete the tasks in relation to all four staff roles. The questionnaires were also sent to all the 108 mentors and 21 professional tutors in schools currently involved in the scheme and which had also been involved in the 1992–3 year, and to the 39 higher education (HE) staff currently acting as curriculum and/or general tutors. Mentors and curriculum tutors were asked to complete the set tasks in relation to their own and each other's roles, and so were professional and general tutors. A 60-percent response rate was obtained by the given deadline, with very little variation across the different categories of respondents.

A simple check on the reliability of the data collected is in the relationship between responses to the two tasks. The activities rated as of highest value within a given role should generally be those least likely to be nominated by the same set of respondents for omission, and vice versa. The extent to which that was so was checked using the Spearman rank-order correlation coefficient, and this revealed very high levels of consistency, with correlations around 0.9 for all four roles and all five sets of respondents. Because the two tasks therefore generated very similar information, only the results for the rating exercise will be reported here.

In order to distil the rating information into a manageable form and a relatively small space, only one set of figures will be presented for the ratings of the 18 role activities of each role by each set of respondents. These figures will be the percentage of each group giving ratings of four or five on the five-point scale, i.e. the percentage of the group who judged the activity to be of high value.

RESULTS

Overall evaluation of roles

A simple indication of how highly a role is valued by a particular group – taking all activities and all respondents from the group into account – is given by the median of the high-value percentage ratings by that group of the 18 listed activities for that role. These medians are given in Tables 3.1 and 3.2. From these tables it may be seen that:

- for all four roles, according to the majority opinion of each of the groups rating them, the majority of activities listed are of high value;
- although generally positive about the four roles, ex-interns are less positive than are the four staff groups;
- ex-interns are most positive about the mentor role, and there appears to be most consensus in the overall evaluation of this role; and
- the greatest divergence of opinion appears to be in relation to the curriculum tutor role.

Further light will be thrown on these summary figures by the more detailed examination of the several roles which follows. At this point, however, it is appropriate to emphasize the first of the above conclusions, and to elaborate upon it in the light of respondents' back-page comments.

These comments – made by over half the respondents – inevitably ranged

TABLE 3.1
Medians of 'high-value percentage ratings' for the mentor
and curriculum tutor roles

	EX-INTERNS	MENTORS	CURRICULUM TUTORS
Mentor role	67	72	76
Curriculum tutor role	58	62	88

TABLE 3.2

Medians of 'high-value percentage ratings' for the professional tutor and general tutor roles

	EX-INTERNS	PROFESSIONAL TUTORS	GENERAL TUTORS
Professional tutor role	59	76	78
General tutor role	52	75	71

from the highly critical to the highly enthusiastic. The two poles were distinguished, however, by the specificity of most criticisms and the overall nature of most praise and support. Generalized support for internship was expressed by respondents from all five groups. Many ex-interns stressed their belief that their training had prepared them far better for teaching than had that of other newly qualified teachers whom they had recently met. The views of the ex-intern who wanted to take the opportunity '. . . to thank OUDES for starting my career in such a positive way by making me a thinking, critical professional' were typical of such responses.

Mentors were equally inclined to express generalized support, with comments such as 'The whole thing feels like a proper professional training scheme'. This widespread (though far from universal) sense of general approval is reflected in the responses to the task of identifying five activities for each role which could be abandoned with relatively little loss. Large proportions of respondents failed to identify as many as five activities; and this was true of responses to all roles by all groups. The difficulty of identifying five such activities was frequently commented on and was much the most frequent criticism of the questionnaire made by respondents.

The mentor role

Table 3.3 shows the percentage of ex-interns, of mentors and of curriculum tutors rating each of the listed mentor activities as of high value (4 or 5). Five mentor activities are rated as of high value by 80 per cent or more of the exinterns. These are as follows:

7 Observing interns teaching and providing feedback (95 per cent).
5 Discussing with interns teaching methods for their subject (89 per cent).
15 Planning individual interns' programmes for teaching and learning, and discussing their progress (82 per cent).
8 Discussing with interns lessons they have observed in school (80 per cent).
11 Organizing interns' timetables for J-weeks and S-weeks (80 per cent).

TABLE 3.3
Proportion of responses 4 or 5 on mentors (%)

ACTIVITIES	INTERNS	MENTORS	CURRICULUM TUTORS
1. Attending meetings at OUDES for the planning, monitoring and evaluation of the curriculum programme	41	57	76
2. Involvement in selection procedures for prospective interns	44	36	38
3. Co-ordinating interns' tasks in school with their OUDES-based activities	57	65	86
4. Discussing with interns the philosophy of the teaching of their subject	46	59	43
5. Discussing with interns teaching methods for their subject	89	84	86
6. Discussing with interns contrasting perspectives on the teaching of their subject	63	81	57
7. Observing interns' teaching and providing feedback	95	96	100
8. Discussing with interns lessons they have observed in school	80	91	95
9. Collaboratively planning and teaching particular lessons with interns	71	91	76
10. Guiding interns' planning of their lessons	72	90	95
11. Organizing interns' timetables for J-weeks and S-weeks	80	87	90
12. Providing interns with guidance concerning practical arrangements in school	60	42	48
13. Explaining the internship scheme to colleagues	41	46	67

(*continued over*)

ACTIVITIES	INTERNS	MENTORS	CURRICULUM TUTORS
14. Negotiating with colleagues about interns' involvement with their classes	73	74	76
15. Planning individual interns' programmes for teaching and learning, and discussing their progress	82	88	100
16. Helping interns to develop the criteria through which they will be able to learn from the critical self-evaluation of their own teaching	61	68	62
17. Holding profiling meetings with interns and curriculum tutors	53	57	76
18. Responding to problem situations	73	70	76

All of these activities were also rated as of high value by more than 80 per cent of mentors and more than 80 per cent of curriculum tutors. In addition, more than 70 per cent of each group rated the following activities as of high value:

9 Collaboratively planning and teaching particular lessons with interns.
10 Guiding interns' planning of their lessons.
14 Negotiating with colleagues about interns' involvement with their classes.
18 Responding to problem situations.

There is, then, a high degree of consensus not only on the value of mentors' work in general but also on the value of a broad set of specific mentor activities concerned with organizing and guiding interns' learning, teaching and existence in schools. There is also a rather more modest consensual enthusiasm across the groups for mentors helping interns to develop the thinking they need to be self-evaluating teachers (item 16).

There is, moreover, a high degree of consensus across the three main groups in giving relatively low value ratings to three mentor activities:

2 Involvement in selection procedures for prospective interns.

4 Discussing with interns the philosophy of the teaching of their subjects.
13 Explaining the internship scheme to colleagues.

Some divergence is apparent in curriculum tutors' greater enthusiasm for mentors' joint activities with the university department (items 1, 3 and 17), in ex-interns' greater concern with school practicalities (item 12) and in the distinctive importance which mentors attach to 'Discussing with interns contrasting perspectives on the teaching of their subject' (item 6).

The substantial consensus about the relative value of different mentor role activities is reflected in the Spearman rank-order correlation coefficients for the percentage of high value ratings given to mentor activities by different groups:

- Correlation between ex-interns and mentors: .84.
- Correlation between mentors and curriculum tutors: .76.
- Correlation between ex-interns and curriculum tutors: .74.

The mentor role was the one which elicited significantly more comment than any other, and this reflected its perceived importance in the scheme: 'the key figure' and 'the most important relationship' were common expressions from ex-interns, while 'at the sharp end of internship' (professional tutor) typified many other comments. Mentors and ex-interns in particular emphasized the importance of the mentor role in giving practical guidance, and the centrality of this to the concerns of beginning teachers.

A major complementary theme that emerged from interns' comments on the mentor role was that of the variability of their experiences of their mentors. This concern was also evident in the comments of curriculum and general tutors, and those of mentors themselves, who advocated more training as a way to ensure more 'parity and quality of experience'. Commitment was also suggested by both ex-interns and tutors as a crucial factor in effective mentoring. Some ex-interns pointed out that while the mentor–intern relationship was intrinsically the most important, it was when the mentor was not 'up to standard' that relationships with others, especially the curriculum tutor, became especially important.

Among mentors themselves the aspects of their role most commonly commented on was that of curriculum-area mentor meetings at OUDES. The 'questionable value' of these meetings 'in their current format' was raised as an issue, both by experienced mentors and by some new to the scheme who felt that their concerns about starting out as a mentor had not been addressed. Detailed analysis of mentors' ratings of attendance at such meetings revealed substantial differences according to subject areas.

The curriculum tutor role

Table 3.4 shows the percentage of ex-interns, of mentors and of curriculum tutors who rate each of the listed curriculum tutor activities as of high value

TABLE 3.4
Proportion of responses 4 or 5 on curriculum tutors (%)

ACTIVITIES	INTERNS	MENTORS	CURRICULUM TUTORS
1. Preparing the draft curriculum programme for consideration at meetings with mentors	50	54	87
2. Preparing for and attending meetings with mentors for the planning, monitoring and evaluation of the programme	56	52	83
3. Planning and implementing selection procedures for prospective interns	74	58	87
4. Co-ordinating interns' tasks in school with their OUDES-based activities	58	59	65
5. Discussing with interns the philosophy of the teaching of their subject	65	62	87
6. Discussing with interns research on the teaching of their subject and guiding their reading	57	59	91
7. Discussing with interns teaching methods for their subject	75	71	91
8. Discussing with interns contrasting perspectives on the teaching of their subject	69	70	96
9. Observing interns' teaching and providing feedback	81	70	71
10. Collaboratively planning and teaching particular lessons with interns	30	41	30

(continued over)

ACTIVITIES	INTERNS	MENTORS	CURRICULUM TUTORS
11. Discussing with the curriculum group the implications of their experience in schools	54	62	87
12. Supporting mentors in their work in schools	55	70	83
13. Giving particular support to new mentors in school	65	68	96
14. Explaining the internship scheme to mentors' colleagues	20	35	48
15. Setting, and providing feedback on, curriculum and self-evaluation assignments	58	65	78
16. Helping interns to develop the criteria through which they will be able to learn from the critical self-evaluation of their own teaching	73	70	87
17. Holding profiling meetings with interns and mentors	56	59	74
18. Responding to problem situations	67	61	74

(4 or 5). Curriculum tutors themselves rate the value of their own activities very highly: 11 of the 18 listed activities are rated by over 80 per cent of them as of high value, and as many as 16 of the 18 activities are rated as of high value by over 60 per cent of them. Also, although there are minorities both of ex-interns and of mentors who are less enthusiastic, almost all the curriculum tutor activities are highly valued by between 50 and 75 per cent of ex-interns and of mentors. Thus the wide divergence of opinion between groups that was noted earlier does not arise from a rejection of some curriculum tutor activities by a majority of any group. It arises instead from the near unanimity among curriculum tutors about the value of the listed activities in contrast to the lack of enthusiasm for many of these activities on the part of minorities of the other groups. There is in fact approval by the majority of all groups for nearly all curriculum tutor activities.

The dissent of minorities is, however, considerable. Seven of the listed activities stand out as being highly valued by virtually all curriculum tutors (average, 90 per cent) but by many fewer ex-interns (average, 60 per cent) and mentors (average, 61 per cent). These activities are as follows:

1 Preparing the draft curriculum programme for consideration at meetings of mentors.
2 Preparing for and attending meetings with mentors for the planning, monitoring and evaluation of the programme.
5 Discussing with interns the philosophy of the teaching of their subject.
6 Discussing with interns research on the teaching of their subject and guiding their reading.
8 Discussing with interns contrasting perspectives on the teaching of their subject.
11 Discussing with the curriculum group the implications of their experience in schools.
13 Giving particular support to new mentors in schools.

Thus substantial minorities of ex-interns and of mentors seem to put less value on curriculum tutors' planning in advance of mentor meetings, on their discussion activities with interns at the university, and on their support for new mentors. In contrast, there is one of the listed activities which ex-interns and mentors both value highly more frequently than do curriculum tutors:

9 Observing interns teaching and providing feedback.

There is then little relationship between the relative frequency with which different activities are valued by curriculum tutors on one hand and by ex-interns and mentors on the other. This is reflected in the Spearman rank-order correlation coefficients between different groups' high value ratings for curiculum tutor activities:

- Correlation between ex-interns and mentors: .66.
- Correlation between mentors and curriculum tutors: .43.
- Correlation between ex-interns and curriculum tutors: .36.

On the other hand, there is a very strong consensus across the three groups as to which activities are of little value. There are only two activities which less than 50 per cent of any group rates highly and both of these receive similarly low ratings from all three groups:

10 Collaboratively planning and teaching particular lessons with interns.
14 Explaining the internship scheme to mentors' colleagues.

The general lack of consensus about the relative value of different curriculum tutor activities is reflected in the comments made on the role. The lack of any clear consensus emerged most strongly in concerns expressed about the nature and purpose of school visits made by curriculum tutors, especially when interns are working full time in schools. Some saw these visits as a prime target for reductions in order to save money, while other ex-interns and mentors wanted more structured programmes and more frequent visits. The common concern was that these visits should be a useful deployment of time and resources, with the usually implicit suggestion that that is not always seen to be the case.

The work of the curriculum tutor, and their own relationship with the curriculum tutor, was clearly for many of the ex-interns a valuable aspect of their training, with the organization into curriculum groups commented on as allowing constructive feedback and useful sharing of experiences. As was the case for mentors, divergence of experience among the interns in their contact and work with their curriculum tutors was a significant factor in their evaluative comments.

The professional tutor role

Table 3.5 shows the percentage of ex-interns, of professional tutors and of general tutors rating each of the listed professional tutor activities as of high value (4 or 5). Most professional tutor activities, like those of curriculum tutors, are valued highly by the majority of ex-interns but are rated as of relatively little value by a substantial minority. Thus 12 of the 18 activities are valued highly by between 50 and 75 per cent of ex-interns, and only one activity by a larger proportion. There is much more of a consensus among both professional tutors and general tutors: 13 activities are highly valued by over 70 per cent of professional tutors, and as many as 16 by over 70 per cent of general tutors. Thirteen of the professional tutors' activities are highly valued by the majority of each of the three groups.

The two activities most frequently rated highly by ex-interns, and also by almost all professional tutors and general tutors, are as follows:

3 Organizing the school-based programme.
7 Discussing with interns the particular school's approach to a range of educational issues.

In contrast, the two activities for which the tendency is greatest for a smaller proportion of ex-interns than of either of the other two groups to give high ratings are as follows:

12 Holding meetings for mentors in the school.
14 Involving and briefing other members of staff regarding their contribution to the whole-school programme.

TABLE 3.5
Proportion of responses 4 or 5 on professional tutors (%)

ACTIVITIES	INTERNS	PROFESSIONAL TUTORS	GENERAL TUTORS
1. Participating in meetings with professional tutors at OUDES	34	47	78
2. Liaising with the general tutor to prepare the school-based programme	61	76	96
3. Organizing the school-based programme	74	88	91
4. Regularly participating in school-based seminars for interns	62	94	78
5. Encouraging interns to participate in critical discussion about a range of educational issues	59	94	74
6. Discussing with interns research on educational issues and guiding their reading	29	12	17
7. Discussing with interns the particular school's approach to a range of educational issues	78	94	96
8. Organizing and monitoring interns' experience of school-based pastoral activities	67	88	87
9. Providing guidance and making practical arrangements for interns' research for their assignments and their dissertation	48	35	48

(*continued over*)

ACTIVITIES	INTERNS	PROFESSIONAL TUTORS	GENERAL TUTORS
10. Providing interns with feedback on their general professional progress including their work as form tutors	58	76	70
11. Taking care of the general well-being of the interns in the school group	64	100	74
12. Holding meetings for mentors in the school	37	71	78
13. Keeping other members of staff informed about the school's involvement in the internship scheme	59	65	70
14. Involving and briefing other members of staff regarding their contribution to the school-based programme	50	82	78
15. Co-ordinating the school's relationship with OUDES	62	88	74
16. Helping the school to develop as a context for ITE	59	71	78
17. Holding profiling meetings with interns and general tutors	32	59	74
18. Responding to problem situations	68	76	78

The following are activities about which general tutors are much more enthusiastic than professional tutors and ex-interns:

1 Participating in meetings with professional tutors at OUDES.
2 Liaising with the general tutor to prepare the school-based programme.
17 Holding profiling meetings with interns and general tutors.

The two activities which fewer than half of each of the three groups rated highly were as follows:

6 Discussing with interns research on educational issues and guiding their reading.
9 Providing guidance and making practical arrangements for interns' research for their assignments and their dissertation.

The correlations between the rankings of the three groups reveal that, although professional tutors and general tutors tend to agree in giving much higher ratings to professional tutor activities than do ex-interns, it is the ex-interns and the professional tutors who are in greatest agreement in their relative ratings of the different activities:

- Correlation between ex-interns and professional tutors: .77.
- Correlation between professional tutors and general tutors: .44.
- Correlation between ex-interns and general tutors: .59.

There were fewer comments about the professional tutor role than about other roles. Ex-interns seemed to have only shadowy ideas about the professional tutor's contribution except in relation to seminar programmes on whole-school issues, which will be discussed below.

The general tutor role

Table 3.6 shows the percentage of ex-interns, of professional tutors and of general tutors rating each of the listed general tutor activities as of high value (4 or 5). The pattern of responses to the general tutor role is very similar to that for the professional tutor, but slightly less positive. Thus 13 of the 18 activities are highly valued by over 60 per cent of both professional tutors and general tutors, and some by much larger proportions. Also the majority of ex-interns give high ratings to 11 activities, all of which are also highly rated by most general and professional tutors; but again there is a substantial minority of ex-interns who do not rate these activities highly and indeed no activity is highly rated by as many as 70 per cent of ex-interns.

The following are the four activities most frequently rated highly by all three groups:

5 Encouraging interns at OUDES to participate in critical discussion about a range of educational issues.
6 Discussing with interns at OUDES research into educational issues and providing guidance for their reading.
14 Setting and providing guidance and feedback on assignments.
15 Providing feedback and guidance on the dissertation.

TABLE 3.6
Proportion of responses 4 or 5 on general tutors (%)

ACTIVITIES	INTERNS	PROFESSIONAL TUTORS	GENERAL TUTORS
1. Overseeing travel and other practical arrangements	39	17	4
2. Liaising with the professional tutor to prepare the school-based programme	52	67	92
3. Planning and preparing materials for seminars and workshop activities at OUDES	55	83	77
4. Regularly participating in school-based seminars for interns	45	67	62
5. Encouraging interns at OUDES to participate in critical discussion about a range of educational issues	69	100	96
6. Discussing with interns at OUDES research into educational issues and providing guidance for their reading	61	100	92
7. Discussing with interns their particular school's approach to a range of educational issues	44	25	69
8. Monitoring interns' experience of school-based pastoral activities	34	25	23
9. Taking care of the general well-being of interns in the school group	52	67	54

(continued over)

ACTIVITIES	INTERNS	PROFESSIONAL TUTORS	GENERAL TUTORS
10. Setting and helping to negotiate topics with the school for the dissertation	50	75	73
11. Attending school mentor meetings	25	33	46
12. Attending other school staff meetings	13	0	12
13. Holding profiling meetings with interns and professional tutors	36	75	77
14. Setting, and providing guidance and feedback on, assignments	66	83	88
15. Providing guidance and feedback on the dissertation	69	83	88
16. Supporting the professional tutor in the development of the school as a context for ITE	55	75	69
17. Co-ordinating OUDES' relationship with the school	62	75	77
18. Responding to problem situations	57	100	69

There is also a consensus across the groups on those activities that are not of high value. Four activities are not rated highly by the majority of any of the three groups:

1 Overseeing travel and other practical arrangements (although this is more frequently valued by ex-interns than by others).
8 Monitoring interns' experience of school-based pastoral activities.
11 Attending school mentor meetings.
12 Attending other school staff meetings.

There is less consensus on a small number of activities. Thus almost all general tutors, but smaller numbers of the other groups, place high value on the following:

2 Liaising with the professional tutor to prepare the school-based programme.

Professional tutors are unanimous, but general tutors and ex-interns far from so, about the value of the general tutor activity 18:

18 Responding to problem situations.

Finally, interns are much less enthusiastic than the other two groups about activity 13:

13 Holding profiling meetings with interns and professional tutors.

The overarching pattern, however, is one of substantial consensus on what is more or less valuable in the general tutor role, as is reflected in the correlations between the rankings of the three groups:

- Correlation between ex-interns and professional tutors: .84.
- Correlation between professional tutors and general tutors: .78.
- Correlation between ex-interns and general tutors: .76.

Many ex-interns made comments questioning the value of the general tutor's role and of the programme concerned with whole-school issues for which they were jointly responsible with professional tutors. The lack of perceived 'practicality' of this programme (i.e. its lack of direct relevance to classroom teaching) appeared to be the major factor underlying such comments.

This view of what was 'practical' was far from being shared by everyone. Nor were conceptions of what was 'useful' closely related to school–university differences: school and OUDES-based seminars were variously described as 'useless', the main complaint being of the 'woolliness' of the input of professional tutors or general tutors or both. Differences in intern perspective also seemed to interact with the quality of general tutors' contributions, with some being described as 'inspiring'; and some interns and school-based staff were in agreement about the crucial dependence of the programme on university perspectives in order to foster theorizing and critical reflection.

None the less, despite the diversity of experiences and perspectives, there were a good many comments from all groups questioning the need for both professional tutor and general tutor to be in regular attendance at school-based seminars; and this was a view expressed even by those who emphasized the importance of the contribution which each of them had to make.

CONCLUSIONS

Among the clearest conclusions which can be drawn from the evidence presented are the following:

- Most of the suggested activities of the four key internship roles are highly valued by the majority of all groups of respondents.
- For each of the four key roles, there is consensus on a small set of activities which is not valued by the majority of any group.
- Systematic differences in perspective between the groups of respondents are apparent in relation to all four roles, but these systematic differences relate to quite a small number of activities.
- Consensus is most complete in relation to the value of the mentor role and a broad set of activities associated with it.
- While almost all curriculum tutor activities are valued by the majority of all groups, there are substantial minorities both of ex-interns and of mentors who do not place much value on curriculum tutor activities.
- While there is a considerable consensus among professional tutors and general tutors in valuing most of their own and each others' activities, there are substantial minorities of ex-interns who do not place much value on professional tutors' or general tutors' activities.
- There appear to be large variations in the quality of interns' experiences, both in the schools and in the university, and in relation to all four roles.
- There is considerable scepticism, especially among ex-interns, about the value of general tutors' participation in school-based seminars and more generally about their role in the school context.
- There is a good deal of questioning about the precise nature of the role which curriculum tutors should be playing in the school context.
- Among the activities least valued by ex-interns and by school staff are those involving mentors' and professional tutors' visits to OUDES, either for regular meetings or for intern selection interviews.
- School-based communication activities such as mentors' or curriculum tutors' explaining of internship to other teachers, and general tutors' attendance at mentor or other meetings, are not generally highly valued.
- Profiling meetings are not generally highly valued except by OUDES staff.
- Members of all groups found it difficult to identify as many as five activities which could be omitted without much loss from any of the key roles.

Four themes seem to be especially important. First, as could be expected with so many staff involved, there is evidence of considerable variation in their interpretation of their roles, their standards and their commitment; and there is a consequent unacceptable variation in the quality of interns' experience. Some of this variation in practice clearly stems from a lack of clarity in the overall conceptualization of the scheme. The purposes of curriculum tutors' visits to schools is the most striking example of this. From the beginning, the frequency of these visits has been more a result of pragmatic readiness to respond to the considerable demand from schools, together with many tutors' enthusiasm for spending time in schools, than it has been a coherently theorized part of the scheme. The evidence of this study shows that clear guidance is needed about the range of functions that such visits should serve, and about the implications of that for practice.

Other variations in practice, however, have occurred despite a very clear conceptualization of role responsibilities, and detailed guidance about how these responsibilities can be met. Such detailed guidance is clearly, therefore, not enough. Probably fuller, or different kinds of, induction and support for those in all the key roles is necessary; and certainly, better monitoring mechanisms are necessary for ensuring that all interns' experiences, in working with staff in all four roles, meet basic standards of adequacy.

A second major theme is that of using time effectively. Meetings and administrative activities involving school staff tended to receive low ratings, and were the focus of questioning comments, especially from mentors. While working on classroom teaching with the interns in a variety of ways is almost always seen to be of value, the usefulness of time spent on other activities is frequently questioned. The same kind of message emerges in relation to the three-way profiling meetings between interns, mentors and curriculum tutors and between interns, professional tutors and general tutors: is this an efficient use of everyone's time? Similar considerations were apparent in relation to visits by university staff to schools, widely seen as having considerable potential value, but also as being often wasteful and inefficient in their use of time. A second area of concern for a review of internship – one directly relevant to the problem of reduced resources – has to be that of making more careful use of the time of all those involved.

The third theme that comes through strongly from both the quantitative data and respondents' comments is that parts of the programme are perceived by substantial minorities of interns and of mentors as lacking in practical usefulness. This is a complaint made by some about parts of the university-based curriculum programmes and by rather more about school and university elements of the whole-school programme. These complaints must be taken seriously, but the reasons for them seem far from straightforward or simple. In part, they seem to stem from practices which diverge from a fundamental principle of the programme, that all elements of it should be directly relevant to the day-to-day work of teachers. In part too, however, they seem to stem from narrow preconceptions on the part of some respondents about the functions of ITE, showing a lack of concern to question established practices in schools or to consider aspects of teachers' work beyond the classroom. It seems that a more consistent realization of internship principles needs to be combined with redoubled efforts to persuade all interns and mentors to recognize that ITE must mean more than inducting interns into established classroom practices.

Finally, the fourth main theme apparent in the evidence is a widespread satisfaction with, and indeed enthusiasm for, the existing internship scheme. This was apparent in the high value attached to most activities by the majority of each category of respondents: over 80 per cent of the figures in Tables 3.3 to 3.6 show majority responses assessing the role activities as 'highly valuable'. The same satisfaction and enthusiasm was apparent in the large numbers of the comments written on the back page of the questionnaire. In particular, a widespread resistance was expressed to significant cutbacks in the scale or range of activities currently engaged in.

This research project was undertaken with the very specific and practical purpose of facilitating an informed review of the Oxford Internship Scheme: its primary purpose was an internal one. We believe, however, that the concerns and satisfactions expressed by participants in the Oxford scheme, and the problems identified, are likely to be of relevance to all those attempting to develop partnerships to provide school-based ITE of high quality.

CHAPTER 4

Communication and Innovation

NICHOLAS FOSKETT, MARY RATCLIFFE
and DAVID BRUNNER
University of Southampton

INTRODUCTION

In response to DFE Circular 9/92, the University of Southampton negotiated a partnership with schools to support a secondary-phase PGCE course that commenced in October 1993. The partnership engaged 40 schools and colleges in Hampshire, Dorset and the Isle of Wight in the initial training of an intake of 193 students.

In developing the new course, both the schools and the university had misgivings about many facets of the course. The literature on the successes of partnership-based courses was limited by the small number of institutions that had developed school-based training under previous initial teacher training (ITT) criteria (e.g. Benton, 1990a,b; Wilkin, 1990), and the initial analyses of the proposals of Circular 9/92 raised more concerns than optimism about the operation of such schemes (e.g. Gilroy, 1992). Beyond the inevitable questions of resource transfer to schools, concerns focused upon the difficulties of interpreting the requirements of Circular 9/92, particularly with regard to assessment, the challenge of developing shared views of the content and process of an ITT course and the problems of communications and administration in such a large, devolved partnership.

Existing research has emphasized the importance of the development of good communications to the success or failure of partnership. Lucas (1990, p. 12) has emphasized the centrality of building up good relationships in ITT partnerships to the point where the community is '. . . properly critical . . . with all the members committed to criticism'. Duquette (1993) has confirmed the views of Williams (1993) that developing time to communicate within the partnership is difficult and that there is a key need, for example, to provide training for mentors about their role. Duquette (1993) also identified the need for continuing conferencing during the programme to reinforce the links between partners.

These views supported our own experience of curriculum development in schools, for we perceived the establishment of school-based ITT as having many of the characteristics of the diffusion of curriculum innovation. Rogers (1983) has considered some of the perceptual processes in adopting innovation. He identified, following the work of Rogers and Shoemaker (1971), that key dimensions in mediating successful adoption include the complexity of the innovation and the difficulty of its implementation. Complexity of innovation is seen by Rogers as having two components: ease of performance and ease of understanding. We perceived that successful PGCE implementation would depend on the effectiveness of the communications which enable understanding by all partners. It seems reasonable to assume that the overall interpretation of the policy documentation from government is made initially in the higher education institution (HEI). The HEI's ability to develop this into a comprehensible and well communicated format is crucial.

In general terms, therefore, we wished to focus on issues of communication within the PGCE partnership. More particularly we wished to test the conclusions of researchers examining partnership schemes that were developed prior to Circular 9/92. As course co-ordinators we identified a number of research foci for consideration during the evaluation of the new course. In particular, these included the following:

1 *Administration* – i.e. evaluating the importance of effective administrative communication in the system in building up confidence in the overall effectiveness of the scheme.
2 *Interpersonal relationships* – i.e. evaluating the importance of good, positive and effective communications between tutors and mentors in developing confidence in the scheme and positive attitudes towards it.
3 *Shared understanding* – i.e. identifying the most effective mechanisms for ensuring that ideas and perspectives on teacher education can be shared between all the partners.

COMMUNICATION SYSTEMS WITHIN THE PARTNERSHIP

We need to consider at this point the communication systems built into the Southampton partnership. The organization and operation of the students' course was designed jointly by the partnership, with responsibility for implementation of each course element allocated either to schools or to the university. The curriculum programme covers teaching issues and methodology in the student's main teaching subject and is jointly planned by the university curriculum tutor (CT) and the school's nominated curriculum mentor (CM). The programme is then delivered in the university by the CT, and then followed up in school by the CM, providing, in theory, an integrated and coherent programme. The professional themes programme addresses broad educational issues (e.g. language in the classroom), and is delivered in the university by a lecture or workshop and developed by activities in school, coordinated by the professional mentor (PM) – a senior member of staff in the school. For two-thirds of the course students are based full time in school and the organization of their programme of teaching, observation and other activities is the school's responsibility within a framework of guidelines.

The ITT curriculum is delivered and the students are supported and assessed, therefore, by 40 PMs (one per school), 13 CTs from the university, some 120 CMs in school, and 13 professional tutors (PTs) from the university. The role of the PT is to liaise with specific schools and to monitor the progress of the students in those schools. Preparation for these roles was undertaken through

- planning and preparation meetings between CTs and CMs in each main teaching subject;
- planning and preparation meetings between PMs and university colleagues in an overall PGCE Management Group;
- regular meetings of mentors throughout the operation of the course; and
- the production of detailed handbooks for each main subject curriculum course and for the professional themes course. These indicate the programme of work to be followed, the operation framework within which it must be implemented and the assessment system.

RESEARCH METHODOLOGY

The research was designed as an integral part of the evaluation system within the new course. At the end of each phase of the course a comprehensive evaluation is undertaken to solicit the views and comments of all participants within the course – students, tutors, mentors and headteachers/principals. The research instrument comprised an evaluation sheet which each participant was given to complete and return. For students this was in the form of a semi-structured questionnaire, which invited them to comment separately on each facet of the course they were experiencing, e.g. curriculum work within the university. For all other participants the evaluation sheet was entirely unstructured, and simply invited respondents to comment in whatever way they deemed appropriate. At each evaluation stage, therefore, responses were available, potentially, from 193 students, 200 PMs and CMs from schools, 26 CTs and PTs from the university and the 40 headteachers from the partnership schools. This chapter is based on the responses one-third of the way through the first year of the course, with replies from 96 students (49.7 per cent response), 27 PMs (67.5 per cent), 92 CMs (76.7 per cent), 13 headteachers (32.5 per cent), and 6 PTs (46.2 per cent) and 8 CTs (61.5 per cent).

For the focus of this chapter on communications issues, the data was analysed by grouping together comments into three categories:

1 Comments that were positive about communications within the course.
2 Comments that were negative about communications.

3 Comments that were neutral in judgement, either because a 'satisfactory' judgement was made or because no value judgement could be identified, or because the comments were a mixture of negative and positive in a more or less balanced proportion.

A summary of the results is shown in Table 4.1.

TABLE 4.1
Overall judgements about communication issues (%)

RESPONDENT GROUP	POSITIVE JUDGEMENTS	NEUTRAL JUDGEMENTS	NEGATIVE JUDGEMENTS
Students	50	20	30
Professional mentors	30	41	30
Curriculum mentors	28	40	32
Headteachers	31	46	23
Tutors	60	40	0

ANALYSIS AND COMMENTARY

In general terms the data demonstrated that the effectiveness of communication was important in the perception that participants have of the overall effectiveness of the partnership. Within the Southampton scheme there were approximately equal numbers of mentors recorded as perceiving communications as positive (8 PMs and 26 CMs) or negative (8 PMs and 30 CMs) with 11 PMs and 37 CMs making neutral judgements. Student perceptions were more favourable, with 39 students making negative comments, 66 expressing positive comments and 27 being neutral. While interpretation of this evaluation may be related to specific management issues that pertain simply to the Southampton course, more detailed analysis of the comments revealed a number of generalizations which appear to be more generic to the concept of partnership in ITT. We can identify a number of key principles from these observations.

A clear written framework for each element of the course provides security of interpretation, by removing from individual mentors, tutors or schools the responsibility for translating policy documents into practice. In the Southampton partnership this documentation was provided through the course handbooks, which were seen to be the most effective means of communication within the partnership. They provide negotiated, agreed programmes and act as a consultation document for the implementation of potentially problematical areas of course design. Their value was commented on positively by 23

CMs (24.7 per cent) and by 11 PMs (40.7 per cent). Only 2.5 per cent of respondents made any negative comments.

Principle 1, therefore, might be: *Support the course with accessible printed handbooks.*

It is clear that continuous and unambiguous dialogue across the partnership is essential, and where this is not present then a number of problems arise. This communication would appear to have two elements: confidence in the other members of the partnership through the existence of positive interpersonal relationships, often at the level of individual tutor–mentor relationships, and the content of communications. Even where good interpersonal relationships exist, however, there may be difficulties in the following areas:

1 There may not be agreement on fundamental principles in the operation of the course. For example, seven mentors expressed the view that schools do 'practice' while the university does 'theory', a view that course designers had striven to dispel.
2 There may be a feeling that each partner is not aware of what the other partners are doing. A large number of mentors (17; 18.2 per cent) expressed the view that they did not know what tutors in the university were doing with students on university-based days. This is despite the fact that the handbooks and mentor training produced agreed programmes for each element of the course.

A second principle might be, therefore: *Build on strong interpersonal relationships and ensure frequent dialogue between the participants.*

The organizational complexity of any partnership scheme raises concern about the achievement of communication between partners. Two dimensions of this may be important:

1 For the individual student the existence of four people supporting their work may be a mirage of support. Among their PM, CM, PT and CT there may be substantial sharing of information and good monitoring of progress, but it may also be that they feel that no individual provides the lynchpin of the scheme. Nine per cent of students, for example, commented on an apparent lack of concern for their progress by CTs when they are in school full time.

A third principle might be: *Ensure that students have a key tutor with whom they build up a strong relationship throughout the course.*

2 The other dimension relates to assuring that communication occurs at all. Under the new structure, some documentation is disseminated to the 15 PTs within the School of Education, but also by post to 35 PMs in schools, who may then disseminate materials further within their own school. The logistical task is immense, and time lags in the system require much more sophisticated forward planning among the generators of the

materials. Furthermore, particularly in the first year of operation, the need to interpret materials across a diverse range of school environments makes the gap between intended practice and actual outcome potentially much greater. For example, comments from some CMs (10 per cent) revealed a lack of knowledge of some aspects of the scheme's operations.

A fourth principle, therefore might be: *Provide substantial administrative support and ensure that communication time lags are understood and allowed for in the operational system.*

A key focus of courses under Circular 9/92 is the assessment process relating to the competency-based model that underpins the new schemes. Effective conduct of this system is dependent on clarity and consistency of interpretation within schools, between schools and HEI, and across all the schools in the scheme. The conduct of the assessment process in schools was illustrated by the 15 schools that commented on this element of the scheme's operation. In particular, many (10) of the CMs in these schools, who have responsibility for implementing the assessment process, found difficulty interpreting competencies in the context within which they were operating. However, many (14) also found the profiling system linked to the competencies to be very useful as a focus for communication with students and as helpful with supporting student development. The students in these 15 schools were generally positive (81 per cent) about the usefulness of the profile and the feedback that they were receiving from mentors in relation to it. It was noticeable in three of the schools in particular that large numbers of positive comments on assessment by mentors were matched by large numbers of positive comments by students.

A fifth and final principle might be, therefore: *Ensure that there is a shared perception of the nature of assessment between the partners from the outset.*

CONCLUSION

The evidence from initial evaluations of the Southampton partnership suggests that attention to developing effective communication systems is essential to effective innovation. The use of jointly prepared handbooks and continuing dialogue reduce the possibility of the innovation being rejected by the partners. In those areas of the course where this occurred we observed strong positive comments about the partnership and the effectiveness of the scheme from mentors, tutors and students. Where the communication was weakest, the comments were less positive. Our analysis supports the conclusions of Williams (1993), Lucas (1990) and Rogers (1983) in terms of effective communication providing a key to success. The five emergent principles outlined above represent broad conclusions in relation to our three research foci – administration, interpersonal relationships and shared understanding. The maintenance and development of these principles to a consistent high standard, within resource constraints, will be a continuing challenge to ITE schemes.

CHAPTER 5

Managing Further Professional Studies

HUGH BUSHER and PETER KING
Loughborough University

THE TEACHER EDUCATION CONTEXT

PGCE students have traditionally brought a variety of attitudes and commitment to their training. Many arrive on their courses preoccupied by notions of teaching their subjects, a view which this survey suggests persists in a small proportion of student-teachers, and have over-riding concerns about coping with pupils in classrooms (Waterhouse, 1993). On the other hand, many student-teachers in this study, when still only part way through their course, recognized the range of knowledge of whole-school issues needed by teachers, which is discussed by Mortimore (1993) and elaborated by Waterhouse (1993) into a national curriculum for preservice teachers, to meet the demands of corporate school development envisaged in *Better Schools* (DES, 1985) and enacted now through school development planning. To overcome the potentially narrow focus of trainee teacher concerns, prior to 1993 Loughborough University required student-teachers to undertake an education studies course, successor to the 'four disciplines' courses of an earlier era, which encapsulated a range of knowledge of wider educational issues with which, Barrow (1990) argues, it is essential for student-teachers to become familiar.

The issuing of Circular 9/92 (DFE, 1992d) led to the creation of a new PGCE course under the supervision of a PGCE Partnership Committee composed of school-based teachers and university tutors. The new PGCE course is divided into two phases. Phase 1 lasts from mid-September through to the end of the following February, during which student-teachers pursue a sandwich course in a partnership placement school, undertaking a six-week block practice before Christmas in between two periods of serial practice (two days a week in school and three days in the university). Phase 2 consists of a 12-week block practice in a second partnership school from March to May followed by four weeks in the university. The 153 student-teachers on the course are placed in schools in subject pairs (in groups of between two and ten students) in one of the 46 schools in the partnership scheme, under the supervision of a school co-ordinator, who is usually a deputy head.

Within this framework the education studies course was re-examined by a working party of university tutors and school co-ordinators. It was decided to reinforce its importance by transforming it into a common core course called Further Professional Studies (FPS), closely related to the competences listed in DFE Circular 9/92, and designed as an integrated course to be delivered in both university and placement schools for six hours a week during Phase 1. During Phase 2 students have to gather information from their placement schools and undertake whole-school activities. The assessment processes reflect this integration, the four assignments requiring students to consider the wider issues of being teachers in schools. For example, the second assignment asks students to learn a computing skill, helping them to reflect on the problems which pupils face when learning. This is described in more detail in Simmons and Wild (1992).

FPS is delivered by lecture and seminar in the university during serial practice and, in schools, by students working from self-study guides supervised by a school co-ordinator. Each week a lecture focuses on a topic and the relevant study guide encourages students to gather information from school. The study guides provide background reading and information as well as suggestions for inquiries on a variety of topics, such as how pupils learn, pastoral care, school organization and communicating with parents. The seminars, held in groups of about 24 student-teachers with mixed subject specialisms under the supervision of a university tutor, encourage students to reflect on their experiences in schools in a structured way, a process Schon (1983) described as developing professional reflective practitioners. Jaworski (1993) perceives reflection as the crucial link between experience and learning in the development of professional teachers. This reflexiveness is reinforced by the final assignment for FPS, a presentation by students relating to their school experiences, discussed elsewhere by Busher and Simmons (1992).

In the partnership schools the School Co-ordinators are responsible for ensuring student-teachers can take part in whole-school activities (attached to tutor groups, attending parents, consultations, extracurricular activities) and have opportunity during Phase 1 for weekly discussions with themselves or with other staff. School Co-ordinators are supported by university link tutors and the FPS study guides. Link tutors usually work with four or five schools each and also run an FPS seminar group, to which students from their link schools are allocated. The course is supervised by an FPS group of school co-ordinators and university tutors.

EVALUATING THE MANAGEMENT OF THE FPS COURSE

To maintain quality and the collaborative nature of the course after its inception, a review group of teachers and university tutors was established. This decided to survey student and School Co-ordinator opinion of the manage-ment of FPS. Some 37 of the 46 School Co-ordinators responded to this survey and 120 of the 153 students on the course replied. Responses were gathered at the end of the autumn term of the first year when students had completed 10 of the 17 weeks of the course and experienced both serial and block teaching practice. The survey was carried out using open-ended questions.

The support which schools gave student-teachers can be classed broadly into two models: the proactive or professional development model and the reactive or self-development model. The professional development model consisted of weekly timetabled school-based sessions on FPS topics for all the students in a school together led by the School Co-ordinator (18 of the 37 schools) or by specialist staff brought in by the School Co-ordinator (12 of the schools). In 15 schools this programme was supported by School Co-ordinators being avail-able to students whenever they wanted to see them. Some 73 of the 120 students confirmed that these sessions continued during block teaching prac-tice in the autumn term.

The timetabled sessions often represented the major effort which student-teachers committed to FPS during their school-based work. In 20 of the 37 schools, these lasted for approximately one hour a week, although in nine schools it was longer and nine had none at all. On the other hand, 58 of the 120 students spent one hour a week or less on FPS outside these sessions, a figure that did not alter substantially between serial and block practice, al-though 37 spent more time on it than this. Ten (16 during block practice) students worked on FPS during lunchtimes, at weekends and in the evenings. Where schools did not provide timetabled sessions for FPS there is some evi-dence that neither did the students spend much time on it, 17 reporting spend-ing less than one hour a week in these circumstances during serial practice.

Student-teachers strongly preferred the professional development model. All the 42 students who claimed that they received excellent guidance and support in schools related their comments to a structured programme of school-based FPS sessions. Some 43 students thought that the delivery of FPS would be improved if schools' discussion sessions followed the same programme as the topics discussed in the university and a further 28 wanted School Co-ordinators to receive additional briefing on their role in FPS so that the school-based element of the course could be more carefully articulated with the university element. This points to the importance of an integrated approach in developing teachers' professional understanding, a view endorsed by Nichol (1993) in his description of the school-based PGCE course for history run at Exeter University.

The self-development model relied on student-teacher initiative. In the six schools where it operated, School Co-ordinators arranged meetings between student-teachers and relevant staff when students requested them or simply told students which staff to meet for which FPS topic, leaving the students to organize formal sessions if they would or could. As the students were not always timetabled together for their non-contact time it was difficult for them to organize formal sessions and they seem, often, to have worked individually rather than in groups on FPS. This last finding stands in opposition to students' preferred means of working. Although 22 student-teachers preferred to work singly, 82 preferred to work in groups on FPS, perceiving it as easing the workload and improving the quality of learning through discussion.

Direct evidence of student-teachers' dislike of the self-development model is more difficult to discover, especially as some students said that they preferred working alone and others emphasized the importance to them of subject teaching at the expense of FPS. Nearly half the students who might be said to have been disaffected with FPS (i.e. those who perceived it as of little value or help) are to be found in four of the six schools which left it entirely up to students to take the initiative in gathering information for FPS.

The central figure in effective school-based FPS programmes was a proactive School Co-ordinator who organized timetabled sessions to meet student needs and was approachable and relatively easily available to give advice and help when necessary (81 of the 120 students). As important was the culture of support for student-teachers which these postholders helped to foster, with some School Co-ordinators claiming that students were 'absorbed into the school ethos'. Busher, Clarke and Taggart (1988) pointed out the impact on beginning teachers of the environment and culture in which they worked. Some 46 students remarked on the willingness of teachers to discuss educational matters when approached by students, although a few students felt awkward about taking up the time of busy teachers for this. Student-teacher involvement in school-wide activities (School Co-ordinators listed 26 different types) perhaps helped to sustain this supportive ethos. In 30 of the 37 schools, students took part in staff meetings of one sort or another, in 22 in lunchtime activities and sports, in 13 in INSET days and in 37 in after-school activities, such as parent consultations.

These findings fit in well with the recommendations of the DES for inducting newly qualified teachers, given in Administrative Memorandum 1/83 (DES, 1983), and with HMI recommendations (DES, 1988, para. 1.44) and perceptions of good school practice (para. 5.17), as well as with Barber's suggestions (1993) of how schools should support student-teacher development by providing an opportunity to talk with experienced colleagues; mentoring, advice and support on classroom matters; understanding of the school as an organization; and experience of teaching and of the wide range of views held by teachers.

WHAT RESOURCES WERE PROVIDED BY SCHOOLS TO SUPPORT FPS?

The School Management Task Force (DES, 1990) thought it important for school leaders to create an environment in schools which would enable teachers and pupils to learn effectively, a view referring not only to the culture of a school but also to the physical and social resources available. Respondents in this study made reference to two major categories of resources: room space for personal professional work and staff expertise.

About a half of all students had access to shared temporary space for personal professional work, either empty classrooms (27 of the 120) or a school library or subject preparation rooms (34). A few had access to a staff workroom. Although 25 students professed to be happy with the accommodation provided by their placement schools, 38 students wanted their own designated room or reasonably sized desk because they found staffrooms noisy and distracting places in which to work. This last point raises broader issues about the resources schools are able to commit for helping temporary (part-time) teaching staff to carry out their professional work. Farrar (1992) points out that at its best teacher education through partnership schemes should involve the whole school and embrace the training needs of all staff.

Staff were the important resource for supporting FPS programmes, School Co-ordinators listing 28 different types of staff involved, with deputy heads/ vice principals, heads of special needs departments, heads of pastoral systems and heads of department of IT playing important roles in many schools. In 15 of the 37 schools subject teachers also played a valuable support role, while in 17 schools form tutors were among those staff listed. Regrettably, 17 of the 120 students thought they received little support from staff outside their subject areas.

Other resources to which students referred included computers, to which 28 students claimed they had difficulty gaining access, and personal access to photocopying. The computer access problem seems to have been most acute during block practice (17 students) and to have been compounded by three factors: technical problems with software (28); students' poor typing skills (12); and the distant location of some students' placement schools from the university (13).

INTERACTIONS BETWEEN FPS AND TEACHING SUBJECTS

Some 43 of the 120 student-teachers thought FPS and their teaching subjects supported each other, 41 referring particularly to the work on classroom management and control; 32 thought FPS raised their awareness of what people needed to know about in schools. As one explained, '. . . teaching the subject-matter is only part of the job and FPS helped identify other areas within teaching'. Conversely, 40 students thought that their teaching subjects provided FPS with examples of practice or arenas in which to carry out FPS activities. One student said: 'Everyday life in the classroom has reflected work in FPS. There seems to be a reflexive relationship between the two.'

Although 57 students thought there was a shortage of time for preparing FPS and their teaching subjects, a view in keeping with the work of Hannam, Smyth and Stephenson (1976), only 22 students thought FPS of little help in supporting their teaching and even fewer thought their subjects offered little help to FPS. Of the students, 28 ascribed their perceptions of the insufficiency of time to the educational values they espoused, preferring to allocate more time to subject-based activities and less to FPS than the partnership PGCE course allocated.

ARTICULATION OF THE FPS COURSE BETWEEN SCHOOLS AND UNIVERSITY

The two main mechanisms in FPS for linking partnership schools and university are the link tutors and the FPS study guides. The survey did not ask about the workings of the FPS review group as it is not visible to students. Of the 120 students, 51 welcomed the work of link tutors, finding them supportive and accessible, and 27 students thought the two scheduled visits to schools in the autumn term adequate. On the other hand, 40 students were dissatisfied, claiming to have had insufficient contact with their link tutors. In part this might be because, to make contact loads feasible, link tutors only visit those schools (25 of the 46 taking 120 of the 153 students) in which four or more students were placed in Phase 1, although all schools had a link tutor available by telephone for consultation.

Students perceived link tutors having two main aspects to their role, a pastoral one of offering support to trainee teachers (36 of the 120), and a task-oriented one of observing lessons (13) and briefing School Co-ordinators to help them structure the school-based element of the FPS course (25). Some 26 students thought that link tutors should be more involved in the latter, especially during block practice.

Both groups of respondents thought the FPS study guides valuable sources of information but preferred that fewer be given out at one time (47 students). Although some students (22) preferred fewer topics for inquiry in each guide, in particular they pointed to the work involved in making a selection of these into a folder of school-based activities for the third FPS assignment but this was not a view generally shared by School Co-ordinators.

CONCLUSIONS

The successful management of a course, such as FPS, which is an element within a broader PGCE course, depends on the quality of partnership between schools and university and the quality of in-school support. The former involves two types of integration: institutional collaboration, and the integration of student-teachers' understandings of FPS with their teaching subject methodologies to create the sort of holistic understanding of teaching and learning in schools which Waterhouse (1993) recommends in her national curriculum for preservice teachers, and the DFE (1992d) elaborates in its list of competences in Circular 9/92. Integration of student-teachers' understandings can be achieved through school-based teachers and university tutors encouraging students to reflect in a structured way on their practical teaching experiences (Jaworski, 1993; Nichol, 1993), as the FPS course appears to do.

Institutional collaboration can be facilitated through organizational mechanisms such as the five identified as operating effectively in the Loughborough partnership scheme: the role of the link tutor; the use of study guides; formally structured in-school programmes of study; the role of the School Co-ordinator; and the work of the FPS review group. These, in turn, raise important issues about the costs of resourcing partnership courses in times of economic stringency; about how to make such courses sufficiently flexible but sufficiently well structured to meet the competing needs of students, different schools in the partnership, and the accreditation and certification requirements of the DFE; about the status and influence which School Co-ordinators and university tutors need to lead such courses effectively; and about the interpersonal qualities which effective School Co-ordinators and link tutors need to have.

The quality of in-school support is determined by the training culture of a school (Shaw, 1992). The FPS programme is not only dependent on School Co-ordinators' interpretations of their role but also even more crucially on the attitude of the rest of a school's staff towards this part of the PGCE programme and to involvement with teacher education in general. It takes time for Co-ordinators to build such a supportive consensus in schools. It also requires, as Barber (1993) suggests, schools and university to go through an evolutionary process of creating a partnership through genuinely shared exploration, planning and delivery of all aspects of the course.

The management of an element such as FPS can only be effective where it interlocks university and school inputs, constructs positive values and beliefs in school staff both for FPS and for school-based teacher education, promotes understanding in a university about the needs and limitations of its partner schools, and provides the level of support that students say they need in both schools and university.

CHAPTER 6

Students' Perceptions of Consistency and Coherence

NIGEL WRIGHT and JEFF MOORE
University of Hull

Partnership-based training for PGCE began at Hull in September 1993 with the university working formally with a group of 34 schools. This represented a significant development for what was a conservative department operating a recognizably traditional PGCE. Partnership training was designed to include a number of structures and procedures to ensure quality in consistency, coherence and manageability. This chapter outlines these structures and procedures, reports initial survey data collected to examine the efficacy of joint training and draws conclusions.

The secondary PGCE at Hull is designed in two major sections reflecting the requirement in Circular 9/92 that '. . . students should have the opportunity to practise teaching in at least two schools during their training' (DFE, 1992d, para. 3.4.2). Each section contains a substantial block of eight weeks when students practise teaching. These blocks are preceded by a period of preparation, designed and delivered jointly by tutors and mentors. The key features of this joint training are derived both from experience with articled teachers and based on recommendations made by Ofsted in their report on the articled teacher scheme (Ofsted, 1993a). These are as follows:

- A division of each week into three days spent in the university and two days spent in schools (a concurrent model).
- The stipulation of an agreed weekly focus theme to underpin the joint training.
- The use of a series of handbooks for students jointly prepared by tutors and mentors.
- The designation in each school of a senior member of staff to act as 'co-ordinator'.
- The assigning of a university tutor to each partner school (as 'link tutor') to undertake a weekly liaison visit to the school to see the co-ordinator, mentors and students.

- A weekly seminar held at the university between the 'link tutor' and the group of students from his or her partner schools.

An intensive period of precourse subject-application planning, mentor development and co-ordinator briefing was undertaken in the summer term. Colleagues from both sides of the partnership were involved. Mentors in subject areas where schools had contracted to take students were specifically targeted. In excess of 2,000 mentor/tutor hours were invested in the programme. Further termly meetings of mentors and co-ordinators have continued after the course commenced.

Internal evaluation of the course has been undertaken by the authors as the course has unfolded. The principal concerns reported in the rest of this chapter are consistency in training across the partnership and coherence and progression within the programme elements. Both of these raise important management issues.

Investigations have focused particularly but not entirely on the responses of students during the joint training. As both the recipients of this training and those who have to put what they have learnt into practice, their views on the consistency and coherence of the programme are essential. Students have completed two detailed questionnaires on a range of aspects of the provision. The first examined time devoted in schools to initial teacher training (ITT) and was completed during the jointly delivered training. The second explored student views on the coherence of the joint training and was completed shortly after that period was over. Given the centrality of the roles of the school co-ordinator and the 'link tutor' in the joint enterprise, their views on their developing roles were elicited during the joint training phase of the course. The responses to these four surveys are shown in Table 6.1.

CONSISTENCY

Each student on the course is entitled to consistency in the provision, tuition, support and experience they receive, within the parameters that no two schools

TABLE 6.1
Respondents to surveys

	STUDENTS FIRST SURVEY	STUDENTS SECOND SURVEY	LINK TUTOR SURVEY	CO-ORDINATOR SURVEY
No. replying	152	161	14	32
Total possible (%)	84	91	87	94

Note: Between the two student surveys, five students left the course

was reported as 18 per cent receiving no extra time, 15 per cent up to an hour, 14 per cent about an hour, 22 per cent over an hour and just over 30 per cent indicated that time was 'as needed' or in breaks and lunchtimes.
the partnership model, where more trainers are involved, it was considered important to maintain as much consistency as possible – hence the extensive precourse planning, training and structuring.

Students were asked about the amounts of time they spent during the joint training with the co-ordinator, their mentor and other teachers. (Out of a total of 152 students, 70 per cent received a school-based seminar, 29 per cent did not.) Table 6.2 shows the amount of time devoted to these weekly seminars. Student negative replies were confirmed by the co-ordinators' survey, where five said they did not hold a seminar and a further three did not reply. This raises important quality and management issues for course design and monitoring.

TABLE 6.2
Time spent in school-based seminars (n = 152)

	%
Less than 1 hour	14
About 1 hour	43
Nearer 2 hours	16
No reply	27

Students were also asked about any extra time they spent with co-ordinators. This is summarized in Table 6.3. The student responses show that, on average, about 20–25 minutes a week of extra time was spent with their co-ordinator. Similar questions were asked about time spent with mentors. Of the 152 students, 95 per cent had regular contact with mentors, and 5 per cent did not. Extra time spent by students with mentors beyond regular weekly contact

TABLE 6.3
Extra time spent with co-ordinators (n = 152)

	%
None	37.5
Up to half an hour	19.0
Half an hour–1 hour	12.5
1 hour	9.0
Over 1 hour	5.0
'As needed'	6.0
In breaks/lunchtimes	11.0

was reported as 18 per cent receiving no extra time, 15 per cent up to an hour, 14 per cent about an hour, 22 per cent over an hour and just over 30 per cent indicated that time was 'as needed' or in breaks and lunchtimes.

Contact with co-ordinators and mentors was what was required to deliver the training, but students were also asked about how much time they spent with other teachers for ITT matters. Two-thirds of the students said that they had time with other teachers, 9 per cent having less than an hour, 21 per cent about an hour, 24 per cent more than this and 12 per cent in the 'as needed' category. These last data indicate some of the difficulties in trying to establish a managed and consistent structure and system. Students and teachers will respond outside structures to meet needs and opportunities. It makes detailed specification in contracts and costings rather difficult and inaccurate.

'Link tutors' were instituted as a further means of delivering support and enhancing consistency. Regular visiting was stressed by Ofsted (1993a, para. 53). The 'link tutor'/co-ordinator liaison developed with some variation, and students perceived this in their responses. Table 6.4 shows the regularity of contact between students and their 'link tutors'.

TABLE 6.4
Student contact with link tutors in schools (n = 158*)*

TIMES SEEN	%
Never	0
Once/twice	22
Several times	16
Every week	62

Clearly, the majority received regular contact. Where less contact was made, this was in part the result of placements in small schools where weekly contact could not be maintained on the grounds of distance, time and tutor availability. 'Link tutors' interpreted their role quite widely, undertaking a range of tasks in and for schools. Where tutors undertook some teaching in the school, they clearly had less time available for students, co-ordinators and mentors. Some schools were keen to have tutors teaching as this provided extra resources! The range of tutor time is summarized in Table 6.5. Seven tutors indicated 'other'. Five of these indicated that they were teaching in the school and that this was taking between 30 and 40 per cent of their time in schools.

Of some concern is the smaller level of contact between 'link tutor' and co-ordinators and mentors. Students saw 'link tutors' as coming to see them, and their replies to a free-response question showed that many good relationships had developed, as the following extract demonstrates: '. . . extremely helpful –

TABLE 6.5
Link tutor time for tasks in schools (n = 14*)*

	%
Seeing students	66
Seeing mentors	10
Seeing the co-ordinator	10
Other	14

at university they knew what you were talking about because they had been there. At school it was like having a portable educational compendium!' (English student). A managerial concern must be that the interface between school and university needs to be developed by changing the emphasis in the role of the 'link tutor' to spending more time with mentors and co-ordinators and less in school with students.

Student perceptions of the consistency in provision across the group of schools show that there is very evident variation. This is in spite of the planning, preparation, training and structures. Students will inevitably seek out extra help from whatever sources they can and no amount of rubrics are likely to prevent them, nor perhaps should they. What is more serious is that it was possible for some schools not to provide what was expected and for this to emerge only in response to an evaluative questionnaire. Any new venture is bound to generate teething troubles and take time to 'bed' down. A period of stability in partnerships, working with regular and increasingly known personnel to ever more familiar requirements, will undoubtedly help. Whether such time will be allowed is another matter (Wright, 1993a).

COHERENCE

An associated issue in partnership training must involve achieving coherence between the respective training inputs. One attempt to ensure this was through the stipulation of a series of weekly focus themes, joint training materials and regular monitoring meetings. Students were asked to respond to a number of items relating to course coherence. Table 6.6 reports student ratings of the coherence of school-based seminars to the focus lecture, university seminar and work in schools.

Students were then asked to concentrate on the focus lecture and its coherence with the university seminar and the school seminar. Table 6.7 shows their responses. Finally, students were asked to rate the coherence of university-based method work with school-based method work. Responses are shown in Table 6.8.

TABLE 6.6
Coherence issues, school seminars

RATING SCALE (%)

High rating	1	2	3	4	5	6	7	Low rating
Comple-mented university seminar	29	29	17	17	3	3	1	Repeated university seminar ($n = 135$)
Match to focus lecture	24	35	16	16	6	3	—	Poor match to focus lecture ($n = 139$)
Well related to work in school	33	35	17	8	6	1	—	Poorly related to work in school ($n = 140$)

TABLE 6.7
Focus lecture: coherence (%)

LEVEL

	Very high	High	Moder-ate	Low	Very low	
With university seminar	19	45	35	1	—	($n = 140$)
With school seminar	9	45	34	9	2	($n = 134$)

Student responses broadly indicate that a substantial degree of coherence between the respective parts of the course had been achieved. Coherence was asserted by three-quarters of respondents to the relationship of the school-based seminar to other key aspects of provision. On the five-point scale, the focus lecture achieved between half to two-thirds rating it as high or very high and a solid third of respondents rating its coherence as moderate. Most disap-

TABLE 6.8
Method work: coherence between university-based and school-based training (%)

LEVEL					
Very high	High	Moderate	Low	Very low	
9	28	39	17	6	(n = 137)

pointing, especially in terms of the person-hours invested in preparation and materials, is the stated coherence between university-based and school-based method training. That nearly a quarter rated the coherence as low or very low is plainly not good. This must be counterbalanced by noting that in excess of a third rated it as high or very high. Some explanation is to be found in student replies to a free-response question on this point. Many underlined the age-old tension experienced between what method tutors suggest and what students find at the 'chalkface' in a particular school. The following examples illustrate:

> Some sections of the university course were too obviously derived from theory rather than practice.
>
> (Maths student)

> Practical guidance from the university was often in cloud cuckoo land when faced with the reality of classroom teaching.
>
> (Geography student)

Yet many others perceived the rationale for what was being attempted:

> It was a very organized phase filled up with lots of information which was well prepared and explained and became clearer on the block practice.
>
> (German student)

> University method sessions were relevant to what we did in school on TP.
>
> (English student)

Workload was criticized by many as working in joint training for two masters, which increased burdens.

Disappointing reactions to joint method training are in part a result of the expectations of some students who see a training course as providing tools for a 'concrete operator'. This may therefore lead to a reaction against the wider context and exposure to rigorous scrutiny offered in a university course (Wright, 1993c). Equally, there are some departments in a few schools where a similar understanding of training exists, underlined by this student comment: 'What is school method work?' (Maths student). University tutors are not exempt from some responsibility in the disappointing reactions to joint method training. Clearly more mentor development work is needed. This year's experience and more stability in future may assist.

A solution to this problem is not made easy in the new market created in ITT. Higher education institutions (HEIs) have not been inundated with requests from schools to participate in training; in fact, there are concerns that offers of places will decline (*The Times Educational Supplement*, 1994a; 1994b). Usually, just enough places have been offered and HEIs have found themselves in the role of 'beggars can't be choosers'. Inadequate levels of resourcing (Wright, 1993b) will perpetuate this situation and, with the end of the transitional funding, further resources to continue the necessary mentor development work will be very hard to find. The conclusions of HMI in 1991 (DES, 1991, para. 76) are still valid:

> The concept of school-based training should not be merely a quantitative one but should include also the quality of teacher involvement in planning, providing and assessing training and the quality of co-operation between higher education and schools. That said, it is quite clear that the amount of time students spend in school already differs quite considerably from one course to another and that some of the courses with more generous amounts of school experience provide better than average training. The main caution is that some do not . . . What is needed is a clear definition of the respective responsibilities of the participants . . . and assurance that appropriate resources accompany those responsibilities.

If experience in our course is one example, then achieving consistency and coherence in partnership training is developing. It is going to take much more than a contract, mentor training and course materials to achieve it.

CHAPTER 7

Lessons Unlearnt?
Aspects of Training Licensed Teachers

CONOR GALVIN
University of Cambridge

INTRODUCTION

Since the spring of 1990, about 60 English LEAs have operated a scheme which provides two-year, school-based training for roughly 300 licensed teachers per year. The fundamental differences between licensing and other entry routes into teaching are that licensing leads only to Qualified Teacher Status (QTS) and, unlike short-course entry (e.g. PGCE or a two-year BEd), licensees need not be graduates. Moreover, all other routes are organized by institutions of teacher education or formalized consortia of higher education institutions (HEIs) and associate schools while licensing is run solely by LEAs or by grant-maintained schools (GMS).

An important issue in the context of ongoing debate on teacher education reform in Britain is whether licensing constitutes a fundamental challenge to existing practices in the initial professional preparation of teachers. This may seem strange considering that the number of teachers under licence stood at about the thousand mark at its highest point and has since declined. But in the light of recent moves to reconstruct radically the initial teacher training (ITE) relationship between teacher training institutions and the school, it is possible to appreciate that there may be some valuable lessons to be learnt from research into the scheme.

It is all the more jarring, then, to realize that the licensing experiment has been marked by a significant absence of research that documents and evaluates the scheme; both of the major reports commissioned to this end by the government have seen misadventure. The HMI report – eventually released by Ofsted in 1993 – was disappointingly vague and seemed to have suffered from the attenuation of the original HMI research team in the transition to the new regime. But it was at least published: the NFER report was not. So it has fallen instead to a relatively subsidiary component of the Modes of Teacher

Education Project (MoTE) – published as Barrett and Galvin (1993) – to supply the bulk of publicly available data on practice and provision across the scheme nationally.

An examination (necessarily brief in the context of this publication) of certain specific aspects of the licensing scheme, drawing upon research findings from the national study on which the MoTE report was constructed, may go some way towards illustrating just how important the lessons of the scheme are. It may also suggest why so little research on licensing has actually come into the public domain.

THE BACKGROUND TO THE LICENSED TEACHER SCHEME

To contextualize with any degree of completeness the thinking behind the initiative requires acknowledgement of the profoundly anti-professional and anti-theoretical aspects of the ideological voice that came to be known in Britain and elsewhere as the New Right (Levitas, 1986). This discernible voice was arguably of considerable significance in the decision to make so radical a departure in initial teacher preparation in Britain. Since the late 1960s the Right has consistently denigrated many aspects of contemporary educational practice and – since the mid-1980s in particular – the 'collusion' of higher education set teacher preparation in perpetuating such practices. What was formidable about these attacks through the mid- to late 1980s was the undoubted influence of the groups involved on the making of policy at the very top levels of Conservative government (Ranelagh, 1991; Chitty, 1992).

A particularly frustrating feature of this presence during the consultation process that preceded the introduction of the licensing scheme was the way in which the Right consistently attempted to conflate the debate on reforming routes to QTS with calls for licensing to mean a total restructuring of teacher training along apprenticeship lines (see, for example, O'Hear, 1988). It became increasingly difficult to separate out the two issues because of this politicization. What should have been essentially an administrative reform became an ideological battleground.

That briefly is the background against which the licensing initiative may best be set and understood. It is important because it highlights what is perhaps the key characteristic of the licensing scheme – its origins as a political rather than professionally led initiative.

Some measure of the antipathy that this engendered among teacher educators can be gauged from reactions to the scheme throughout and immediately following the consultation period. A consensus quickly emerged among those in the teaching profession most centrally involved in the day-to-day business of educating teachers: licensing was to be regarded as a 'cheap-fix' and an infinitely poorer alternative to properly resourcing the training and retention of teaching professionals (see, for example, Reid and Newby, 1988, or Smithers,

1989). What was seen to be at stake was the very principle of the liberally educated, all-graduate teaching profession; a principle in which teacher educators, practising teachers and teachers in training had invested very considerably over the years.

This returns us to the original consideration: the significance of licensing in the wider context of teacher education reform.

THE SIGNIFICANCE OF THE LICENSED TEACHER SCHEME

The licensing scheme certainly had some impact in opening up a route to QTS for overseas trained teachers and for secondary school instructors, but it could be argued that these would have been working in their respective sectors anyway; all that had changed was that they could now do so with the status and pay of a teacher. In addition many licensees came from ethnic minority groups (as much as 75 per cent of intake on some of the London schemes, 41 per cent nationally) and almost two-thirds were women. In all of this licensing proved laudable and in no way exceptionable to teachers and teacher educators at large.

However, the woolly central administration through which the scheme was introduced and financed left licensing open to diverse interpretations at provider level. A wholly idiosyncratic training provision resulted which varied widely in terms of selection process, on-site and off-site support for licensed teachers, mentor selection and training, payment patterns, assessment and accreditation arrangements, and even QTS requirements. (See Barrett and Galvin, 1993, for a full discussion of these issues.) This led to as many variations of the scheme as there were LEAs and schools participating. All they had in common was that they differed, which represents an almost impossible context against which to evaluate a policy initiative, especially one which has at its heart so radical a change in the initial preparation of teachers. Despite this, certain aspects of the scheme as it was implemented over the first two years of its existence are of significance for what they tell about school-based teacher training on the licensing model. These are to do with the localization of the scheme's impact, the cost of provision and the quality of training and support offered through the scheme.

Localization

The impact of licensed teacher training on teacher shortages was highly localized. LEAs which in the late 1980s had had the most chronic teacher recruitment and retention problems were quick to exploit the scheme, hiring locally to fill local needs. As a result, licensed teacher training matched the pattern of recruitment and retention difficulties of the late 1980s not just in some broad sense but also down to the level of phase of training and specific location: primary phase in the greater London area and in some other large urban centres; secondary phase in the rest of England, though mainly in the south east. No schemes were established in Wales during 1990–2.

It was not therefore just a case of most of the LEAs with substantial numbers of licensed teachers being in the south east of England, as the Ofsted report suggested (Ofsted, 1993b). In fact, eight out of every ten licensed teachers – whether on schemes of substantial size or otherwise – were in training in the south east; and six of these were in the London area specifically.

But this linkage between teacher shortage and licensed teacher recruitment, though predictable, was unfortunate. It meant that licensed teachers were most likely to be appointed directly against vacancies in schools where staffing difficulties in shortage subjects meant that these schools were probably among the least likely to be able to provide the necessary training and support for a licensed teacher. They often did not have mentors who were confident enough in the subject (or age phase) involved, and even when potential support existed, many schools found it inordinately difficult to allow release time for staff to train as mentors or carry out mentoring activity. This had inevitable implications for the quality of on-site support and training that licensees received.

Cost

Economies of scale also proved extremely difficult across licensed teacher training provision. Of the 59 licensing LEAs in 1990–1, 41 catered for less than ten licensees but each of these was obliged to provide on-site and off-site training that would typically involve LEA inspectorate and advisory staff as well as those at school level and those providing the necessary administrative back-up. It would also involve a range of 'hidden costs' usually carried by HEIs as part of their teacher training function. These include the expense of recruiting and interviewing, course materials, training co-ordination, assessment and quality assurance, facility use and necessary travel and cover costs.

Furthermore, the range of licensees' training needs varied widely within and between schemes. Four our of every ten licensed teachers on the schemes surveyed were in fact first degree holders and almost 8 per cent were higher degree holders. In addition there was significant variation between London and the rest of England in the distribution of these qualification holders (Barrett and Galvin, 1993). Matching this diversity of training needs against training provision was clearly a most difficult proposition and costly in terms of resources and personnel.

The complexity of fully costing the necessary training provision was such that none of the LEAs surveyed for the MoTE project had formally attempted to do so. However, 26 scheme co-ordinators were prepared to offer a rough indication of overall outlay based on LEA-level expenditure. These varied from £3,065 per licensed teacher per year (over two years) where minimal training occurred to £9,000 per licensee per year for a highly sophisticated programme of training which was in all but name a PGCE course. The majority of respondents placed their estimates at around £6,500 per licensee per year over each year of training. In addition, the licensee drew a full salary as either an instructor or teacher. It is stressed, however, that these figures are only indicative and that all that could be concluded with any certainty from the survey returns was that running a licensing scheme cost significantly more than had originally been estimated or budgeted for through LEATGs/GEST funding. This meant that it was next to impossible to calculate with accuracy the true cost of implementing the licensing scheme nationally.

The quality of training

As far as the quality of training was concerned, the only consistency in licensing was again its inconsistency: not only between schemes – which offered very different training experiences according to levels of LEA and school interventions – but also even within schemes where licensees were often effectively on different routes because of school-level training and mentoring arrangements. Considerable differences also emerged between schemes regarding the personnel involved in licensed training provision and the level of their involvement as well as in the ways through which training was actually delivered and the readiness of trainers to deliver school-based training (Barrett and Galvin, 1993).

Given the importance of the mentor in sustaining the school-based core of licensed teacher training provision, it would seem reasonable to expect that mentors would be trained to undertake, and supported in exercising, this new and complex function. Indeed, the notion of mentoring has been linked to licensed teacher training since the scheme was first introduced; the term 'mentor teacher' appears explicitly in the implementing circular (DES, 1989d), and almost every licensed teacher had a designated 'mentor' from as early as the spring of 1990 (Galvin, 1992; Ofsted, 1993b).

But having a designated mentor did not mean being mentored in the sense of receiving some sort of appropriate support and training – arguably because the training and support of mentors was not generally effective. Consequently, the Ofsted report could reasonably describe mentoring arrangements within the licensed teacher training as '. . . the weakest link in most schemes' (1993b, p. 15). When considered with reference to the training of licensed teacher mentors, the truth of that claim becomes only too apparent.

Nationally, provision for the training and support of licensed teacher mentors was patchy and variable in both quantity and quality. Inconsistency of content, structure and access marked the training experiences of mentors on almost every scheme surveyed. At one extreme some mentors had the opportunity to undertake a rolling programme of professional studies centring on the mentoring of a licensed teacher and laid on in conjunction with a local polytechnic or college. At the other, no formal training whatever was provided; in the words of a mentor on one such scheme, 'It was just something to be got on with; sink or swim'.

Arrangements relating to the accreditation and payment of licensed teacher mentors also varied greatly. But accreditation of the training given to the mentors of licensed teachers was marked by its absence rather than its prevalence. Only seven schemes in all provided mentors with the opportunity to gain any sort of accreditation for their work in schools with licensed teachers. Three LEAs offered their own accreditation in the form of mentoring certificates; two of these overlapped with credits towards HEI awards of various sorts. Decisions whether to pay mentors were mostly taken at LEA level, though schools were said to have the main say in this in a little more than one in three instances. Only 17 schemes paid the mentor for work undertaken in conjunction with the training of the licensed teacher. None of the larger schemes were among this number.

The result of this was that the quality of training provided for licensees on many schemes came to rely heavily on the personal qualities of individual, untrained, unpaid mentors and the enthusiasm or otherwise they brought to their work. And as has been said, many of the mentors were teachers in schools which were seriously under pressure from the shortage of appropriately qualified staff.

COMMENT

Licensing has had only limited and localized success as a measure to counteract teacher shortage problems by 'opening up' teaching posts to non-graduates through legislation, due largely to its failure to take root among its main target population: middle-aged 'career changers'. That in itself is an interesting research finding.

But the cardinal significance of research into the licensed teacher scheme is that it illustrates at the very least the questionable nature of recent hasty moves towards school-centred initial teacher training. Even within the relatively small-scale numbers of the licensing scheme, few schools were found to be capable of offering high-quality ITE or had the infrastructure in place to do so. Consequently, most licensing schools could not provide well structured training for their licensed teachers. And in addition the training and on-site support of mentors was wholly inadequate for the task they were being asked to undertake. In short, the keystones of the licensing scheme were missing or fundamentally flawed.

In any rational analysis of policy and policy implementation in teacher education reform this would give pause for thought. There are clearly issues of responsibility, direction and resourcing involved in school-centred initial teacher training which have not been resolved. The experience of the licensing scheme suggests that these include the hidden costs of recruiting, course provision, training co-ordination, providing high-calibre trainers, training facility use, quality-control mechanisms and appropriate travel and cover for teachers in training and their mentors. More importantly, they include issues of leadership, due process of training and licensee evaluation, and the unambiguous assignment of appropriate responsibilities of all parties in the process. Without these clear lines of accountability, purpose and commensurate resourcing – far in excess of that offered in support of licensing provision – the quality of teacher education in England and Wales may be seriously threatened by the proposed shift to school-centred initial teacher training.

Sadly, research evidencing this danger has been ignored and even suppressed in a climate of adversarial relations between successive Secretaries of State for Education and those who work to provide professionalizing education in the teacher training sector.

CHAPTER 8

The Extra Pair of Hands Comes with a Free Brain

DEREK HAYLOCK
University of East Anglia

This chapter describes a small-scale, local study of why primary schools take students on teaching practice. The results of the study may confirm some generally held perceptions about the benefits to schools of participating in initial teacher training (ITT) and provide a useful background for institutions and schools involved in the development of new forms of professional partnership in training.

THE CONTEXT FOR THE STUDY

At the University of East Anglia (UEA) we train about 100 primary student-teachers a year on the PGCE course, split between an early-years course (4–8 years) and a middle-years course (7–12 years). Typically for primary PGCE courses in Britain, the students are well qualified and highly motivated. The average age of the primary PGCE students at UEA is consistently around 27 years. The students we offer to schools are generally good honours graduates, with some degree of maturity and often with experience of the world of work outside schools and higher education.

For teaching practice placements we approach local schools, mainly in Norfolk and the northern area of Suffolk, and in the past have always had little difficulty in securing placements for students on teaching practice. Each year a number of schools who show willingness to take students are disappointed that we are unable to take up their offer, often simply for geographical reasons.

Circular 14/93 (DFE, 1993c) sets a new context for the relationship between higher education (HE) initial teacher training institutions and primary schools, with para. 37 requiring negotiation over 'transfer of resources' to partnership schools. Effectively, 'transfer of resources' means money, of course, and paras 38 and 39 of Circular 14/93 seem almost to anticipate, if not to encourage, a spirit of confrontation between HE and the schools with which they work over the level of payment to be made.

THE PURPOSE OF THE STUDY

The purpose of the study was to establish a base-line for negotiations with schools who work with us in our existing primary ITT programmes. Recognition by schools of the benefits which they perceive in taking student-teachers is likely to be an important component of our negotiations with them. Part of the context for the implementation of the requirements of Circular 14/93 is the extent of the difficulties associated with the earlier implementation of the corresponding secondary ITT Circular 9/92 (DFE, 1992d). It could be argued that insufficient recognition of the positive benefits for secondary schools of being involved in teacher training has contributed to a level of transfer of resources which has put an undue strain on the ability of HEIs to maintain their commitment to secondary ITT.

METHOD

The method of the study was straightforward. The headteachers of 18 schools which currently take primary PGCE students on teaching practice were interviewed by a UEA tutor, normally visiting them in the course of their work with students in schools, and asked simply why they agreed to take students in their school. Similarly, the teachers in each of these schools who supervised students undertaking teaching practice were asked why they had agreed to take a student in their class. In some instances headteachers and teachers were encouraged to expand on their responses. The responses were written down, collected and analysed to identify any recurring themes.

ANALYSIS OF RESPONSES

In some cases the headteachers and teachers interviewed referred to the burden associated with supporting a poor student-teacher. In fact, the negative experience of dealing with a weak or uncommitted student who fails to measure up to their expectations occasionally leads to a school deciding to decline the invitation to be involved with students on the course in subsequent years. But such responses were isolated and, on balance, it is clear from the interviews that schools perceive that the benefits associated with successful students outweigh the potential burdens associated with the weak ones. If this were not so, then it would seem logical that the supply of schools providing regular teaching practice places would have dried up long ago.

The analysis suggests four categories of reasons why schools and teachers are apparently so willing to take primary ITT students on teaching practice. These broad categories are benefits to the children, benefits to the teachers, benefits to the school and commitment to the profession.

Benefits to the children

Many teachers clearly perceive that there is potential benefit for the children in their school from having students on teaching practice. Sometimes these benefits are expressed in terms of expectations that students will bring fresh ideas and enthusiasm into the classroom:

> Students come with a fresh input which can benefit the children. After you've been teaching for as long as some of us here have you get a bit stale. Students bring in more exciting things for the children to do. And they can sustain this over a period of six weeks in a way which we can't, because we're here with the class for the whole year.
>
> (Teaching head of a rural primary school)

> Students bring a bit of life and colour to the school . . . new ideas and methods. We feel we get a bit out of touch sometimes or stuck in our rut. It's good for the children to have contact with someone coming in from outside with a fresh approach.
>
> (Headteacher of a large urban primary school)

A benefit perceived frequently by the teachers who take students into their classes is the value of an extra pair of hands. This seems to be particularly important in classes where the teacher has to employ complex organizational strategies, for example in order to cope with a significant number of children with poorly developed basic skills in reading and writing, or in small primary schools where one class may have pupils from two or three year groups:

> The children will always benefit from having an extra person in the classroom, whoever they are. I'll take any help that's offered. I have to organize different activities for the different year groups anyway and with a student we can share the responsibility.
>
> (Supervising teacher, mixed years-4–6 class in a rural primary school)

> This is a demanding class with lots of special needs. I've got about a dozen children for whom English is their second language and several non-readers. Extra pairs of hands are always helpful. The student and I can work as a team much of the time. The children get more help than I can normally give them.
>
> (Supervising teacher, year-3 class in a city primary school)

> When I have a student in my class I can give more time to my special needs pupils.
>
> (Supervising teacher, year-4 class in an 8–12 middle school)

The staff of one small rural primary school actually approached us recently about the possibility of taking students on extended periods of teaching practice because they saw this as a possible solution to the problems they had identified in the teaching of mathematics to mixed-age classes. There was obvious disappointment that the school was too remote geographically for us to be able to respond positively.

Some teachers perceived the contribution of PGCE students as being at a different level from that of other helpers, such as parents:

> It's not just an extra pair of hands. As someone once said, the extra pair of hands comes with a free brain.
>
> (Headteacher of an 8–12 middle school)

> It's really useful to have someone to talk to professionally about a particular child. After all, a student teacher is a fellow professional, not like a parent helper.
>
> (Supervising teacher, year-5, in an 8–12 middle school)

Benefits to teachers

Some teachers openly admit that they like to have a student working with their class because the student's presence in the classroom can generate time for the normal class teacher to make progress with tasks which require their attention. This is in no sense an implication of laziness or lack of professionalism, but a recognition that, particularly in the primary sector, there is just not enough time available to deal to their own satisfaction with the many demands of the job:

> It's been great having the student this half-term. I've had time to prepare some work for the children on the computer that I've been wanting to do for ages.
>
> (Year-6 supervising teacher in a city primary school)

> The student's given me the opportunity to get on with other things – like policy documents and sorting out staffing problems – as a teaching head I don't get time to do these properly.
>
> (Teaching head in rural primary school)

In addition, a number of teachers made comments suggesting that their interactions with student-teachers are perceived as being of value to them in their professional development. Sometimes this kind of comment is merely at the level of picking up ideas:

> The student brings new resources from their university course which I find useful in my own teaching.
>
> (Year-3 supervising teacher in a primary school)

> We see their enthusiasm and new ideas and unashamedly plagiarize!
>
> (Headteacher of a 5–8 suburban first school)

But other comments focused on the benefit associated with being put in a position where issues and practicalities of teaching had to be addressed and analysed. This was a view supported by a number of headteachers who felt the professional contact with students would benefit their staff in this way:

> It makes you think about your own teaching in a way you don't normally have to do.
>
> (Year-4 supervising teacher in a suburban 8–12 middle school)

> I like my staff to work with students because it makes them stop and think about their own teaching. When they have to assess the student's preparation and organization it raises questions about their own work. Then the student wants to talk about things like classroom management and how to control children, and so on. It's all good experience for the teacher as well.
>
> (Headteacher, suburban 8–12 middle school)

> It's a two-way thing. The student learns from us and we learn by helping them to learn. It's an enriching experience.
>
> (Year-2 supervising teacher in a suburban 5–8 first school)

> I thought I was getting a bit stale, so when the head asked me if I would take a student I thought, well, why not, it'll do me a lot of good.
>
> (Year-5 supervising teacher in an urban 9-13 middle school)

Benefits to the school

A number of headteachers in particular perceive some kind of value in the ongoing link with the university through the contact provided by teaching practice arrangements. They appreciated the regular visits from tutors and their professional interactions with them. Comments in this category tended to be fairly unspecific, indicating rather just a general feeling that it was a good thing for the school to have this ongoing contact. The existence of a higher education base supporting the work of practitioners in the field is traditionally seen as one of the features which distinguishes the professions from other forms of employment. Maintaining a link between schools and HE by one means or another is therefore significant in the protection of the status of teaching as a profession. As is shown below, a sense of commitment to the profession is an important aspect of teachers' involvement in ITT. This sense of what it is to be professional could therefore be what lies behind such typical comments as follow:

> I appreciate the contact with the university. It's nice sometimes to have someone to talk to about education who's outside of the school.
>
> (Headteacher, suburban 8–12 middle school)

> Part of the reason for having students here is that it keeps us in touch with what's going on at the university. That's got to be good for us as a school.
>
> (Headteacher, urban 8–12 middle school)

It's a partnership isn't it, so we all benefit from working together.

(Headteacher, urban 5–8 first school)

In some cases, this contact leads to special opportunities for the school to be involved with the university. One school regularly sends its year-7 class into the university one morning a week for half a term to do work in art and computer-based mathematics with specialist groups of students and their tutor:

We've really appreciated the link with the university. Our year-7 children have done some wonderful work in art and maths. It's got back to the parents and they've been really impressed with what the children have been doing. We've had lots of positive feedback.

(Headteacher, suburban first and middle school)

'Perks' such as this, which obviously cannot be available to all schools, are nevertheless a genuine incentive for some to maintain the link with the university through the teaching practice arrangements. Two headteachers mentioned particularly another significant benefit which accrued to the school from taking students on teaching practice – the potential for recruitment of new staff:

Half my staff are ex-UEA students. We always try to have six students on TP over the course of the year, then if there are any jobs coming up . . . In the last couple of years I've appointed four students who actually did their TP with us. It's ideal really. We get a good look at them and they get a good look at us. And we know already how they'll fit in with our staff.

(Headteacher, 8–12 middle school in a market town)

Even if you can't appoint the student you've got for some reason, they can pass the message back to other students . . . tell them this is a good school to work in and what we're like. Some teachers are a bit wary of applying for a job here because we've got a council-estate image. But the students tell other students we're OK. I've picked up some good teachers that way, by word of mouth.

(Headteacher, city 8–12 middle school)

In our own institution, over the last two years, out of 230 PGCE primary students who qualified for teaching, 66 first appointments were to schools which we regularly use for teaching practice, and 28 of these were actually to schools in which the students had themselves undertaken teaching practice.

Another small but not insignificant benefit was mentioned by one deputy headteacher: 'We organize our summer term field-trips on the assumption that we'll have students to call on' (deputy headteacher, 8–12 middle school in a market town).

Finally in this section it should be recorded that the existence of a close professional and personal relationship between the university tutor and their colleagues in schools can sometimes exert a mild form of blackmail on schools approached for teaching practice places. Several headteachers asked why they had taken a student simply replied: 'Because you asked me and I don't like to say no.'

Commitment to the profession

Particularly impressive in the responses made by both headteachers and supervising teachers is the sense of having a commitment or obligation to the profession. The status of teaching as a profession, with the associated understandings of autonomy, rigorous training through higher education and progress towards an all-graduate workforce, has been won through a process of struggle during this century. In the context of the current government's assertion of central control and their promulgation of policies which might undermine or threaten features of the educational system which underpin the status of teaching as a profession, it is admirable that the notion of there being a commitment or obligation to serve the profession comes through very strongly in the responses of headteachers and classroom teachers in primary schools. Almost every headteacher or teacher spoken to made some comment of this kind when asked why they take students on teaching practice:

> Students are the future for the profession, aren't they?
>
> (Year-2 supervising teacher, suburban 5–8 first school)

> I like to help people starting out in the profession. It's nice to have the chance to put something back.
>
> (Year-1 supervising teacher, city 5–8 first school)

> It's important for the profession that schools like ours participate in training.
>
> (Headteacher, urban primary school)

> It's just something we ought to do, unless you've got some particular reason sometimes why you can't.
>
> (Headteacher, rural primary school)

> The profession needs new teachers and you can't train teachers without them doing teaching practice in schools, can you? We have a responsibility to the profession to be involved.
>
> (Headteacher, suburban 8–12 middle school)

> My memories of being a student on TP . . . I didn't get much help from my class teacher and I've always thought I could do better. I'm looking forward to giving better support than I had to someone coming into the profession.
>
> (Supervising teacher, year-3, in an urban primary school)

Finally, it is interesting that many headteachers clearly feel that their school has something special to offer to new entrants to the profession. The following responses are not untypical:

> We're a good school with a lot to offer. Students will learn a lot from coming here. It's important for the profession that schools like this one are involved in teacher training.
>
> (Headteacher, urban primary school)

I think we give students a good chance here. The staff are very supportive.

(Headteacher, city 8–12 middle school)

CONCLUSION

This sense of commitment to the profession, of course, embraces all the previous categories of responses. It is, no doubt, because teaching, to those engaged in it, is not just a job but also a profession that teachers are characteristically so open to opportunities with perceived benefits for their pupils, their personal professional development and for their school. This local study has been undertaken in a context in which ITT in HEIs has been under threat with the recent advent of government initiatives such as school-provided ITT and the proposals for a Teacher Training Agency (DFE, 1993a). However, if such a sense of responsibility to the profession as emerges from this study were to be widespread among headteachers and teachers in primary schools seeking to be involved in ITT partnerships with HE, then the prospect of HEIs being able to sustain primary teacher training would perhaps be more secure than some of us might have dared to hope.

The data from this small-scale study may be some encouragement for HEIs as they enter into negotiations with partnership schools. But there still remains the tricky problem of the benefits perceived by teachers in working with students being quantified in terms of cash equivalents which can form part of the delicate equation of costs, benefits and responsibilities which, in the future, must inevitably be involved in determining the level of transfer of resources from HE to partnership schools.

CHAPTER 9

I'm Sorry, but There's Not Enough Money for a Third Teaching Practice Visit

DYLAN WILIAM
King's College London

INTRODUCTION

This chapter presents a summary of the current funding arrangements for initial teacher education (ITE) and outlines the development of a model that provides an estimate of the teaching time that can be justified for a given course on the basis of its recruitment. While many of the assumptions within the model are open to question, the model itself is quite robust: even big variations in the assumptions on which the model is based do not produce big changes in the results.

The model indicates that once central overheads, academic services such as library and computing, and the costs of clerical and technical staff are taken into account, a 'pre-9/92' PGCE course is resourced sufficiently well to provide just under 30 hours of tuition per student. The model also shows that if payments to schools are to be made from income that has been 'top sliced' for central overheads and academic services, then no ITE course could be viable. If, however, the payments to schools are made before any 'top-slicing', then the amount of tuition generated by each student is around 23 hours. Nevertheless, with college-based tuition being given in groups of 20, with 25 per cent of college-based time given over to students' unsupported study, there just isn't enough money for a third teaching practice visit.

BACKGROUND

The bulk of the income of each higher education institution (HEI) in England comes from two sources. The first is in the form of tuition fees which, for most home and European Union (EU) students, comes from LEAs, and the second is in the form of a block grant from the Higher Education Funding Council for

England (HEFCE), partly to support research, and partly in recognition of the fact that the tuition-fee income does not cover the cost of teaching.

In the past, the block grant, as its name suggests, has been a single un-differentiated amount of money, but over the years of its existence, the HEFCE has moved towards an increasingly 'transparent' model for funding the ac-tivities of HEIs. What this means in the context of the current 'reforms' in ITE is that it is possible to examine, with much more precision than was possible before, the financial basis of ITE.

This chapter outlines a model that has been developed in one HEI to esti-mate how much teaching time is made available by the government for the tuition of students on ITE courses. The purpose of developing such a model is to assist those involved in the planning of activities within an HEI to determine whether the gains likely in pursuing an activity outweigh the costs, thus enab-ling more rational decision-making. However, I do not want to suggest that a course generating enough income to cover the cost of its teaching is the sole criterion that determines a course's viability. Some courses may, on paper, appear to 'run at a loss' but bring in other benefits, such as providing a focus for scholarly activity that leads to enhanced research selectivity ratings in the future.

In this sense, the *viability* of a course is a much more complex notion than whether income generated exceeds costs. A 'reductionist' approach to ac-counting – i.e. making sure that each course runs 'at a profit' – fails to recognize the complex inter-relationship between teaching activities, and be-tween teaching and research, and has the effect of creating artificial barriers between activities. On the other hand, an holistic approach to the determina-tion of viability allows a much more complex set of factors to be taken into account. However, this does not remove the requirement to make some tough decisions. If a course is viable only because it is believed that students subsequently go on to take other, more 'profitable' courses, then a case will need to be made that this is likely to happen. Decision-making thus becomes more difficult rather than easier, since there is no 'off-the-peg' method for determining viability.

The next two sections outline the basis of how both teaching and research are funded in HEIs in England, and the following section shows how the details of the funding model can be developed in order to relate income genera-tion to individual courses. This is followed by sections illustrating the applica-tion of the model to a 'pre-9/92' PGCE course (i.e. one that does not conform to the requirements of DFE Circular 9/92), which and showing the impact on PGCE courses of making payments to schools.

The earlier sections of this chapter, which develop the financial model, are necessarily somewhat technical. The reader who is prepared to take the de-velopment of the model on trust could skip to the section entitled 'Time available for teaching and research', which presents the results of the modell-ing exercise. The subsequent sections, which show how the model can be applied to courses, should then be largely self-explanatory.

TEACHING RESOURCE

Although the money that pays for teaching in HEIs has always come jointly from tuition fees and a central grant, the balance between these two has varied over the years. Until 1993, the trend had been to increase the proportion of the total provided by tuition fees and to reduce the proportion funded centrally through the block grant. This made it increasingly attractive for HEIs to take on extra students even if there were to be no more money from the HEFCE (i.e. taking students on a 'fees-only' basis). As institutions were prepared to take more and more students on a fees-only basis, the number of students grew rapidly and the government realized it had no way of controlling the numbers of students or the costs of higher education. The government's response was to reverse the trend of recent years and, from 1994–5 onwards, it will provide a greater proportion of the teaching resource centrally, with a smaller amount coming from tuition fees.

The actual level of fees and of central support also varies from subject to subject and with the level of the course. In the HEFCE's funding model there are two academic subject categories (ASCs) related to education: initial teacher training (ITT) education and non-ITT education, and each ASC is funded at three levels: undergraduate (UG), postgraduate taught (PGT) and postgraduate research (PGR). In education, not all of these are used, since there is no ITT course delivered via research! The amount of the tuition fees for the various levels for 1993–4 is shown in Table 9.1.

As noted above, for most students (usually called 'funded students') the fee income is augmented by the block grant. Since the block grant for each institution was determined largely on the basis of historical factors, this led to huge variations in the amount per student given by the HEFCE to support the tuition-fee income. For most HEIs this additional amount for ITT students was between £1,300 and £1,600 (median = £1,468), but some got as much as £2,200 and some as little as £470 for each ITT student (HEFCE, 1993).

RESEARCH RESOURCE

Each HEI is notified directly by the HEFCE of the total research income for each one of its ASCs. This total income is made up of three components: QR

TABLE 9.1
Tuition-fee levels for education subjects, 1993–4

	UG	PGT	PGR
Non-ITT education	1,300	2,260	2,260
ITT education	1,300	2,770	—

(quality research), CR (contract research) and DevR (development research), although in future years there will be a new category related to initiatives from the Office of Science and Technology (OST) called GR (generic research).

QR research component

Most of the research income (about 97 per cent) is allocated in the form of QR income. The amount is derived by allocating a certain-sized 'cake' for research in each subject across the whole country (£28 million in the case of education in 1993–4, out of a total QR allocation of £585 million), and by sharing this out in proportion to each institution weighted by the *quality* and the *volume* of research. The weighting used for the quality of research is J–1, where J is the research assessment rating, so that departments in the lowest category (a rating of 1) will get no QR resource at all. The volume weighting is based on the number of research active staff, the number of research assistants, the number of research students and 'charitable equivalent income', weighted at 1, 0.1, 0.15 and 0.05 respectively. The 'charitable equivalent income' is obtained by dividing the income from charities for research by £25,000 to give a notional number of full-time equivalent staff employed on the contracts.

The effect of this in 1993–4 was that each 'research-active' member of staff in a '5'-rated department generated around £18,000 of QR income, with those in '4', '3' and '2'-rated departments generating £13,500, £9,000 and £4,500 respectively.

CR and DevR research component

Nationally, these two components together account for about 3 per cent of the available research resource. CR is distributed in proportion to the income earnt by departments for contract research and the DevR component, as its name suggests, is intended primarily for 'pump-priming' in those HEIs where there is little existing research. In future, an increasing proportion of the money currently allocated under CR will be distributed under the 'GR' heading.

DEVELOPING A MODEL

Although the basis on which money is given to HEIs is now almost completely transparent, there is great variation in the extent to which this transparency is continued in the funding of individual faculties and cost centres within institutions. However, whether or not an institution chooses to tell each faculty how much income its activities generate, individual faculties can now calculate the income generated by its students by looking at the HEFCE data.

At King's College, London, it has been college policy for many years that the allocation of resources to departments should, as far as possible, follow the activity that generated it, and that the method of doing this should be completely transparent. The next subsection details the various sources of income of the Faculty of Education.

Teaching and research income in the Faculty of Education

The Faculty of Education has a planned load of 214 funded ITT students (nine undergraduate and 205 postgraduate) and takes another 24 postgraduate ITT students on a 'fees-only' basis. The planned load of non-ITT students is for two undergraduates and 113.5 postgraduates fully-funded, with another 11.5 undergraduates being taken on a fees-only basis. The income generated by these students is shown in Table 9.2.

In addition to this income, the faculty also generates income by teaching students from outside the EU. These students (often called 'overseas' students)

TABLE 9.2
Income generated by the various categories of students

TYPE OF STUDENTS	NO.	TUITION-FEE INCOME (£)	HEFCE INCOME (£)	TOTAL INCOME (£)
Undergraduate-funded ITT students	9.0	1,300	1,458	24,822
Postgraduate-funded ITT students	205.0	2,770	1,458	866,740
Postgraduate fees-only ITT students	24.0	2,770		66,480
Undergraduate non-ITT students	2.0	1,300	1,166	4,932
Postgraduate non-ITT students	113.5	2,260	1,166	388,851
Undergraduate fees-only non-ITT students	11.5	1,300		14,950
Income from service teaching				19,391
Total				1,386,166

are charged at a uniform rate of £6,200 (the 'high-fee' rate), and since we have 44 such students in 1993–4, they generate an income of £272,800. This, added to the £13,880 which we expect to earn from teaching non-award-bearing courses (e.g. INSET), results in a high-fee income of £286,660.

The research income in the Faculty of Education comes mainly from QR. The faculty has a quality rating of '5' with a volume rating of 40. The 200 'shares' in the £28 million education research 'cake' were worth £744,200, but in order to soften the extent of the changes, the HEFCE imposed a 'safety net' for institutions whose income dropped too sharply. The education faculty's QR was therefore capped by £18,298, yielding an actual research income of £725,902 which, together with £44,000 for CR research, resulted in total research income of £769,902.

This new 'transparency' in the funding arrangements enables the value of scholarly activity to an HEI to be seen much more clearly. For example, although the education panel involved in the last research-assessment exercise did not use mechanistic formulas, it seems reasonable to assume that if each member of academic staff published two scholarly papers in academic journals each year, and the department was awarded a reasonable number of research grants, then that department would probably get a '5' rating. Since the '5' rating brings in over £18,000 per member of staff, then it does not seem unreasonable to conclude that each paper published in an academic journal brings in around £8,000 to the faculty.

In addition to teaching and research income, many institutions receive an element of 'non-formula funding' to support, for example, special libraries, subjects in low demand and inherited liabilities. For King's College, the most important element of non-formula funding is that which supports the additional costs associated with being in London. The total of these non-formula funds for education is £225,045. Allocating this amount in proportion to the net income generated by each of the various activities produces the gross income shown in Table 9.3.

TABLE 9.3

Allocation of non-formula funding to other income

	NET (£)	GROSS (£)
Non-formula funding	225,045	
Teaching income	1,386,166	1,513,871
of which: (non-ITT)	(411,516)	(449,429)
(ITT)	(974,650)	(1,064,443)
High-fee teaching income	286,660	313,070
Research income	769,902	840,832
Totals	2,667,773	2,667,773

Deductions

Having determined how much of the college's income can be attributed to the activity of the Faculty of Education, the next step is to make deductions from this gross resource in order to pay for centrally provided administrative and academic services, such as finance, personnel, registry, library and computing services. The details of how these are allocated are contained in a more technical paper (Wiliam, 1993), but broadly, the principle used is that teaching activity makes about four times as much use of space, library and computing services as does research, while other deductions (for personnel, finance, etc.) are levied as a proportion of the income.

Table 9.4 shows the income generated by the four kinds of activity undertaken by the faculty (row 1), the deductions that can be attributed to each kind of activity (row 2) and the net income actually coming in to the department (row 3). Before the amount of teaching time can be estimated, some allowance for non-pay costs (resources, photocopying, etc.) and clerical and technical staff time must be made. These are distributed in the same 4:1 ratio assumed

TABLE 9.4
Allocation of deductions to income

ITEM	LOW-FEE NON-ITT TEACH- ING	LOW-FEE ITT TEACH- ING	HIGH-FEE TEACHING	RE- SEARCH	TOTAL
1. Income	£449,429	£1,064,443	£313,070	£840,832	£2,667,773
2. Total deduc- tions	£216,835	£513,559	£158,249	£299,237	£1,187,879
3. Net income	£232,594	£550,884	£154,821	£541,595	£1,479,894
4. Non- pay	£54,096	£128,122	£36,008	£54,556	£272,782
5. C+T staff	£46,598	£110,363	£31,017	£46,994	£234,972
6. *Acad- emic pay*	*£131,901*	*£312,398*	*£87,797*	*£440,045*	*£972,140*
7. **Acad- emic ftes**	3.9	9.1	2.6	12.8	28.3

for teaching and research and are shown in rows 4 and 5 of Table 9.4. The amounts left for academic pay for each of the four kinds of activities are shown in row 6, and the number of average full-time equivalent (fte) staff supported by each activity (row 7) is found by dividing the amounts in row 6 by the average academic staff cost (including superannuation and National Insurance).

TIME AVAILABLE FOR TEACHING AND RESEARCH

The last line of Table 9.4 shows how the costs of the 28.3 fte staff members in the faculty can be attributed to the four kinds of teaching and research activity. The data suggest that about 45 per cent of academic staff time (12.8 ftes out of a total of 28.3) is supported by research income, and 55 per cent of staff time is supported by teaching. However, part of this 'research' time is generated by the contribution of research students to the 'volume' factor of QR (see above). It seems more reasonable, therefore, to count the research income generated by research students as teaching rather than research income.

Out of the 113.5 postgraduate non-ITT students (Table 9.2), 33.5 are 'research' and 80 are 'taught'. Since research students are weighted at 0.15 of a 'research-active' member of academic staff for the calculation of the 'volume' weighting for QR, the 33.5 research students are equivalent to just over five members of research-active staff, which accounts for about 12.5 per cent of the block-grant research income (say £55,000). Table 9.5 shows the effect of

TABLE 9.5

Calculation of number of half-days of teaching generated by each student

	LOW-FEE NON-ITT UGT AND PGT	LOW-FEE NON-ITT PGR	LOW-FEE ITT TEACH-ING	HIGH-FEE TEACH-ING	RE-SEARCH
1. Academic pay	£83,087	£48,813	£312,398	£87,797	£440,045
2. Adjustment		£55,000			(£55,000)
3. Adjusted pay	£83,087	£103,813	£312,398	£87,797	£385,045
4. Academic fte	2.4	3.0	9.1	2.6	11.2
5. Teaching half-days	600	750	2,275	650	
6. No. of fte students	93.5	33.5	238	44	
7. Half-days per fte	6.5	22	9.5	15	

disaggregating the £131,900 available for teaching postgraduates into 're-search' and 'taught' courses in proportion to student numbers (row 1), and the effect of treating the £55,000 of *research* income generated by research students as *teaching* income (row 3). The revised number of fte staff supported by each kind of activity is shown in row 4.

The next step in the development of the model is to derive an estimate of the teaching time available for the three kinds of teaching activity. Within the Faculty of Education, it has long been the practice to compare the teaching loads of all academic staff by making known within the department each person's teaching commitment in standard units. The unit chosen, because of its wide applicability across different courses, is a notional three-hour 'half-day' teaching session, which can be a morning (9.30–12.30) or afternoon (1.30–4.30) session for full-time courses or an evening session for part-time courses (5.30–8.30).

If we assume that a research-inactive member of academic staff would be expected to undertake a teaching load of 250 half-days per year, then the number of half-days of teaching supported for each of the kinds of teaching activity is shown in row 5. This can then be divided by the number of fte students for each type of course (row 6) in order to find the number of teaching half-days generated by each student (row 7). The most important feature of the model encapsulated in row 7 of Table 9.5 is that it allows very quick estimates of the amount of teaching that can be justified for a course based on its recruitment.

For example, a non-ITT 'taught' course (e.g. a masters) that recruited 12 'home' and 6 'overseas' students would generate income to cover 168 (= 12 × 6.5 + 6 × 15) half-days of teaching time. This does not mean that such a course would be unviable if it needed 200 half-days of tuition to be run at an acceptable quality. What it does mean is that if significantly more than 168 half-days were needed, then additional arguments would have to be made for why the course should run.

The other important feature of the model is that it allows very quick projections to be made of the impact on ITT courses of payments to schools. For example, if the money for payments to schools for teaching practice placements is to come out of the money for academic pay after all the deductions detailed above, then it is clear that no PGCE course would be viable. Row 3 of Table 9.5 shows that there is £312,398 available for the tuition of the 238 ITT students at King's in 1993–4. If payments of £1,000 had to be made to schools for each student, then this would have left just under £75,000, or just over two fte academic staff, to do *all* the college-based teaching of these 238 students.

However, the model also allows us to estimate the impact of making the same size payments (i.e. £1,000 per full-time student) out of the *gross* income, before any deductions are made. The details of the calculations are not reproduced here, but the effect is, put simply, to reduce the number of half-days of teaching per student from 9.5 to 7.5.

APPLYING THE MODEL: COSTING A 'PRE-9/92' PGCE COURSE

In this section, the implications of the model are followed through and applied to a large PGCE course. The work of college-based staff in most PGCEs can be classified under three main headings:

1 Individual supervision of teaching practice.
2 'Methods work' (i.e. subject-specific studies).
3 'Foundation studies' (i.e. non-subject-specific studies).

If we have a full-time PGCE course with 200 students, then, according to the model, these students generate enough income to support just under 1,900 half-days of teacher time. If we assume that each personal tutor is given five half-days per student for four half-days' TP supervision, assessment, writing references, etc., then 1,000 teaching half-days are given over to this purpose.

In the 'pre-9/92' King's PGCE, students spent about 20 weeks (i.e. 100 days) out of the total 36 weeks of the course in schools, and the remaining 80 days were divided roughly equally between subject-specific and generic teaching sessions. This would suggest 450 half-days of teaching available for the methods work, and the same for the other 'foundation' teaching.

Once these data are followed through, it is clear that even 'pre-9/92' PGCE courses were subsidized to a substantial extent. If we assume that the 40 days of 'methods' work done covers 10 different subject groups with 20 students in each group, that allows only 45 half-days of teaching for the 80 half-days of methods work in each subject. This is an average figure. If we also take into account that some subjects are not likely to recruit 20 students, then other groups will either have to be larger, or have even less contact time.

LOOKING FORWARD: COSTING A 'POST-9/92' PGCE COURSE

The fundamental assumption underlying the shift in government policy signalled in Circular 9/92 is that schools can take over a substantial proportion of the teaching that has, up until now, been done by HEIs. The preceding section showed that even before Circular 9/92, there was not enough money to support teaching in groups of 20, and yet, 'post-9/92', it is supposed that it somehow makes financial sense to teach them in groups of five or six in a school. When one adds in the fact that much of this teaching will tend to be done by deputy headteachers, who are paid more than the college staff that are typically involved in PGCE, the scheme is clearly disastrously ill-founded on financial grounds alone.

The model developed above showed that, provided the payments to schools are taken out of the resource attributable to the Faculty of Education *before* any deductions for central services, each full-time PGCE student will generate enough revenue to support about 7.5 half-days of teaching. Since HEIs will still be responsible for a substantial amount of assessment and record-keeping on students, at least one half-day will need to be given over to this. Since the typical group of 20 referred to above now generates only 150 half-days of teaching time (20 × 7.5), 130 half-days of tutor time are available for the tuition and teaching practice supervision of the group.

A post-9/92 PGCE will have at most 60 days, or 120 half-days in the HEI. Even if we assume a contact ratio of only 75 per cent for a group of 20 students (i.e. only 75 per cent of the college-based sessions are tutor-led), this will require 90 half-days of tutor time. This leaves only 40 half-days for the teaching practice supervision, or two half-day visits per student.

Any more tuition than this means that the HEI is subsidizing the PGCE from other sources. Since the time demands of other teaching commitments are fairly inelastic, the extra time needed to deliver the PGCE effectively is likely to come from research income. The consequence of this will, in all probability, be a drop in future research ratings, which will reduce the income of the HEI still further, resulting in a slow but inevitable move towards a 'teaching-only' department, with no research income at all. An alternative strategy, which may well be followed by some HEIs, will be to get out of ITE altogether, preferring instead to concentrate on higher degree teaching and research.

PART THREE

Mentoring and Supporting Student-Teachers

CHAPTER 10

Mentoring Articled Science Teachers

BOB CAMPBELL and ALASTAIR HORBURY
University of York

It was really hard work at first, unbelievably time consuming but I suppose you could say there was a movement from a parasitic to a symbiotic relationship.

(Articled teacher mentor)

INTRODUCTION

The articled teacher scheme was introduced in 1990 to provide two-year, 80 per cent school-based courses of initial teacher training (ITT) delivered through a partnership between LEAs and higher education institutions (HEIs).

Articled teacher courses must be accredited by the Council for the Accreditation of Teacher Education (CATE) and successful completion leads to the award of a PGCE. During their training, trainees are supernumerary to the staff of their schools but are termed articled teachers rather than students. A key feature of the articled teacher scheme is that LEAs have had to bid for earmarked government funding. This is used to help provide LEA support, to pay articled teacher bursaries, tuition fees and travel costs, to put additional resources and staffing into training schools and to help meet the costs incurred by HEIs in developing courses and supporting school staff.

Though no longer available for the secondary sector, articled teacher courses remain as a training route into primary schools. HMI have reported that '. . . the levels of competence demonstrated by most articled teachers were generally similar to those of students who have followed a one-year PGCE course' (Ofsted, 1993a, p. 3) and that 'All articled teachers had attained a better understanding of the pattern of school life and the role of the teacher than students trained by other routes' (*ibid.*). Crucial to this success has been the acceptance, interpretation and execution by school staff of new roles and responsibilities. The same will be true of the new school-based models of ITT. This chapter is based on a series of taped, semi-structured, individual interviews with five teachers who took on key roles in an articled teacher course for secondary-school science teachers. The points emerging from the analysis of the interviews have informed the development of the PGCE at York and are considered to be of importance to others involved with or interested in school-based ITT.

CONTEXT

The Department of Educational Studies at York is part of an articled teacher-training consortium and, in partnership with LEA-nominated training schools, provides a PGCE in secondary school science. Each training school has a professional tutor and one or more science mentors. The professional tutors are deputy headteachers or senior teachers with considerable experience of working with students and beginning teachers. They contribute a professional studies element to the course and have overall responsibility for the school-based activities. The science mentors are, likewise, experienced teachers holding promoted posts as heads of faculty or heads of department. All have supervised students on teaching practice and inducted new colleagues. They have responsibility for the subject-related elements of the course and the day-to-day supervision of the articled teachers. In order to establish joint ownership of the course, this group, along with the tutors in the Department of Educational Studies, who would work with the articled teachers, shared the task of course development and documentation and, together, worked through a training programme to prepare themselves for their new roles. The first cohort started in September 1990, a second in September 1991 and a third in September 1992.

THE MENTOR INTERVIEWS

All the science mentors were interviewed. The interviews covered three areas. These were:

1 the range and dimension of the role of mentor as perceived and carried out;
2 the perception of personal effectiveness at mentoring and the criteria employed to make this judgement; and
3 the factors which they considered facilitated and hindered effective mentoring.

Mentoring

Analysis of the interview transcripts identified four functions which mentors considered they fulfilled. These were as (1) an organizer, manager and administrator; (2) a personal tutor; (3) an ITT-INSET provider; and (4) an assessor of professional competence.

Organizer, manager and administrator

Although described as very time consuming, all mentors considered efficient organization, management and administration essential to the smooth running of the course. In addition to the fact that the mentors 'had to develop a handbook' for the articled teachers in their schools, mentors took on a range of organizational, management and administrative tasks well beyond what they had anticipated. Particularly at the start of the course, which in the words of one mentor 'needs an awful lot of administration', they devoted a considerable amount of time to this aspect of their role. All gave particular attention to communication within school to try to ensure that colleagues knew about the course, understood the position of the articled teachers and recognized the school's corporate responsibility for their training (but see later). The complexity of organizing an apparently simple element of the course in which articled teachers shadowed various staff members and pupils is illustrated by the following interview extract:

> . . . the programme involved teacher pursuit, shadowing of the head of faculty, the school office, caretaker, lab technicians, pupils. Spending days with them so that they could see what the whole system is about. All of that had to be programmed, timetabled. The various people, and every pupil that they were pursuing, have to be contacted. You've got to look at the pupils and get their permission and you've got to then look at what classes they're going to be in and consider if the teachers they are going to be with are suitable role models to see at such an early stage and, having established that, would the members of staff mind an AT being in there?

> (Interview transcript, mentor 1)

All mentors reported that the most demanding organizational, management and administrative task over the two years was setting up and monitoring individualized programmes of classroom experiences so that each articled teacher gained a deepening insight into practice, a wider view of the curriculum and greater opportunities to develop their teaching skills at a pace appropriate to their growing confidence and competence. One mentor noted that 'Every term we've got to arrange a new timetable, to negotiate a timetable with them, so that took up time.' This required him '. . . to liaise with the staff whose lessons they were taking'. His practice was that 'Once a week or once a fortnight we go and see the staff and see that everything is okay'.

A further organizational dimension recognized as very time consuming was the regular monitoring, recording and discussion of progress. Mentors had helped develop a lesson observation schedule and an end-of-term record of achievement document which aided these tasks but, as one mentor reported, it was not just a matter of making sure that information came to him, but it was demanding of time in '. . . talking them [the articled teachers] through it, and then it's got to be typed, then copies sent here, there and everywhere. Copy to university tutor, copy to the head, copy in their file.'

Mentors also reported that they had to establish good communications with other schools and outside agencies. This was to ensure that elements of the course, such as '. . . visits to industry, visits to primary schools, visits to special units [hearing impaired and visually handicapped], administration of the teaching practice at the sixth-form college', took place successfully. The arrangements for such activities demanded detailed planning and careful organization so that all parties shared a common view of their purpose.

Personal tutor

Mentors willingly accepted the role of personal tutor. They saw themselves as offering both professional and pastoral support. They were conscious that articled teachers were very different from PGCE students. One mentor described his group as '. . . three raw products which have never been in school before and they're just helpless, you've got to look after them'. Part of this initial looking after involved simple, but thoughtful considerations, of '. . . getting keys for them, stationery for them, establishing their room, making sure they could get coffee, all these little things to make them welcome, such as pigeon holes in the staffroom'.

Working with articled teachers in the classroom was seen as central to the mentoring role. One mentor made it quite clear that, in the early stages, despite the programme of preparation, he was learning to be a mentor 'on the job'. Initially, he considered that an articled teacher would learn simply by observing teaching. He later changed his practice as he realized that it was insufficient just to observe teaching. It was necessary 'to spell it out'. He reported that '. . . it really wasn't enough to let them watch. They might get a sense that this is a good lesson but the mechanics of its achievement can be tacit.' Related to this perceived need to help articled teachers understand classroom practice and identify the factors which led to good practice, all mentors voiced a concern that the articled teachers might actively try to replicate or inadvertently acquire a mentor's own particular teaching style or idiosyncratic traits and become 'mentor clones'. Mentors were also concerned that by being based in one school, while they might become skilled practitioners there, articled teachers could be less well prepared to be successful elsewhere. For these reasons, the personal development plan for each articled teacher incorporated classroom work with a variety of staff in the school, teaching placements in other schools, exchanges with other articled teachers and a programme of visits to schools and colleges.

Mentors reported that, over the two-year period, they progressively changed the balance between their levels of classroom support, criticism and challenge. Simply put, as the articled teachers gained experience and grew in confidence, mentors felt able to engage more in critical but constructive debate on their professional skills and to encourage them to tackle more challenging teaching tasks.

Weekly tutorials were considered by all mentors to be very important. Tutorials had two purposes. First, mentors used tutorials to discuss topics of immediate concern, such as lesson planning, classroom management, discipline, questioning techniques, exposition, teaching approaches or choice of curriculum materials, and often grounded this in observations made over the previous week. Tutorials acted, therefore, both as a vehicle for planning and as an arena for informal discussion of progress. Secondly, tutorials allowed mentors to cover the ITT syllabus by providing information and discussing science education topics, such as assessment, differentiation, laboratory safety and schemes of work, and link these to university-based elements of the course. These meetings also allowed discussion of contemporary issues as they hit the headlines. Tutorial sessions required mentors to clarify, organize and articulate their professional knowledge in a way which had not been demanded by teaching practice students.

All mentors were sensitive to the need to provide comprehensive training and considered it important to organize experience in areas other than science teaching. One mentor makes the point when he said: 'Rather than just develop them as science teachers we want to try and make them into whole teachers.' They recognized that to do this required the co-operation of colleagues: '. . . It has to be subcontracted.' This requirement led to the need for mentors to take on ITT-INSET.

ITT-INSET provider

Mentors reported that, initially, their colleagues were neither as committed to the articled teacher course as they were nor did they have much understanding of how it was to work. Consequently, mentors noticed that staff did not always provide the level of lesson support and supervision they did or that colleagues had done previously with students on teaching practice. Mentors stated that they had to remind colleagues that the articled teachers were not staff but students and, as such, needed support and encouragement. One mentor frames the sentiment thus: 'The other staff weren't so involved. I had to remind them that they weren't just on a freebie and so they could just go and have a coffee somewhere. They should be working with them. They should be helping all the time' (interview transcript, mentor 2). Consequently, despite their efforts at the start of the academic year, mentors had to brief staff on the course, explain their expected contribution and outline the potential benefits. They also had to provide INSET sessions on working with articled teachers and monitor how well staff did this.

Assessor of professional competence

Mentors readily accepted a responsibility for assessing professional competence. Assessment was done both formally and informally. Formally, it was embodied in a termly, negotiated, record of achievement. Informal assessment was ongoing. Mentors spoke of regular informal lesson observations and feed-back discussions. As noted above, feedback on informal assessment was often left until tutorial time. There was no doubt, however, that despite their exten-sive experience of working with PGCE students and the precourse preparation, it was in the role as assessors that the mentors felt least secure. While mentors spoke of the support given to them by university tutors and valued peer-group discussion of the issues involved, when it came to actual assessment they felt vulnerable. As one interviewee explained, '. . . there was nobody to watch the mentors making judgements'.

Mentor effectiveness

When asked for a perception of effectiveness, one mentor had 'no idea about that', another was 'unsure' but other mentors considered themselves 'relatively successful', 'effective' or 'very effective'. Mentors used three criteria to judge their effectiveness. The first and simplest of these was whether and how quickly the articled teachers got jobs. This external benchmark was considered to be a palpable testimony to effective mentoring. The speed with which the articled teachers gained teaching posts implied a comparison with other routes into teaching. The second criterion was based on a notion of a value-added change from the 'raw recruit to the finished article'. Mentors spoke of attempt-ing to identify the professional knowledge and competencies of the articled teachers at the end as compared with the beginning of the two years. Three indicators were suggested to determine this. These were: (1) an analysis of the records of achievement; (2) gleaning comments from other staff; and (3) noting comments made by parents at parent evenings. It is interesting to note that two of these ways of evaluating the 'value-added' dimension drew on the judge-ments of others. The third criterion, like the second, was comparative in na-ture. Here, mentors claimed to judge their success by comparing the performance of articled teachers with one-year PGCE students on teaching practice. Another form of comparison was with staff. This may be considered somewhat demanding in the light of the comment on articled teachers made by HMI (Ofsted, 1993a, p. 3) that '. . . a small minority (around 10 per cent) was performing at the level expected of an experienced teacher', but it does indicate that the mentors set high standards.

Facilitating mentoring

The overwhelming message from mentors was that mentoring was time consum-ing. None had anticipated the amount of work that would be involved. While mentors had a reduced teaching timetable, that was insufficient to cope with what they felt they had to do. Autonomy and flexibility were reported as vital to their role. Autonomy was created when budgets were controlled directly by the mentors. One way in which this was important is illustrated by a mentor thus: 'I accrue the money and then maybe have two days off and have a supply teacher in and get on with things I'm going under with. But a period here and there would be no good. I wouldn't get much done and it would disrupt my class' (interview transcript, mentor 1). While such flexibility was seen to be important, blocking off time in this way was used more as an emergency survival system than as a routine event. What mentors reported as a regular occurrence was the need to take home 'volumes of school administration'. As the mentors had to run departments or faculties it was the paperwork associated with these responsibilities which was put on one side to give school time to mentoring.

There was, however, a change in the time required of mentors during the course. They reported that they devoted much time to the articled teachers in the first months of the course but, as the articled teachers acquired more skills, the time demand of mentoring lessened.

One of the most striking aspects of the mentor interviews was the transmission of a sense of sheer dedication and commitment to mentoring and, despite some self-doubt about their abilities as assessors, their firm belief in the value of what they were doing. With this was a recognition that they were not 'ordinary teachers' but experienced and confident teachers able to reflect critically on practice. One mentor stated how '. . . it's important to get critical purchase on one's own practice so helping to identify the needs of the articled teachers'. Another expressed a similar view in stating, 'To do this job you have to be a confident sort of teacher. You mustn't mind having adults in your room watching you. You must be able to criticize yourself, make explicit what you're trying to achieve and how you will do it' (interview transcript, mentor 4).

IMPLICATIONS

The perceptions presented above reflect a reassuring, self-critical openness and flexibility of approach and a ready acceptance of a responsibility to provide a supportive base for professional development. Mentors accepted roles as teacher trainers requiring them to deliver a curriculum. They were aware of the potential insularity of the experiences they could provide and took steps to avoid this. Perhaps, above all, the mentors saw a need to support beginning teachers in more ways than in the acquisition of basic classroom knowledge and craft skills. This is in contrast to Jacques (1992) who, while also reporting that the mentors she worked with saw mentoring as more than dealing with practical craft skills, noted that they did not regard themselves as teacher trainers but as facilitators. The professional values emerging from the mentor interviews reported here are seen as essential to successful mentoring and, as school-based ITT is extended, providers will need to ensure that mentoring practice embodies such values.

What cannot be ignored as a major finding of this study is the considerable demand made on mentors. Mentors are seen as of crucial importance in helping develop student-teachers' professional skills and confidence (Booth, 1993). They need the time to do this. Mentoring articled teachers took experienced teachers away from classes and away from administrative work and, although the articled teacher scheme is generously funded in comparison to other ITT programmes, being a mentor resulted in extra (and not just different) work. Mentors choose to resolve the organizational conflicts of mentoring noted by Watkins and Whalley (1993) by taking work home. This cannot be a satisfactory long-term solution. As the demands of school-based ITT are recognized by teachers and school managers alike, HEIs are likely to be put under severe pressure to release an ever-increasing proportion of their ITT funding to support school-based work. There is a real danger that if teachers and schools reject the notion of apparently subsidizing ITT, professional integrity and economic reality will cause the emerging school-based system of ITT to collapse before it is built.

Finally, it needs to be noted that while the mentor interviews presented an overall picture of professional confidence, mentors were open about their feelings of insecurity in assessing competence. It is suggested that while the mentors had experience of observing student-teachers and had written teaching practice reports for HEIs, they had seen themselves as contributors to a process which was controlled by the HEI and where the reports of significant others (visiting HEI tutors) were of greatest importance. With articled teachers they were the significant assessors: they had to accept more of the responsibility. Looking at early models of school-based ITT it is of note that in the Leicester course described by Everton and White (1992), assessment stays with the HEI subject tutor while in the Oxford Internship Scheme (Benton, 1990b) the responsibility for assessment appears to be shared equally between four people: the school mentor and professional tutor and the HEI curriculum and general tutors. Accepting a greater responsibility for student assessment will be an important change of practice in all school-based ITT courses (Wilkin, 1992b). Our study leads us to recommend that special attention will need to be given to building up the self-confidence of mentors so that they can accept their new responsibility without undue concern.

CHAPTER 11

'In at the Beginning'
A Pilot Partnership

KATH ASPINWALL, VIV GARRETT and
GWYNETH OWEN-JACKSON
Sheffield Hallam University

This chapter focuses on recent changes in initial teacher training (ITT). It is based on the findings of an evaluation of one university's response to the DFE's Circular 9/92 requiring that secondary PGCE students spend 24 weeks of their training year in schools. Sheffield Hallam University School of Education elected to pilot this process immediately. Their students already spent 60 per cent of their time in schools, and the new initiative involved two changes to existing arrangements: the mentoring programme and the School Based Initiative (SBI). The findings of the evaluation were largely positive, and the majority of the students had both enjoyed and benefited from their experience. However, close examination of the evidence revealed that their positive experience was the result of considerable effort from others. In order to explain the nature of the task facing schools and higher education institutions (HEIs), we have drawn together what emerged as the ten key elements of an 'ideal' mentoring experience for students; an explanation of these forms the substance of the chapter.

The first of the two new developments, the mentoring programme, involved 12 volunteer schools already providing teaching practice placements for students at the university. Each school took four students as two pairs placed together in a particular subject department or faculty, each pair being placed with one mentor who took responsibility for teaching practice supervision and assessment. These mentors were either generic or subject focused and a sum of money was made available to each school to support the process. In addition, funding was provided for teaching cover to enable both mentors to attend a mentoring training programme at the university.

The largest eight of these schools were also asked to be involved in the SBI. These schools were given an allocation of 10 to 12 students, who spent two days per week in school over the spring term carrying out a variety of tasks. One of the mentors was also asked to act as liaison teacher for the SBI programme.

Two evaluators were appointed in January 1993 to report on the effectiveness of the pilot programme; they were subsequently joined by an MEd student who was studying this development for her final dissertation (Owen-Jackson, 1993). Data was gathered from questionnaires, interviews, observation, review meetings and evaluation activities, and documentation from the DFE and the university.

At the end of the pilot the evidence showed that the mentoring scheme was generally accepted to have been a success, although there were some reservations about longer-term implications. The picture concerning SBI was more mixed. Most students felt they had benefited from the experience, some did not. It was also the part of the initiative which came closest at times to pushing teacher goodwill to (although not beyond) the limit. Certain questions kept recurring in different contexts throughout the year:

- How many students can a school cope with, at once, and over a year?
- How much initial training can schools be expected to provide in addition to the teaching practice experience?
- How far can access to up-to-date, quality subject knowledge be guaranteed in all schools?
- How far can teacher goodwill be stretched?

Evidence from other evaluation studies indicates similar findings (for example, Everton and White, 1992; Harvard and Dunne, 1992; Booth, 1993). There is much to be positive about but also caution: 'how far can this go?' It is important to remember that these schools, mentors and tutors were all experiencing the development for the first time. However there were considerable advantages in this situation. The schools and mentors had all volunteered for the process and they had some feeling of being selected. There was the important sense of being part of a new initiative, of being observed and being in a strong position to influence the shaping of the programme. As the teachers involved recognized, such enthusiasm and energy may be difficult to ensure more widely across schools in the future, particularly in times of rapid change when new priorities are constantly being set. There are also doubts whether the level of funding will be sufficient to provide all the support necessary for students (see, for example, Wright, 1993b, p. 156).

The evidence from all the schools was consistent. Although student experience had varied to some extent from school to school, it was possible to identify a series of key elements which were necessary to provide what we might call an 'ideal' mentoring process. What then were these key elements?

1 The mentor has chosen the task and feels that it has been given a legitimate place in his or her workload with some time allowed.
2 The subject department is willing and able to support students and some time is available for this process.

Mentors were asked why they and their schools had chosen to become involved in the mentoring programme. Their reasons were clear and consistent. All expressed a desire to be 'in at the beginning' of the new developments because 'it's the way things are going'. This desire was founded on several factors: a sense of responsibility or even duty to be more closely involved in teacher training; previous good experience and a sense that students bring energy, life and up-to-date ideas into a school; a belief that the school knew how to be helpful to students; a desire to further the links with higher education in general and Sheffield Hallam University in particular; and the wish to keep the school on the map and to attract promising students to apply for jobs.

Most (but not all) mentors were members of the senior management teams in their schools and all had volunteered or been selected for the role because of past or potential interest in this area of work. Existing responsibilities, a position enabling an overview to be taken, personal qualities and the availability of more discretionary time were seen to be key factors in selection. Schools had also considered the 'readiness' of individual departments to give students the necessary support. Sometimes mentors were selected from these departments and were therefore 'subject mentors'. Others were not and were 'generic'.

The need for both subject and general support is demonstrated by the assessment process. All students received five formal assessments with written and verbal feedback and reports to the university. Some had a good deal more. Class teachers were also involved in informal assessment and feedback, 'the more eyes the better', and some were part of the formal assessment procedure, in particular where it was felt necessary to check the student's subject knowledge and expertise, for example, in a foreign language. In one school, three of the formal assessments were carried out by subject teachers. In addition, where the mentor's role was generic, subject teachers also often took on some of the tutoring and supporting role with the mentors focusing on general issues, such as classroom management. In one school each student was designated to a member of their subject department. In lessons such as technology, class teachers had to be present in all lessons and some other students were observed all or most of the time. A small number of students reported having received little subject support during their first non-mentored teaching practice. One claimed to have lacked access to any plans or coherent materials. This was not true in any mentored school in the pilot study because departments had been chosen for their perceived ability and inclination to support students. However, this quality of support may be more difficult to assure for all students in all schools in the future. Of course this has always been true but the more student experience is delegated to schools the more critical this dimension will become.

The time given to students was considerable and in all schools far outreached any that was designated. Fifteen of the mentors had no specific time allowance and seven had time that varied from 40 minutes to four hours per week. In practice, mentors reported spending between two and six hours a week with the students; some of this time was for formal observations and feedback. Mentors found the time quite difficult to calculate as they responded as was needed, in break and lunchtimes and after school. For example, one mentor said: 'I look at their faces in the staffroom at break and I can tell if they need to talk something over.' Another mentor said: 'This role takes more time than any other of my management responsibilities.' In most cases subject teachers were not given any extra time to spend with students, although some cover was provided in some schools.

Students agreed that mentors and other teachers had given an enormous amount of their time. Most reported that their mentor was always there when needed, some using words like 'brilliant' and 'fantastic' to describe their appreciation. One or two reported less satisfaction. For example, one student who had also been mentored on the first practice had been very surprised by the amount of support available on the second: 'Last time my mentor was always too busy to see me. This time the mentor is actually much busier but always has time for me.'

3 The mentor (and others) give clear, constructive and regular feedback to students about how they are progressing and what else they might need to do.
4 The student is able to build a good relationship with the mentor and teachers and able to take and learn from advice and guidance given.

During the interviews, which took place during the second teaching practice, mentors often cited developing their skills in giving constructive feedback to students as one of their main pieces of learning from the first teaching practice. The issue also formed part of the discussion on the mentors' training days. In addition the university provided criteria for assessment which were used extensively by the schools. Most students spoke of receiving detailed and thorough written and verbal feedback, often immediately after the lesson, and also copies of the reports sent to the university. They placed a very high value on clear and helpful feedback and, unlike the students in some other studies (see, for example, Booth, 1993, p. 193), they felt that they were given the information which they needed to know how they were doing. They particularly valued being given a small number of clear targets to work on for the next observation. One student who had received almost constant observation, and who '. . . would not have opted for mentoring if I'd known I'd feel I was in a goldfish bowl', found the consequent feedback very helpful.

Calderhead (1988) suggests that teachers have traditionally found it difficult to offer systematic, diagnostic appraisal to student-teachers. The evidence from this study would suggest that the key responsibility for student assessment, helped by the mentor training, developed the mentors' ability to give effective feedback. Several mentors also referred to building on their experience from appraisal and records of achievement.

However, there were some problems. It emerged that it was most difficult for the mentors to give unequivocal feedback when students were at risk of failure. Some teachers found it hard to be clear about what was at stake. Supportive warning messages and clear guidance on what aspects needed to be improved were not always given early enough, nor clearly enough documented. The evaluators were not able to speak to any of the small number of students who failed their teaching practice after the event and so do not know how this affected them. It was, however, clear that the mentors did not enjoy the experience: in the final mentors' meeting this was a major item for discussion although only a small number of mentors had had to deal with failure.

5 The whole school staff (or at least a majority) are welcoming and helpful to students.

As the schools, mentors and departments had volunteered their involvement, this was not on the whole a problem in the mentoring programme. However, relationships with school staff in general, rather than whether a practice was mentored or not, was of central importance to students when describing their experiences. There were more problems in this area in the SBI. Twelve students is a considerable number for even a large school to absorb and sometimes students reported that a proportion of staff had seemed unwelcoming and that they had been made to feel intrusive and demanding. Conversely it was reported that some students had seemed to be 'unaware how busy teachers are'.

6 The school is not overburdened with students in a way that is detrimental to pupils.

This point is clearly connected to the above. There is a limit to the number of times a class of pupils can be taught by students. If there is a constant succession of students in school, which is quite possible when a number of HEIs are seeking placements, some students may have to teach classes that it would be fairer to everyone to avoid. The time mentors spent with students was considerable and took them away from other tasks, sometimes teaching or other aspects of work connected with pupils. Shaw (1992) stresses that the primary purpose of schools is to teach children, not to train teachers, and the possibility of being able to strike a balance must depend to some degree on the number of students in a school over a year. Some schools in the study were taking students from four different HEIs and some mentors were considering having to set a limit on numbers in the future.

7 There is a balance of practice/reflection and theory.

HMI (DES, 1991) suggest that, in their initial training, students learn the practical and management skills necessary to provide learning opportunities matched to individual needs principally in schools, while, in HEIs, they undertake rigorous study of various relevant issues and are given the opportunity to reflect. Others (for example, Elliott, 1991c) dispute that theory, reflection and practice can be so neatly divided. Some tutors wondered if the new assessment process sufficiently stretched and challenged good or excellent students. If a student is working in a department that is well run, picking up on already well planned and resourced programmes, assessment could focus on little more than classroom management skills. A teacher committed to the materials being used might find it difficult to challenge a student about what they were teaching and why. There could even be a tendency for students under this system to become 'clones' of a mentor with whom they had continuous, close contact. However, one mentor felt that in this tension lay important potential for staff development. The process of having to assess students against clear criteria and carry out systematic observation had 'given an edge' to discussions and heightened everyone's awareness of 'how the school works'; unexamined assumptions were necessarily challenged to the benefit of the whole institution.

8 A well informed tutor is available to ensure moderation is correctly and fairly applied and is readily available to provide a second opinion and help where relevant and appropriate.

In most instances in this study things went extremely well, with respect and understanding on both sides. Mentors and tutors carried out a shared observation of a lesson, the mentor gave the student verbal feedback with the tutor observing, after which the tutor gave the mentor moderation feedback. However, some moderation visits were found to have been 'too late'; one student attempted to play tutor and mentor off against each other; not all tutors observed students teaching and some who did interpreted the event in the terms of traditional teaching practice visits rather than moderation; some teachers wanted the tutor to make up their minds for them, 'what grade would you give this student?' It would seem that old habits were, to some extent at least, dying hard.

Students generally felt that teachers who 'know the pupils and know the school' were in the best position to make an informed judgement about how a student was performing. However, they liked to know that they could call on a tutor if they felt the need, although very few did so in practice. A tutor's knowledge of a student is bound to be fragmented in comparison with someone who is constantly on hand, but will be based on experience of considerably more than one school (see also Furlong *et al.*, 1988). A student who had received excellent support in school on her first non-mentored practice had felt it was a great bonus to have a tutor who was an outsider to the school also available: '. . . she was great, I could ring her any time.' This possibility is becoming less available.

9 There is an effective partnership and trust between a school and the HEI.

Implicit in much of the above is the central contribution made by the establishment of an effective partnership between schools and higher education. This was welcomed by all parties and was one of the reasons given by mentors for their school's choice of involvement in this initiative. Tutors often spoke with enthusiasm of building a more equal relationship with schools and their willingness to give up their previous degree of control over ITT. Booth (1993) describes two differing types of partnership relationship, that of 'equivalence' where both parties share responsibilities equally and that of 'complementarity' where responsibility is distributed according to expertise but balanced overall. The partnership described here was clearly complementary in nature.

A key part of the partnership was the mentor training which was highly valued by the mentors and performed a crucial role in ensuring that the university and schools understood each other. The meetings helped to alert the course tutor to key issues and reassured the mentors that their questions and difficulties were being taken seriously. The mentors shared their perceptions, anxieties and successes with each other and the training days helped to ensure coherence and consistency across the programme. However, these events were dependent on the transition funding, and training is not now as well resourced although more schools are involved.

The need for an effective partnership is widely recognized. Booth *et al.* (1990, p. 108) suggest that the complementary roles in schools and higher education must be clearly defined '. . . to encourage the progressive transformation of the student's knowledge into classroom teaching'. Alexander (1990) notes that partnership operates at two levels: the enabling level with formal structures, designated roles and procedures; and the action level of day-to-day interactions.

10 The management issues raised by the mentoring process have themselves to be managed.

There are clear management implications for schools and higher education throughout this and other studies. If supporting and training students is to play an effective part in enhancing the whole school learning environment, the process must be planned and managed. For example, roles and responsibilities must be clearly defined, mechanisms identified or created for the feedback of information and insight, and the staff development potential needs to be understood and linked into the wider school development plan. However, mentors who were clear about the potential of the process found it difficult to identify the management strategies they had found effective. When asked about this during the last day of their training, they replied wryly that when things had gone well it had been 'a matter of good luck rather than good management'. This was probably overly modest but as schools find themselves under considerable and sometimes contradictory pressures a feeling of being, at best, one step ahead may be inevitable.

CONCLUSION

The mentors in this study consistently reported that their schools had gained a good deal from being involved in this pilot. They were, however, only too aware that this new approach to teacher training has enormous implications for schools. The key elements we have identified call for considerable time, effort and skill from already busy teachers. The balance of responsibility for teacher training may be shifting too far in the direction of schools for them to manage within existing resources. There are early indications nationwide that '. . . many headteachers are considering withdrawing . . . to concentrate their efforts on the main task, which is teaching children' (*The Times Educational Supplement*, 4 March 1994). HEIs are also under pressure and staff find themselves meeting new requirements and renegotiating old relationships almost daily. The redistribution of funding is placing increasing pressure on tutor time (or even numbers) which may alter the balance of the partnerships being created. The needs of students, pupils and teachers must be taken into account. The prevalence of good experience as opposed to less good in this and other studies indicates that, given the will and the creation of effective partnerships, students can be well served. However, it is not enough for government policy to prescribe the amount of time students spend in school. The quality of student experience must be kept under constant and careful review or the early perceived bonuses of current developments will become burdens.

CHAPTER 12

Mentors in English and Mathematics

PAT DRAKE and LISA DART
University of Sussex

Current reforms of initial teacher training (ITT) include the specification of competence for newly qualified teachers (CATE; Circular 9/92) and, in particular, the circular attempts to define the competence in 'subject knowledge' and 'subject application' with which a new entrant will be equipped after 36 weeks' PGCE. Peculiarly, the specification is couched in general terms which take no account of possible differences between subjects.

At the University of Sussex, a range of experiments has been directed towards subject-specific aspects of mentoring and, in particular, towards the two apparently contrasting fields of mathematics and English. At the outset, experienced and less experienced mentors were paired in each discipline, with the latter consulting and drawing on the expertise of the former. Data collected on the transactions was analysed and specific mentoring concerns identified (Dart and Drake, 1993). A noticeable omission during that process was reference by mentors to their own and trainees' subject specialisms.

A second phase of the study is focusing on this phenomenon. A number of English and mathematics mentors have been interviewed, their respective trainees shadowed, and recordings made of the weekly mentor-trainee meetings. This work is in progress; full findings will be described in early 1995. However, it is already possible to identify a number of issues arising from the transcriptions of taped interviews with five English and four mathematics mentors.

Various recent commentators on school-based training have identified practices by which practical and reflective elements of initial training are expedited by school tutors (see, for example, Wilkin, 1992a; McIntyre and Hagger, 1993; McIntyre, Hagger and Wilkin, 1993; Jaworski and Watson, 1994). However, in the field of subject knowledge the evidence is less clear. Ruthven (1993) has suggested that mathematics teachers hold different mental constructs relating to specific mathematical topics, which are rarely if ever made explicit. Cooper (1990) points to specific anxieties on the part of PGCE students in the area of investigational school mathematics. An increase in the time that trainee teachers spend in school to a minimum of 120 days has put increased pressure on school tutors[1] to be systematic in their approach to developing competence in trainee teachers, and in assessing, evaluating and recording the progress made by trainees in their pursuit of newly qualified status. In light of the quest for competence, the articulation by practising teachers of their subject beliefs and philosophies is very important, as is the discourse between them and their trainees.

This short chapter focuses on key issues arising out of preliminary analysis of responses by interviewee mentors to the question, 'What do you think makes a good English/mathematics[2] teacher?' Not surprisingly, it is easy to see contrasts between the group of mathematics mentors and the group of English mentors. Interestingly, there are also significant[3] differences between mentors in the same subject. We suggest that subject-specific differences could lead to a range of performance criteria being developed to evaluate the competence in different subjects. Responses of same-subject mentors suggest a range of philosophies about their subject. Furthermore, mentors articulate beliefs which are rarely communicated with the trainee. This may have consequences on the way trainee performance is evaluated and assessed in school since trainees are under great pressure to conform to departmental norms (Dart and Drake, 1993), which are, it seems, unstated.

The clearest difference between the mathematics mentors and the English mentors was the attribution of qualities of 'a good teacher'. The mathematics mentors were unanimous in identifying personal, albeit generic teaching qualities as vital for mathematics teaching: flexibility, adaptability, enthusiasm for the subject and, most importantly, a liking for the pupils coupled with the capacity to show an understanding of their learning difficulties. In some cases these qualities were stressed more than subject knowledge:

> Somebody who is mathematically quite competent, I think that's very important . . . But generally it's someone who likes being with the children, I think that's fundamentally the most important thing that they do actually like children and they have compassion with them, so they have some understanding of how they learn and the difficulties that they have.
>
> (Mathematics mentor, female, head of department)

Interestingly, although some of the English teachers mentioned these qualities, they were not unanimously cited. In the articulation of their answer, reference to pupils was subordinated to other kinds of emphasis; most often English mentors' initial response was expressed in terms of a teacher's relationship to literature. This was frequently formulated in emotional terms, namely, 'a love of literature' or 'love of the subject' and/or 'love of language': 'I think a good English teacher has got to be able to enjoy reading and be able to communicate not only a love of literature but knowledge about how certain aspects and qualities of that literature have been achieved' (English mentor, female, head of department). The kind of qualities emphasized initially by the mathematics mentors were seen by one English mentor as '. . . the second stage of what I consider a good English teacher to be. Someone who has an ability to put these ideas into practice, someone who is willing to be inventive and disciplined in their approach. Someone who's flexible in the strategies they use' (English mentor, male, head of department).

The different emphasis given by the mathematics and English teachers about the qualities they seek in trainees may be explained in a number of ways. First may be differing ideological assumptions held by teachers about their subject. It may be, for instance, that the reputation of mathematics teaching is such that teachers are anxious to preserve and promote whatever improvements in practice may have developed since the stipulation in 1974 that mathematics teachers have needed to be qualified to teach as well as having a subject qualification. It may also be that the seminal report, *Mathematics Counts* (Cockcroft, 1982), and a range of subsequent publications, consolidated this perception that mathematics teachers need personal qualities as well as mathematical skills. It is also true that school mathematics teaching and learning, mainly through the introduction of investigational work, has undergone considerable change since the mentors, and many trainees, were themselves at school. This development is referred to by all of the mathematics mentors, and forms a second difference between the two groups.[4] The English mentors were able to relate their teaching to their experience of good teaching as a pupil: 'I'm always surprised at how little they need to be weaned into school English as opposed to university English. Now either that's because in some cases they remember their own schooling, certainly I did' (English mentor, male, head of department). In mathematics this practice was specifically warned against:

> So someone comes in and they think a good teacher is the best teacher I had . . . At the moment most people come through a far more traditional system certainly in mathematics teaching than we're offering. So it's unusual for them to think of the teacher not being at the front of the classroom . . . So what they're trying to do is turn into something they have a stereotypical image of, and what we are trying to do is assume that we don't want them to do that. There's a mismatch between our assumptions and their aspirations.
>
> (Mathematics mentor, male, head of department)

It may also be that mathematics teachers are used to reconciling perceptions of the subject as a body of knowledge and a collection of discrete skills in a way that some English teachers (until the imposition of recent, galloping, government-driven educational change) have never done. Paradoxically, English teachers are facing a kind of subject definition, the most obvious being attempts to prescribe what literature is taught and at what stage in the English National Curriculum, while mathematics teachers are grappling with the different pedagogic approaches required by the move towards investigational work. Mathematics mentors vary in the importance they ascribe to mathematical skills that trainee teachers bring with them: 'Someone who can make the subject fun and instil enthusiasm in the children, who obviously knows their material, knows their subject matter' (Mathematics mentor, female, head of department). This contrasts with:

S: It's perfectly possible for people to come in without big rafts of areas, say on IT[5] which is now a major part of the delivery. That's not a problem in the sense that people have got degrees and so we assume are capable of learning.

I: ... What if you had an individual who had all the qualities you're talking about: adaptable, flexible, willing to learn, but say didn't have mathematics at degree level?

S: I've employed people like that.

In particular, investigational work has brought about significant change in the way teachers explain the teaching of mathematics. Inevitably, this has considerable implications for teacher trainees, as mentors' comments reveal:

> 'It's also difficult for some people to let go because they feel they're not in control of what the children are doing, because the children are exploring for themselves. Some teachers feel that they've lost control of what's happening in the classroom' (mathematics mentor, female, head of department).

Inherent in the English mentors' articulation about good teaching of the subject were tensions that surround the teaching of English in university departments, i.e. debates about how the subject English is defined (see, for example, Evans, 1993). English mentors' beliefs were conveyed in terms of: for some, a traditional approach to appreciation of literature; an awareness of the need to teach the National Curriculum and to tackle issues arising from basic skills of punctuation, spelling, grammar, etc., which was often combined with a political sensitivity to the conservative nature of addressing these skills; a knowledge about the impact of theories such as poststructuralism, etc., and their potential for offering different exploration of text; and also the skills of being organized, a manager and an effective member of a team.

For English mentors, 'a love of literature' and 'sensitivity to the language of literature' has its roots in a tradition based on the work of F. R. Leavis which, by implication, carries with it notions about what kinds of reading and writing practices are valued within the school context. However, this initial emphasis became more complex as interviews progressed: 'I think the problem with English is, as the original Cox report pointed out, it means different things to different people' (English mentor, male, head of department).

Contrasts in beliefs between mentors within each subject are significant too, although detailed discussion is outside the scope of this chapter. The point we would make here is that it is apparent that mentors articulate complex individual philosophies of teaching and learning their subject which can be traced or connected with identifiable 'scholarly' traditions, for example the Leavisite tradition mentioned. In mathematics, these beliefs may be linked to a view of the teacher as a facilitator who enables a pupil to construct and control his or her own learning as opposed to seeing the subject in absolutist terms as a form of knowledge. There may of course be irreconcilable tensions between intellectual traditions and theories of learning. From the perspective of ITT, perhaps the issue which this raises is encapsulated by the English mentor in the following exchange:

> *I:* Do you ever discuss this with A? I mean you've obviously got a very considered philosophy of your position from which you teach.
>
> *S:* . . . a lot of the time we actually spend discussing the lessons, what happened in the lessons and why, rather than the philosophy behind them, simply because of the pressure of time . . . you know in a sense the philosophy comes out in what they are doing, in their teaching strategy and their classroom management and their relationship with pupils you can see to some extent their beliefs. They must have those beliefs because if they don't, the kids will know.
>
> (English mentor, male, head of department)

So, although the trainee must demonstrate that he or she is suitably immersed in a subject culture through attitude and teaching style, there is not time to discuss approaches to the subject *per se*, as the pragmatics of classroom management inevitably take priority. This too, suggests that criteria for performance may evolve implicitly and differently from mentor to mentor.

It seems reasonable to suppose that the qualities which mentors believe to characterize good practitioners in English and mathematics teaching respectively are likely to be the ones that mentors look for in their trainees. It is less clear when and how trainees learn what these qualities are explicitly, even though it is likely that they are under pressure to exhibit them. It seems too that some philosophical or theoretical position in relation to the subject is expected of the trainee, and that there are, not surprisingly, differences as well as similarities between different subjects. It is difficult to describe competence, though, when there are substantial differences in implicit expectation between teachers of the same subject.

NOTES

1. In the plethora of models for PGCE resulting from reform, a two-tier structure for school-tutor support is emerging. Typically a trainee can expect in-school training from a mentor, who is a teacher of the same subject as the trainee, and from a general tutor, usually known as the professional tutor. This individual is frequently a member of the school senior management team and often also has responsibility for newly qualified teachers in the school.
2. There was nothing fancy about this. English mentors were asked about good English teachers and mathematics mentors about good mathematics teachers.
3. Not in the statistical sense.
4. It is also worth noting that school mathematics, despite the introduction of so-called 'investigational mathematics', still tends to be perceived by other teachers as consisting of a collection of right and wrong answers, as a fixed body of knowledge. Indeed, during this study, the interviews of English mentors was carried out by a university mathematics education tutor, and vice versa. Sometimes the descriptions

of English teaching given to the interviewer were couched in terms of what it was not. For example, one mentor declared, 'There are no wrong answers in English, or at least there are lots of right answers.'

5.   Information technology is delivered across the curriculum. In mathematics, school students are required to use a database and a spreadsheet, and to do some simple programming using languages like LOGO or BASIC.

ACKNOWLEDGEMENTS

We are grateful to the Paul Hamlyn and Esmée Fairbairn Foundations for funding the projects, and to Professor Tony Becher, the projects' director, for his help and support.

CHAPTER 13

Positive Mentoring and the Novice-Expert

VAL BROOKS, TERENCE FITCH and MARTIN ROBINSON
University of Warwick

INTRODUCTION

There is an ever-expanding body of literature on school-based initial teacher education (ITE), much of which focuses on the mentor. The nature of the role, the skills, the requirements are expounded in a way which spotlights the mentor and can make the job sound dauntingly onerous. Thus, when the prospect of becoming a mentor is raised, some teachers recoil. One mentor was expressing a common sentiment when he explained: 'No one else in the department wanted to take on the responsibility or to devote the amount of time needed.' Mentoring is sometimes viewed as an essentially one-way process in which the mentee is a complete novice requiring vast inputs from the mentor and offering little in return. However, less attention has been paid to the mentees and the potential they bring to teaching or to ways of enhancing this. As Mountford (1993, pp. 34–5) has observed:

> In this debate on partnership between HEI [higher education institution] and schools the role of a key partner, the ITT [initial teacher training] student, is often neglected . . . A recognition by HEIs and schools of the need to acknowledge the role that students (only) can play in their own professional development and learning extends the partnership into what HEIs and schools can do for (rather than to) the developing teacher.

This chapter seeks to shift the balance by taking a more detailed look at mentees in the role of novice-experts and the way in which positive mentoring strategies can capitalize on the potential they bring to teaching to the mutual advantage of the students and the school.

It is important to acknowledge that the school-based mentor operates in a range of circumstances, such as the licensed teacher scheme, the articled teacher scheme and the secondary PGCE revised in response to Circular 9/92 (DFE, 1992d). Since the role has evolved in response to a range of initiatives, the term 'mentor' means different things in different settings. Therefore, this chapter opens with a brief description of the course on which its findings are based, which is intended to locate the role of the mentor within this particular scheme and to identify those features which may support the mentee in the role of novice-expert.

A formalized use of mentoring was piloted at the University of Warwick in 1992–3 when a revised PGCE(Sec.) course was introduced. The vision of partnership between schools and higher education embodied in this scheme was based on pairing. Thus, schools were paired, School A taking responsibility for a group of students in the autumn term and School B assuming responsibility during the spring/summer terms. The purpose of the pairing was twofold. For the students, it was intended to offer a breadth of experience, allowing them to work in two departments and with different mentors in establishments chosen, ideally, to contrast with one another. For the schools, sharing was intended to lighten the load of ITE and pairing allowed schools to build continuity and progression into their student programmes. In each school, a period of serial practice prepared students for a block practice. The principle of pairing was also applied to the students who entered a school as part of a group – usually eight in those termed principal schools and four in those described as associate schools – but were assigned to departments in pairs. Thus, students were able to offer mutual support and there were opportunities for joint planning, collaborative work in the classroom and peer evaluation as well as the more usual form of self-evaluation. The principle of pairing was extended to the personnel involved in the scheme. Within the school, the mentoring role was divided between a professional mentor (PM) and a subject mentor (SM). The PM had overall responsibility for co-ordinating provision for student-teachers and for attending to aspects of training which had a whole-school dimension or focused on wider professional development. The SM had a subject-specific brief, inducting the student into the department and into subject teaching. These roles had their counterparts within the university: the professional tutor and the subject tutor. Thus, over the one-year course, a student encountered a total of four mentors. Together, they were the principal agents of the student-teacher's professional preparation.

A distinctive feature of the Warwick course was its utilization of the process of managing change and achieving results developed within the Comino Foundation. The GRASP ® principle (Getting Results and Solving Problems) is intended to enable participants to take control of the process of achievement through the establishment of a framework of clear intentions and criteria strengthening the sense of purpose and maximizing success. The GRASP principle '. . . describes a way of thinking which is designed to promote clearer understanding of the processes of getting results. It draws attention to ways in which we can be aware of what happens as we move towards the achievement of clearly formulated objectives' (Comino Foundation Note, 1991).

At every stage, it seeks to encourage trainers and learners to:

- recognize and advance their own power to create opportunities;
- cultivate their ability to construct a clear picture of the results they seek;

- set clear criteria by which they will know they have achieved those results; and
- select the best way of achieving them.

The GRASP cycle of reflective questioning has informed both the mentor training programme and the student record of professional achievement (ROPA) which is intended to foster and track students' professional development.

The sources of the findings reported here are eclectic since the authors have been involved in different ways in monitoring and evaluating the course. The first author is a full-time lecturer who carried out an independent evaluation of the 1992–3 pilot year using in-depth interviews with five PMs, five SMs and five mentees as a basis for formulating a questionnaire which was sent to 164 mentors in 39 schools in four LEA areas. The very high response rate (91 per cent) indicates, perhaps, the level of interest in and concern about this approach to ITE. The second author is a lecturer at the university and School Practice Officer who has undertaken a series of case studies of individual mentor/mentee collaborations. The final author is a deputy head in a partnership school and a PM. He works part time as a PGCE field officer for the university and visited all participating schools in the pilot year to monitor the implementation of the course. He interviewed PMs, SMs and students as well as tutors involved with the course from the university. This year, he has continued to work in a field officer role. The chapter, therefore, draws on all these sources – interview transcripts, questionnaire responses, field officer's notes and case studies. The findings reported here are offered tentatively in recognition of the fact that the course is still at a nascent stage and 'The profession is feeling its way' (Wilkin, 1992a, p. 18). However, evidence from a range of sources does seem to suggest that positive mentoring strategies can enhance the development of the mentee in the role of novice-expert as well as being beneficial to the school.

THE FINDINGS

DFE statistics show that more than one in three recruits on to PGCE(Sec) courses have been classed as mature (i.e. aged 26 or over) in recent years. The figures (DFE, 1994) for the previous three years' total recruitment are as follows: 1990–1 – 41.4 per cent; 1991–2 – 41 per cent; 1992–3 – 38.4 per cent. Be they mature entrants to the profession or 21-year-old graduates, we know that PGCE students come from diverse backgrounds bringing with them a wealth of experiences and skills. Our studies suggest that a positive approach to mentoring recognizes the mentee as a novice-expert, someone who, while a novitiate in the professional world of the teacher, is likely to possess skills which are already highly developed and experiences which could be utilized in an educational setting. Mentors who have recognized the potential for a more reciprocal approach have been flexible, imaginative and opportunistic. They have recognized that part of their role is to identify existing expertise which, if accessed in a sensitive manner, can facilitate the students' professional development as well as vitalizing the school. This is not to deny the demands of ITE on school-based trainers but it requires a shift in emphasis to acknowledge that the relationship between an *adult* trainee and a trainer may be mutual with a potential for giving and receiving on both sides. It is, after all, an established educational principle that new learning should start from the point which the learner has reached, capitalizing on existing knowledge and skills.

Positive mentoring may require a change in the training culture for all concerned. It is often argued that learners fulfil their teachers' expectations of them. Adults who enter into the student role often seem conditioned to become passive and dependent if they perceive that such a response is expected of them. Teachers, too, work in institutions where the child–adult relationships may encourage a culture of dependency regardless of how much teachers seek to promote a spirit of independence and responsibility among their pupils. The following quotations illustrate this point in a variety of ways:

> Naturally, we found our students to be fairly dependent on us for ideas.
>
> (SM)

> The tendency to talk at passive students is overwhelming at times. I learnt more when I listened.
>
> (SM)

> It would have been useful to participate a bit more. At times, we weren't sure whether we were supposed to and the teachers may say we didn't take part much but it wasn't made clear what we were really supposed to be doing.
>
> (Student)

> We're used to constantly being in charge of children and being in a very controlling situation and that position is inappropriate, indeed unhelpful in the role of mentor. I think that dealing with adults is a completely different skill and you need to adapt the way you relate from children to relating to adults which is something which I think teachers don't have enough experience of.
>
> (SM)

> The school was setting up a GNVQ in science and they fell short of industrial experience in knowing where to send students and what they could do when there. I did have the potential to help but didn't feel I could because I was a student.
>
> (Student)

Our findings suggest that mentors who regarded mentees as capable of making a significant contribution to their own professional development and to the life of the school often promoted a two-way exchange of ideas and expertise which was mutually enriching:

They've participated in departmental meetings which are a fairly open forum for discussion of ideas. They've joined in that very effectively. Ideas that they've produced in their teaching which have been particularly effective, we do tend to discuss and utilize. They've added those to the general pool.

(SM)

It's been a shared experience with the students. One or two have come up with some quite innovative ideas. That sort of initiative has gone down well. I suppose the reward has been to see the success of the students.

(PM)

He's got me involved in things. I've been treated as I would have been if I had been a full-time member of staff. He's generally given me as wide a perspective as I can get in six weeks. I've generally felt relaxed and taken care of.

(Student)

Some mentors who had worked in this way regarded their role as that of an enabler. In describing how he had approached the role, one SM argued: 'I very much see enabling as the important one – knowing . . . how to "oil the organizational machinery" is vital if students are to develop new ideas, approaches, e.g. use of IT.'

Despite the tendency towards a dependent relationship between the training institution and the trainee, the course does recognize the value of a more proactive approach among students. They are encouraged to adopt problem-solving methods as a means of diversifying existing skills. To this end, much thought has been given to the student profile as a way of engaging the student in his or her professional development. The ROPA document is underpinned by the reflective questioning cycle known as GRASP (see above). Students have been encouraged to view their own professional development in terms of:

1 defining closely what you want to achieve;
2 describing what the end-product is going to look like;
3 stating clearly the criteria for success;
4 checking progress towards goals; and
5 revising goals.

There have been teething problems associated with this document concerning its structure and the ambiguity of the intended audience and purpose. Despite ongoing problems with detail, the underlying approach appears to provide a worthwhile vehicle for focusing discussion of professional development. The role of the mentor has been crucial in helping the students to practise this mental discipline by providing a source of dialogue and a point of reference. The formative aspect of ROPA has been welcomed by students and mentors alike, especially as the process has become genuinely student driven and students feel more ownership. The cycle of target-setting and review is capable of producing properly structured and meaningful interviews with students.

Enormous paybacks in terms of positive attitudes, shared perceptions, honest self-evaluations and the recognition of strengths as well as weaknesses were sometimes experienced. Many students acknowledged that they still had a lot to work on during their first appointment and that the reflective cycle of inquiry, target-setting and monitoring of progress would continue to be helpful. The following quotations demonstrate the potential for sharpening and systematizing thought and for encouraging a problem-solving approach:

> Having a vehicle through which you can actually organize negotiating sessions – the ROPA has provided quite a nice focus for the activities which you are doing with the students: meeting with them every day to debrief them on lessons that they've taught, to discuss short-term targets for future lessons, to consider long-term objectives . . . We've looked at other ways that they might have approached things, negotiating and evaluating performance.
>
> (SM)

> It's been good to have to write something down because it makes you think about what's going on.
>
> (Student)

> It's a focusing thing really. It makes you realize areas where you are lacking and it's something to refer to and follow up.
>
> (Student)

> It makes you think: 'What could I do?' If I didn't have it, I probably wouldn't do it at all.
>
> (Student)

> Monitoring of progress has been much more formalized and the discussion generated by the ROPA has been valuable.
>
> (SM)

> Use of self-evaluation proformas by students → ROPA worked well.
>
> (PM)

> Obviously, it is important to be a reflective practitioner. A lot of people feel: 'Well, I do that anyway', and some probably do but others don't. Formalizing it in this way does force people into doing it.
>
> (Student)

However, the ROPA culture required a considerable investment of time and commitment on both sides. Students responsible for drafting comments on their own performances needed support and more than a token negotiation. Teachers honing their mentoring skills recognized the links with appraisal training – similar skills were required: '[Negotiating and interpersonal skills] are important because they are connected with other processes which teachers are also engaged with like appraisal and ROA with pupils. They're all in the same family of skills' (PM).

The novice-expert potential could be there whether the mentee enters teaching immediately following an undergraduate degree course or after a period in another field of employment. Students who enter the profession straight after graduation may have an in-service training potential. Their studies may have exposed them to the latest developments in thinking and approaches in their own subject area. Individual teachers and departments can benefit from tapping into this source of ideas developed at university level. In this way, mentees may become a conduit between higher education and subject study at school level. This has been particularly noticeable in science. As one young science graduate observed: 'Having been at university, we're up to date with current thinking and perhaps some of the members of staff aren't – not through any fault of their own but just the system in general' (student). The following comments pay tribute to the presence of students as a stimulus to innovation:

> These particular students have been a fertile source of ideas. They've brought things to the department which we've been able to use so it's been a nice two-way process really.
>
> (SM)

> It has kept me in touch with new ideas. I feel I have benefited greatly from the two science students I was 'in charge' of.
>
> (SM)

> The students still have ideas and ways of doing things which you lose sight of in the daily grind.
>
> (SM)

> I encountered some new ideas on materials/approaches/thinking generally to help prevent the ossification of the department.
>
> (SM)

> It's true to say that existing staff always learn something from students. They bring a freshness. They come in with new ideas. It's easy for staff who've been here for a long time to become rather stale. On an intellectual level, too, people coming straight from university are perhaps at their intellectual peak. That's good for staff who've naturally had to go down to the pupil intellect which is not as challenging . . . The mentors are queuing up . . . others have seen how refreshing it's been and how useful.
>
> (PM)

> Students enrich my department as well as encouraging me to think about my own teaching methods.
>
> (SM)

The message is, perhaps, best summed up by the SM who urged a recognition of the fact that 'There's a huge amount of potential stimulation which comes from students and I think that departments have to be receptive to that.'

This is not an exploitative approach to school-based ITE. Students who feel they have been able to contribute something to a school invariably value the experience. One student described how this '. . . gave me an idea of what it was like to be a teacher rather than a visitor. I felt I had made my mark.' She went on to describe feeling '. . . more professional, more wanted, more confident' as a result of the experience. These feelings of increased self-esteem and professional assimilation were frequently mentioned:

> It integrates you more. You feel as a member of staff rather than a student.
>
> (Student)

> I felt more involved, more part of the school.
>
> (Student)

Mentees are invariably flattered when established teachers use the materials they have prepared and add them to departmental stocks. For them, it is a confirmation that they have something of value to contribute to their chosen profession and helps to build their professional confidence and standing: 'Because the National Curriculum is new to them, there is a void in materials, especially for year 7, so I know that our worksheets have been photocopied and put into the filing cabinet which is nice' (student).

Clearly, teachers who become mentors are often exposed to new ideas and materials, novel ways of doing things. Thus, they are conscious of the dangers of imposing their own practices on others. As a result, they tend to become open and receptive to innovation. Thus, school-based ITE can act as a stimulus to change and revision of their own existing practices. A tonic effect may be felt at various levels – the whole school, the department or the individual teacher – introducing a new vitality. This injection of innovation is especially welcome in a period of contraction for externally provided INSET. Inducting others into a professional activity also produces a climate of reflection in which analysis and evaluation may become the norm. Teachers who act as mentors often become more self-aware, more self-critical, more willing to challenge their own assumptions:

> There are developmental benefits to the staff who are involved because in order to work with trainee teachers you have to reformulate your own ideas and reflect on your own practice which is a good and developmental thing to do . . . I'm getting towards the latter part of my career and it might otherwise have been easy for me to ease back or slow down or just get stuck in a rut. You're not able to do that when you are working with young teachers. They cause you to reflect upon your present practice and to re-examine it and that is a very helpful thing for anybody at whatever stage of their career they are.
>
> (PM)

> Whenever you work with students, it always makes you evaluate your own performance. It's very easy to come out with the rhetoric . . . but it makes you

look at what you're doing yourself . . . It makes you question the reality of your own teaching.

(PM)

You do tend to look back on your own teaching and think: 'Well, is that a good idea?' Personal reflection is the main thing that comes out of it.

(SM)

Discussion of the philosophy of teaching methods of real interest. Also discussing ways of teaching certain topics quite stimulating.

(SM)

I've personally found it very challenging in my own teaching; it's helped me to reassess what I'm doing.

(SM)

There've got to be benefits in that you're actually reflecting quite closely on other people's performances as teachers . . . It's quite a good time for personal reflection and development.

(SM)

It's a two-way thing – both school and student benefit.

(SM)

I felt that having another adult to relate to and share ideas was very enriching.

(SM)

Likewise, another SM asserted that being 'Reflective on own practices and willing to make changes in own work' were essential qualities for a would-be mentor. Clearly, mentoring is, by its nature, intellectually stimulating. It is a thought-provoking and analytical activity which tends to foster self-development.

The leavening effect which the presence of students can have on an institution was also underlined by some of the quantitative data of the questionnaire. Respondents were asked to identify the two main benefits of mentoring from a list of alternatives; they were also asked to prioritize by indicating the main benefit and the second most beneficial aspect. For SMs, the most frequently cited main benefit was the way in which mentoring promoted personal reflection (43.4 per cent). The enrichment of the subject department emerged as the second most important benefit most frequently cited (46 per cent). PMs recorded a somewhat different pattern of benefits. Their most frequently cited main one was a training investment in the future of the teaching profession (38.9 per cent). However, the second most important benefit was equally shared between the promotion of reflection and the enrichment of the school by the presence of students (33.3 per cent). Thus, both groups identified the contribution which students were capable of making to an institution as the most beneficial paybacks of school-based ITE.

Reference has already been made to students for whom teaching is a first career choice following graduation. Our studies suggest that mature entrants to the profession also may have much to offer and to gain from being in the role of a novice-expert. Recent recruits to the PGCE course have been drawn from wide-ranging fields of employment. For instance, foreign languages students often have experience in the travel industry and marketing. Science students typically come from various industrial backgrounds, such as nuclear, gas and British Telecom. English/drama students may have worked as professional actors as well as in theatre management. The list could be extended. Some schools have been flexible and imaginative in capitalizing on these assets as well as enabling students to utilize prior learning as they develop professionally. The input can range from contributing to the development of new vocational courses and special enterprise projects to fostering school-industry links through networking and contacts, giving presentations on areas of specialist knowledge as well as the fund of insights which can inform teaching in the classroom on a daily basis. Each year may bring fresh opportunities with its new cohort of students with a unique range of experiences.

The course attempts to facilitate this approach by sending CVs to schools before the students' attachment commences. In this way, both the student and the school can try to identify areas of special expertise and interest as well as needs and weaknesses so that positive mentoring can take place. The following case examples demonstrate schools enabling mentees to develop in ways which were of mutual benefit.

D's second attachment was to a school which was new to mentoring. A liaison meeting between the school mentors and the university tutor explored the concept of mentoring in relation to the serial practice. The discussion stressed the need to use and develop the student's prior learning and to do this by providing some space in the serial programme for activities negotiated with the student. The mentors and the tutor jointly outlined a provisional series of activities in the school that would be of mutual benefit to the school and the student, such as researching aspects of school life and presenting the evidence to the school or devising work schemes and materials. In an interview, D described the genesis of a project on which he eventually worked:

> Quite soon after I arrived in the school, the mentor talked to me about the idea of working on the software project. The idea is that I'll work on this in the school and spend some time in the university researching the program. I suppose that this was partly because I had put that I was good with computers on my CV. The program is called Omnigraph. It's a graphics package which allows you to take objects on the screen and you can rotate them and see this happening on the screen. It's possible to plot gradients and to show reflections, shears and translations linked to matrices. The age group that I will aim the package at is top GCSE, level 8 and above. I want to work on how to use it and how to use it in the classroom. Normally, what happens in the classroom is that you have a shape like a square and if you're going to rotate it through 90° you don't see the movement.

The new position is drawn on the screen but it's not a continuous movement whereas with Omnigraph you can watch the movement happening so that the kids can actually see the rotation of the objects if the new data is entered. What I'll do now is definitely produce a worksheet guide for the program and, to make it useful for others to use, I'll also put some example data on the computer network for school classes to use and a guide for staff.

A number of points can be made from this interview. Clearly, there were tangible benefits here as the student was involved in passing on expertise and developing curriculum materials and, at the same time, there were intangible benefits for the mentee and the mentor. The student was able to use prior learning and some expertise in a situation where he would have normally expected to be seen as a novice. The status gained from this expertise helped the student socialize himself into the subject department as a colleague, albeit with the ambiguity of a novitiate with expertise. At the same time, this gave the mentor a situation where she could build the mentee's confidence by allowing him to contribute to his own learning.

Another example is M, a mature student of 36 when he came on to the course in business and economics. His prior learning included a wide experience in industry and some time spent as a business consultant. His skills in information technology (IT) were exceptionally good, both in programming and in IT applications. While on the course, he continued to do freelance consultant work. In the first half of the course, he frequently commented on the lack of IT expertise he found in school. During his second practice, M was able to apply his IT skills and adapt them to the teaching situation. He worked with the mentors in the school to devise a range of spreadsheet data applicable to the business situation. At the time, the school was setting up a GNVQ in business studies and he was able to contribute to the IT aspect of the course.

In his first practice school, M was faced with problems with personal relationships in his subject area:

> The problem is that there isn't a department at all, just two warring factions. In fact, the economics people don't talk to the business studies staff. They keep talking about the 'other side' to me and I have to tell them that I'm here to learn the job. I've asked them not to talk about their problems . . . It's not my problem . . . At least I know what it is to be in a department with lots of politics going on and I've learnt to ignore that kind of negative stuff.

Here M was able to work through this complex and difficult situation using his prior experience of working relationships. This is an example of a novice-expert who realized that he still had much to learn but was able to use existing expertise to manage the conflict aspect of working relationships.

A final example of this use of student expertise occurred in a school where two mathematics students discovered that their department made little use of IT in their teaching as a result of, in the main, a lack of time for staff to work on relevant materials. In this school, the mentor worked by negotiating tasks with the students. The students decided to collaborate on the design of a set of materials for the department and to team teach these to a year-10 class. Several of the mentors who have worked in this way have remarked on the speed with which mentees have developed. Thus, one SM observed: 'It's pleasing to see young teachers developing confidence and skill in a relatively brief time.'

CONCLUDING OBSERVATIONS

We can also understand the necessity for student-teachers to bring their own area of expertise to the school and build on it at a more theoretical level. It is increasingly being accepted that complex systems (and few would deny that classroom interaction is complex) show positive feedback – once a historical accident starts a trend, the trend is self-reinforcing (Mitchell Waldrop, 1992). If students have brought skills which are valuable to colleagues, they are more likely to get the support and co-operation of colleagues when they need it – another self-reinforcing system but one which can be tricky to establish (Boyd and Richerson, 1985; Mitchell Waldrop, 1992). This more theoretical level may justify exploration at a later date; at present it provides assurance that there are good reasons for setting up procedures which give student-teachers a foundation of success on which to build – especially to build up reciprocal benefits. The wider situation gives urgency to the task of making these benefits more generally apparent.

Nationally, the future of school-based ITE is uncertain. Schools which had welcomed the principle of school-based training have found the practice less so. Thus, Harrow School found itself in the news recently when it decided to terminate its partnership with London University's Institute of Education. The report notes that 'The decision of a high profile, well-resourced school such as Harrow will sound a warning for others thinking of expanding teacher training' (Pyke, 1994a, p. 3). Several weeks later, another report suggested that 'Many headteachers are considering withdrawing from the Government's school-based teacher training . . . with some schools talking of quitting and others attempting to return to the old arrangements under which they only had a minor role' (Pyke, 1994b, p. 5).

A way forward which offers a more widely acceptable balance between the costs of school-based ITE and its benefits is required. The findings of this chapter are tentative but they do suggest that a more thorough and systematic investigation into the development of this positive approach to mentoring students may provide one such way.

ACKNOWLEDGEMENT

Thanks are due to Sean Neill for his help with the theoretical component of this chapter.

CHAPTER 14

Student-Teachers and their Professional Encounters

HILARY CONSTABLE and JERRY NORTON
University of Sunderland

INTRODUCTION

Initiation into the rights and practices of teaching is a mysterious process. The culture of teaching in schools is absorbed by student-teachers in a variety of contexts through processes which are difficult to analyse. Initial training courses are planned in detail to prepare students for teaching, with apparently little left to chance. However, student experience of the courses, especially the school-based part, is apt to appear unpredictable. At a time of change towards school-based supervision and assessment of students, it is more than ever necessary to understand what happens to students in school. Little is known about the conversations students have in school about their work. What do they talk about and with whom? On the face of it, students might talk to anyone about their work, including teachers of their own or other classes, tutors from the university and other students, or possibly technicians, support and secretarial staff. They might have a brief word about some factual matter or resources, or might have a longer conversation about classroom strategy or work planning. A chance encounter might expand into a far-reaching discussion of radical plans or a time reserved for a planned review might disappear in the exigencies of everyday life in school. Similarly the content of these conversations remained to be investigated.

The research presented in this chapter provides insight into the frequency and type of meetings, professional encounters, taking place in schools which have an influence on the teaching experience of students. A professional encounter is a meeting which includes discussion about the student's teaching. Where these encounters take place, who initiates them and who takes part may vary, and the encounter may be brief, hardly long enough to merit the title 'meeting'. The defining characteristic of an encounter is that it contains some discussion about the student's professional practice rather than say a purely social conversation.

The aim of the investigation was to delineate and analyse this important element of the everyday experience of being a student-teacher. Specifically the research was intended to provide insight into the frequency and content of professional encounters taking place in schools. How much contact takes place? With whom does it take place? From the evidence a picture of interaction patterns between the participants emerged, which may allow a more grounded understanding of how to improve the quality of the experience to be developed.

Studies have highlighted a concern for relevance in the experience of student-teachers and identified a feeling of inadequate training and communication between schools and training institutions (DES, 1988; Shaw, 1992; Wilkin, 1990, 1992b). Furlong *et al.* (1988), among others, have argued that school-based training can help break the perceived divide between theory and practice when learning to teach. Indeed, consideration of the issues of teacher education and possibilities for improvement has taken place over an extended period (see, for example, Lacey and Lamont, 1976).

The School of Education, University of Sunderland, provides access to qualified teacher status via BEd and PGCE courses for primary and secondary education. All courses contain a school-based element. At the time of the research three courses were based on new partnership schemes: PGCE primary, BEd modern foreign languages and PGCE business education. These courses incorporated explicit partnership schemes in which schools had responsibility for the support, supervision and assessment of students. These responsibilities were mediated by recognized school-based tutors (mentors) who participated in a professional development programme. Schools and school-based tutors worked within detailed common guidelines. Although students on the same course followed the same pattern of experience, initial informal feedback was that the implementation of the guidelines and the experience of the students was subject to wide variation. This was in line with student-teacher experience in previous models of teacher education. Nevertheless this was a new approach and there was little information on the support given to students and how they were able to engage with it.

THE INVESTIGATION

A sample of student-teachers was drawn from full-time initial teacher training (ITT) courses in the School of Education. These courses included partnership (mentor) schemes of training as well as more traditional routes to teacher status, with reference to both primary and secondary schooling. This mixture was advantageous in that it included a range of courses including ones based on the newer and more explicit partnerships as well as older ones based on a more assumed and less explicit form of partnership. One disadvantage was that the partnership courses were new, with their first cohort of students, and thus had not had the chance to iron out the wrinkles to be found in all new courses. Hence comparisons were to be treated with caution. Those tutors involved with each student's school experience were also to form part of the research sample. By establishing a student-teacher population to examine, samples of school and higher education tutors were also determined.

Students were asked to record all professional encounters with others in the school over a three-day period. Tutors, whether based in school or university, were also asked to complete a record of their encounters. Students and tutors were each provided with self-report sheets, structured to invite the inclusion of all encounters connected with student-teachers' school experience. Information on the duration and time of the professional encounters was collected using this self-report technique. As near as possible the second last week of a block of school-based experience was used. The tutors', teachers' and students' logs provided cross-checks on what each considered to count as professional encounter. For instance, what a student may consider a significant professional encounter may have gone unnoticed by a teacher. The final sample obtained was 51 student-teachers, 20 university tutors and 51 school staff. Record sheets were initially given to 89 student-teachers, 30 university tutors and 221 school staff. The sample mortality was an expected part of the procedure: all the participants were busy. The final sample consisted of 38 students on traditional courses (27 secondary and 11 primary) and 13 on new partnership courses (5 secondary and 8 primary).

The content of the professional encounter conversations was a further area of interest. What did students talk about with their tutors; was it the same as they talked about with the teachers, and did it make any difference if the student was on one of the new partnership courses or not? A subsample from each group was selected to undergo interviews in which recorded encounters were analysed in greater depth. The interviews were of a standard structure. The logs were used to identify encounters noted by two parties and of sufficient duration to make recall worth while. The interviews were held shortly after the log recordings had been made. In the interviews the content of encounters, as well as the initiation, regularity and arrangement of each interaction was discussed and recorded. The log was used to assist recall.

HOW MANY ENCOUNTERS?

In a three-day period the mean frequency of professional encounters for a student-teacher was ten. During that period, 62 per cent of the student-teachers recorded encounters with university-based tutors and, perhaps not surprisingly, all the students had encounters with school staff. The mean number of encounters recorded by school staff over the three-day period was five. Of school staff, 88 per cent recorded encounters with student-teachers: 48 per cent of such encounters were initiated by school staff and 28 per cent of school staff also met university tutors in this period. The mean number of encounters recorded by university tutors over three days was five. All the university tutors recorded encounters with student-teachers which without exception the tutors had initiated. During this time, 74 per cent of university tutors recorded professional encounters with school staff.

Taken as it stands, the figure of an average ten encounters for a student in three days is a long way from the picture of the lonely student abandoned and without support. Measures of dispersion fill out this picture, with the range extending from one to 25 encounters. The standard deviation was 4.93, in other words two-thirds of the records were in the range 5 to 15 (5.07 to 14.93). The consequence of this is that one-sixth of the records reported a range of above 15 (14.93) encounters. Certainly some students had few professional encounters but most had many encounters. One way of thinking about this is to envisage the school day and the way it structures the opportunity for discussion. Not counting the time before the start of the school day, there are three or four slots available for discussion – morning and lunch breaks and after school, as well as an afternoon break where there is one. Put this way and bearing in mind that some encounters were very short, many students could be seen as using most of these possible spaces in some way for discussion of their work and sometimes several more besides. It is clear that there is some considerable professional dialogue here. What is less clear is how the sum of the encounters adds up or in what way professional development is enhanced.

INITIATING CONTACT

There were no obvious differences between primary and secondary student-teachers concerning the likelihood of their initiating encounters with school staff: 50 per cent of primary student-teachers recorded initiating at least one encounter with a member of staff and 48 per cent of secondary student-teachers did likewise. Of all such encounters, 29 per cent were initiated by student-teachers. Confirming tutors' perceptions, no student reported initiating encounters with university tutors.

In secondary schools the meetings with school staff were more often prearranged, and in primary schools meetings were more often arranged as needed. Some 10 per cent of primary student-teachers' encounters with school staff were prearranged while 90 per cent were organized as concerns arose. In secondary schools, 27 per cent of encounters were prearranged and 73 per cent organized in response to concerns. Doubtless the organization and structure of primary and secondary schools had its effect upon this aspect of professional encounters – primary schoolteachers have a fuller timetable and largely remain with one class while secondary teachers have contact with a series of classes. This will affect the extent to which meetings are prearranged or respond to immediate needs. However it may be that the difference is as strongly affected by habit or by the climate of responsiveness (the way we do things here). In other words, it should not be taken for granted that the difference is fully explained by organizational structures: differences of culture and context have their part too.

Differences between the new partnership schemes and the existing courses were small. For instance, there was little difference between the frequency of encounter between class teachers and students on the two sorts of course. However, student-teachers on traditional courses reported higher levels of interaction with heads of department or senior staff – recording an average of two encounters – whereas new partnership student-teachers reported only 0.2 encounters with such staff. Partnership-course student-teachers had the additional support of their school-based tutor with whom they recorded an average of 1.6 encounters. In this relatively small sample, partnership-course student-teachers appeared more likely to have initiated encounters with school staff for themselves: 62 per cent of new partnership student-teachers reported initiating encounters compared to only 44 per cent of traditional student-teachers.

THE CONTENT OF THE CONVERSATIONS

The content of the conversations recorded by the student-teachers is summarized in Table 14.1. As expected it was found that classroom discipline, organization and lesson evaluation generally featured highly in the professional encounter discussions. Furthermore the responses across the courses and encounters were in general fairly even.

It is possible to note that the content of the discussions broadly reflected the areas of competence since identified in Circular 9/92 (DFE, 1992d). Beyond that one must be circumspect – the content of conversations was derived from the interviews, consequently the numbers were small. Reflection on the data does raise a number of questions worth pursuing. For instance, primary students discussed pupil learning with school staff and with higher education tutors more frequently than did secondary students. The wider range of curriculum subjects dealt with by primary teachers may be one source of this difference, another may be the concern for processes of learning traditionally ascribed to primary schools.

An interesting question for further investigation will be the place of preparation, planning and content. These early experiences of teaching will inevitably reveal uncertainties and confusions. For the beginning teacher, organizing and reconstructing his or her own knowledge so that it can be taught is not merely an exercise in pedagogical planning. Organization of knowledge in this way is in effect the construction of understanding and is an important part of the development of the student's own subject expertise. The manner in which school-based teacher training is to support this crucial, and sometimes difficult, development needs to be fully articulated.

In this investigation, students on the school-based courses initiated encounters with school staff more often than did those students on traditional courses – a predictable outcome of the planned change which may reflect students taking a greater responsibility for their own professional development or a sharper sense of the locus of responsibility for assessment and certification (if

TABLE 14.1

Categories of discussion recorded by student-teachers on mentor and traditional courses with school staff and university tutors (numbers indicate order of frequency of mentions for categories beginning with the highest frequency first)

NEW PARTNERSHIP STUDENT-TEACHER	'TRADITIONAL' STUDENT-TEACHERS
With school staff	
1. (a) Lesson evaluation (b) Preparation, planning, content	1. Preparation, planning, content
2. Classroom discipline	2. Resources
3. Pupil learning	3. Classroom discipline
4. General support	4. Lesson evaluation
5. Resources	5. Pupil assessment
6. Classroom organization	6. Pupil learning
7. Pupil assessment	7. General support
8. (a) Student progress (b) Staff relations	8. Classroom organization
	9. (a) Staff relations (b) student progress
With university tutors	
1. Lesson evaluation	1. Lesson evaluation
2. (a) Preparation, planning, content (b) Classroom discipline	2. (a) Preparation, planning, content (b) Classroom discipline
3. Pupil learning	3. Pupil learning
4. General support	4. General support
5. Classroom organization	5. Resources
6. Pupil assessment	6. Classroom organization
7. Staff relations	7. (a) Student progress (b) Pupil assessment
8. Student progress	8. Staff relations

these are not the same thing these days). Furlong *et al.* (1988) see active involvement as a positive and critical attribute of successful school-based training. If these findings imply a more active role for students in their training then this is another aspect of changes in roles. It is commonly held that active involvement in learning is desirable and sometimes argued that it is necessary.

ONE DAMN ENCOUNTER AFTER ANOTHER?

It is an assumption of the new partnership schemes that a series of discussions can structure the professional development of a beginning teacher and, evidently, student-teachers have a not inconsiderable professional dialogue. However, the extent to which the discussions in the different encounters add up to professional development is not totally clear. How these discussions of beginning teachers' practice draw on and bring in ideas not already familiar to students or their tutors is not known. This is a further focus for investigation. Meanwhile a profile of professional competence provides an agenda for discussion. A significant issue is the management of the development of new teachers using these competence profiles – how can it be done? One of the unresolved issues is how the students' immediate concern may be connected with an overall pattern of professional development. Essentially the answer must contain reflection on, and mental reconstruction of, experience. Stones (1992) notes that the most telling criticism of school-based training is the way students may be confined not only to existing practice but also to thinking about their practice in terms defined only by their own experience or the experience of the few role models they come across. It will be some time before their argument can be either sustained or refuted.

A large proportion of meetings reported in this investigation were relatively spontaneous and at one level this is to be welcomed. On the one hand, from the point of view of the student, receiving support at the moment of needing to know is likely to result in quick and relevant learning. On the other hand, the pressure on students does not leave them scope for generating an agenda concerned with much beyond coping. Coping in teacher training has long been recognized as a problem, not because coping is undesirable, far from it, but because coping can be a barrier to development, an end point rather than a stage. The demand is to construct a dialogue between short and long term and between parts and the whole. Somehow notions of meaningful learning and constructive teaching need to be woven together with information about where the coloured card is kept and how to get the apparatus cupboard unlocked. This makes a heavy demand on teachers to connect the student's immediate concern with a view of overall professional development. Quite what, exactly, the demand upon school-based tutors and institution-based tutors is will start to become evident as partnership schemes develop and are tracked more fully. For the time being it is worth drawing attention to a possible parallel – informal teaching in primary schools. In the debate about informal teaching in primary schools one line of argument has been that a focus on individual needs may be desirable but only exceptional teachers have a hope of pulling it off: others end up losing sight of progress and of the scope and structure of the knowledge to be conveyed. It is arguable that the demand on school-based tutors is similar and likewise difficult to pull off.

Without a clear picture of what goes on and how it takes place, it is difficult to prescribe a programme which will best educate prospective teachers. The new forms of teacher training offer new challenges in particular in the development of new roles, but also in the chance to address systematically issues in the training of teachers which are central in whatever context the training is provided. Consistency and quality are, properly, important concerns (DES, 1991) in the education of student-teachers and in the continuing professional development of newly qualified teachers (see DES, 1988). The professional encounter lies at the heart of the development of beginning teachers, that is the meetings and discussions of the students' professional practice. Insights into student development can be gained by examining what happens in the course of these encounters. In the absence of long-term experience of school-based teacher education, analysis of the content of the professional encounters is a significant source of information for the evaluation of school-based teacher education.

ACKNOWLEDGEMENTS

Thanks are due to Mary Forrest and Rachael Harker for assistance in collecting and collating data, and to Steve Farrow for contributing to the planning stage.

CHAPTER 15

How Teachers Support Student Learning

JILL COLLISON and ANNE EDWARDS
St Martin's College, Lancaster

INTRODUCTION

The quality of initial training depends upon an integrated educational experience being devised and put into action by a formal alliance of school, higher education establishment and student with a shared model of student learning and a mutual commitment to the values of democracy and educational empowerment.

(McCulloch, 1993, p. 302)

McCulloch's teacher-training partnerships comprise integration, alliance, sharing and mutuality. They have student learning at their centre and entitlement and empowerment as their goals. This vision of partnership is not quickly created as it demands mutual adaptation and new ways of conceptualizing and operating. The potential for the transformation of teacher education is, however, enormous if all participants learn as much as they might.

Earlier analyses of training partnerships, for example, Furlong *et al.* (1988), produced more specific breakdowns of the responsibilities of partners in training. In the Furlong *et al.* model, teachers give students support in direct practice and help with developing generalities from that practice. But the authors propose that the major form of assistance as students produce generalization and critique comes from higher education staff.

In a later discussion, Maynard and Furlong (1993) emphasize more strongly the complexity of training partnerships and identify three potential mentor functions as model, instructor and co-enquirer. The third function may impact heavily on the teachers' own learning and is dependent on a willingness and an opportunity to explore jointly the dilemmas of classroom life.

We suggest that reform of initial training provides the opportunity for profound improvements in the ways that student-teachers are supported in the acquisition of their professional knowledge. But if the teacher training partnership is to be implemented as a transformational alliance in which mutual learning occurs those responsible for implementation need to know what teachers currently feel they can offer students. Our experience of the examination of one year of a higher education–school training partnership confirms our belief that attention should be paid to the voices of teachers who have begun to experience an enhanced role in initial training. At the very least these witnesses inform a diagnosis of what might be required if McCulloch's vision is to become reality.

THE CONTEXT OF THE STUDY

The data we discuss were gathered between June 1992 and July 1993 on the experience of one cohort of students in the first year of a pilot BA (QTS) degree validated for the training of infant teachers. The degree has a partnership between a higher education institute (HEI) and schools at its centre. The course is structured so that each cohort of between 40 and 50 students covers half of the validated primary-curriculum subject studies programme and all of the education courses in schools with teachers. The students spend an equivalent of one day a week in school in addition to block teaching-practice placements. Each school selects a member of staff to receive mentorship training and act as an associate tutor. Associate tutors are released from some teaching and co-ordinate the students' school-based learning; they liaise with the other class teachers and work with HEI tutors to develop the partnership. HEI-based link tutors provide support for the associate tutors and act as personal and academic tutors to the students at 'their' schools. The students work in pairs and stay with one class for each year of the course. Regular meetings occur for associate tutors, link tutors and curriculum specialist tutors to plan the students' curriculum work.

THE DATA COLLECTION

Teacher perspectives were gathered from associate tutors and other class teachers in two interviews with up to 17 teachers: the first two months into the course and the second at the end of the first year. In addition, 33 of the 42 participating teachers completed an open-ended questionnaire at the end of the first year. Student views were gathered in one interview two months after the start of the course and in three questionnaires which included attitude statements and open questions, and these were administered at the end of each of the three phases of study during the year.

In addition, 11 hours of classroom observation were made using an adaptation of Sylva, Roy and Painter's (1980) target-child observation method. Five hours of planning and evaluatory conversations between 11 teachers and 20 students were also recorded. The data were collected by two researchers and a third was involved in data analysis for reliability purposes.

Our concern here is to examine what teachers and students perceived to be the contribution of the teachers to the professional learning of students. The observational and conversation data will be used to contextualize the information from the interviews and questionnaires.

THE CLASS TEACHER ROLE

Associate tutors play a central role in the students' professional development, yet the class teachers ultimately determine the students' school experience through daily interactions. Considerable variation in student experience of class teacher support became apparent in student interviews and questionnaires.

At the end of their first school placement, 40 per cent (20 out of 49 students) disagreed with a statement that they had had useful discussions with their class teacher about what they were doing. Similarly after their second placement, 33 per cent of students (13 out of 39) felt that their class teachers had not supported their learning in the primary curriculum subjects they should have addressed in school. In addition, 50 per cent (20 out of 39) said that their class teachers had not helped them to examine classroom experiences in relation to a wider view of children's learning.

Quotes from students illustrate the variation in class teacher interaction and support:

. . . discusses what we have planned but does not overtly influence, she guides rather than dictates. She will discuss what went well and will praise the positive. Her influence and guidance are invaluable.

. . . doesn't really help us plan or evaluate lessons. I'd really like some constructive criticism on lesson plans and organizational skills.

In interviews with 17 class teachers in four schools, we explored the background to these findings. It became evident that the teachers had insufficient time to talk with the students. The metaphor of being 'torn' was repeated: 'I feel torn in two with my class because I want to give my class 100 per cent and my students 100 per cent.' The feeling of being torn appeared to find its strength in the extent to which all of the interviewed teachers indicated that they cared for the students. This caring sometimes included Maynard and Furlong's (1993) notion of teacher as model: 'I see my role as a caring role in a way. Always to be there if needed. I feel responsible for setting high standards within my classroom, to be a good role model.'

In addition to caring, the majority of the teachers saw themselves as guides for the students: 'My role is somebody to guide them in the practical classroom. It's all right knowing theories but when you get down to the actual practice of classroom teaching it doesn't always work, so I've tried to guide them towards a good working classroom where the children are always learning.' Here we can see a separation of theory and practice which is supported by an analysis of teacher talk in the planning and evaluatory conversations between students and teachers. Of teacher statements, 45 per cent carried specific instructions on what to do in the classroom when setting up tasks for the children they would be teaching. Of the remaining 55 per cent of statements, 21 per cent were simple points of clarification (e.g. 'It's in the cupboard') leaving 15 per cent of statements in which the teacher listened to student comments and built on them and 7 per cent of statements where the teachers listened to students, challenged their interpretations and attempted to extend a student's repertoire of responses. The remaining 12 per cent of statements included general references to how children learn; relationships with parents; discipline; the students' future learning; and some waffle.

The 12 per cent of statements labelled as general references were as near as the teachers got to generalizations. It would be difficult to define the statements as making theory explicit. The teachers explained their relationships with parents, for example, in terms of their preferred practice: 'I like to stand at the door to say goodbye and to see the parents.' Statements related to learning were presented as procedural: 'They need to know their colours first.' These guiding teachers were in fact operating largely as instructors. Again this supports the Maynard and Furlong (1993) analysis.

Maynard and Furlong's co-inquirer was not evident in our study, though we found that in 22 per cent of statements teachers either built on student understanding of practice or challenged those understandings. This suggests that some optimism might be warranted for the notion of teacher as challenger as a third element on a dimension of teacher support which runs from carer to guide to challenger.

We felt that the absence of co-inquiry and the prevalence of instruction might be the result of infant school practice. The teachers frequently worked with and gave instructions to other adults in their classrooms. Our observational data showed that the teachers all regarded the students as another pair of hands. Students were given tasks to implement with groups of children while the teachers took advantage of the extra help to work more intensively with other children. In 11 hours of observation of classroom activity, in only six of the one-minute segments observed is there any evidence of teachers talking to the students. These rare conversations were on mundane issues, like checking the availability of a child for another activity.

THE TEACHERS AS MENTORS

The absence of co-inquiry and of shared teaching raises questions about the mentor role of infant schoolteachers and their function in assisting the learning of student-teachers. For Maynard and Furlong (1993) mentoring is an active role in the training process. Part of this role is to guide the students' 'seeing' to highlight, in Doyle's (1986) terms, what is important in the confusing array of classroom life. Practitioners' expertise as class teachers lies in their ability to highlight within the tasks they set for pupils. The same emphasis on and in task-setting was evident in their work with students. The highlighting of issues that lay beyond actual tasks was rarely seen.

An element of expert mentor practice would, in McCulloch's model, be found in the management of the interpenetration of theory and practice. Yet the teachers in our study confirmed our own observations by indicating clearly (22 of 33 questionnaire respondees) that the HEI should deal with this aspect of student learning: 'It is important for students to have time away from the school environment, to learn and discover and discuss educational theory. Class teachers do not have the time to do this nor necessarily sufficient detailed knowledge to do this effectively.' The same teachers also felt that the HEI should prepare students for teaching by giving them initial frameworks for 'planning and content'. An unpacking of what respondees meant by theory reveals that explanatory frameworks might be a close description.

Another barrier to the easy assumption of the mentor role is the extent to which beginning students seek certainty. One advantage of workplace mentoring for more expert learners is the opportunity to deal immediately with puzzlements in practice (Russell and Munby, 1991). Neither the teachers nor the students in the cohort we studied sought puzzlements for examination.

Doyle's (1986) observations of how both teachers and pupils in classrooms collude in bidding down task demand from risky challenge to the safety of closed tasks bound by agreed rules may be a useful starting-point for the analysis of this phenomenon in the mentoring we observed. Unsure teachers may demand less of students as they feel unprepared for coping with the risk involved in seeking the puzzlements that are necessary if the theoretical frames discussed by Barnes (1992) are to be exposed and explored.

The teachers were concerned to create sympathetic and supportive environments in which students may safely operate. All the teachers regarded themselves as carers who could be liked and trusted by the students and saw their role in terms of positive feedback and the encouragement of students.

AN EMERGING MODEL OF PEDAGOGICAL PARTNERSHIP

Our evidence suggests that while there was some variation in the degree of support the infant schoolteachers gave students, the teachers had a clear view of the limits and extent of their role which in fact resembled that offered by Furlong *et al.* (1988). We are therefore still a long way from the integrative mutuality to be found in McCulloch's vision of partnership.

The teachers appeared confident in their performance as carers and guides. Their activities with students parallel the support teachers give children when they are engaged in practical small-group table tasks. These tasks are usually given after language and concept-framing activities have occurred. The table tasks in infant classrooms are generally carefully structured and require little supervision. Consequently they release teachers to work with those who most require help. These tasks serve a valuable purpose. They give the learners the opportunity to move, in semi-private safe contexts, towards an acquisition of the understandings and skills demanded by the tasks (Edwards, 1994). But in table tasks each learner is only moving towards the relatively narrow understanding afforded by a specific task. To maximize learning, new skills and understandings need to be applied in a variety of contexts of which problem-solving is one.

Our data indicate that the caring and guiding teachers we saw were creating safe places for students to test their understandings of how to work with children. At the same time they were carefully structuring the procedural aspects of the situation to protect the students (and the children) from avoidable failure. They were not, however, monitoring the students on task and were rarely giving evaluative feedback which challenged students' interpretations of events. In addition they were not making explicit their own understanding of how children learn in classrooms in ways which took students' thinking on beyond a grasp of procedural knowledge.

We are not arguing that the teachers could not engage in joint inquiry or challenge the students, but that they didn't. Rather, by emphasizing the mundane and procedural both teachers and students appear to be colluding in avoiding the transformational potential of initial training partnerships. Our data also raise further questions most particularly about whether the classroom contexts in which the teacher-student conversations occurred are conducive to the analytic discussion we are indicating is important; whether reflection almost immediately after action is too soon; and whether there are particular aspects of primary practice that militate against teachers giving students the attention that they, as learners in classrooms, require.

CHAPTER 16

Peer Support

KATE HAWKEY
University of Bath

This chapter examines the nature of peer support which arises out of practical, school-based and teaching-focused activities, where one novice teaches while the other observes, and both discuss the lesson afterwards. The approach is based on a principle of 'enactment over precept' (Butler, 1992, p. 226) and, to the extent that both peers are present in the lesson, it is a shared experience which is discussed.

RATIONALE

Moves to school-based courses

The obligation for novice teachers to spend two-thirds of their time on the PGCE course in schools presents some dilemmas. Less contact with both higher education tutor and same-subject novice peers, and school placements spread over geographically wide areas, all suggest that novices may suffer a greater sense of isolation than previously. This may be further compounded by a narrow, institutionally bound view of learning to teach that schools may offer. Teachers do not provide the important perspective that an 'outsider' brings (Zimpher, DeVoss and Nott, 1980; Proctor, 1984; Swanwick, 1990), even experienced mentors have many other demands on their time, and there are concerns as to the level of support that novices receive during the school-based parts of their course.

Tensions in supervisory relationships

There is a tension within the role of a supervisor which arises from the supervisor being there as both 'helper' and 'assessor' (Boothroyd, 1979; Williams, Butt and Soares, 1992). This is evident when either the higher education tutor (Blumberg, 1976) or school mentor (Zimpher, DeVoss and Nott, 1980) is responsible for carrying out supervision.

It is increasingly acknowledged that learning to teach involves a journey of personal growth (Nias, 1989; Butler, 1992), and it is clear that in this process novices need both support and challenge. The tensions in supervisory relationships may undermine this. Moreover, as Maclennan and Seadon (1988, p. 40) note, learning to teach

> . . . demands learning to come to terms with success and failure, with personal strengths, confusions and weaknesses. It demands that students develop a way of voicing these to themselves in a form which is sufficiently acceptable for them to continue to do so when it is no longer a ritual, formally demanded of them by someone else.

Peers: an underused resource?

Research suggests the role that peers play in the development of teaching expertise is underused. Novice teacher 'supervision' in microteaching situations has led to '. . . positive resolution of issues central to student teaching' (Glassberg and Sprinthall, 1980, p. 37). Whether this carried over into 'real' teaching situations is not clear. More recently, research asking novice teachers what they would have missed had their course been more school based found the highest rating given to '. . . sharing of ideas, experience and expertises with other students' (Swanwick, 1990, p. 204), a finding which also echoes Furlong's research (Booth, Furlong and Wilkin, 1990, p. 92).

Collaborative cultures

The value of peer collaborative work among experienced teachers is increasingly acknowledged (Biott and Nias, 1992), with little or no discussion of how this might inform initial teacher education (ITE) courses (Clift, Houston and Pugach, 1990; Day, 1993). For very practical reasons, the plethora of policy changes that have swamped schools over the past few years have necessitated new and often collaborative ways of colleagues working together within schools. The argument that novice teachers should be introduced to these new emerging patterns of working during their ITE year is a compelling one.

THE REFLECTIVE PRACTITIONER MODEL

The design of ITE courses has increasingly been informed by the reflective practitioner model. This has brought with it an approach to supervision as a 'co-operative operation' (Stones, 1984). There has, however, been little attention given to the potential that peer support within this model might offer.

More usually, research has focused on relationships and pedagogy involved in supervision by mentors and tutors rather than on peer involvement. Consider, for example, these common practices in PGCE courses:

1 The opportunities that do exist for reflection with someone else mean with someone in authority, a very useful activity in itself, but one which also carries tensions (Williams, Butt and Soares, 1992).
2 Novices are required to reflect on their teaching by means of ongoing written evaluations. While important, this activity can become arid and mechanical (Rudduck, 1991, p. 327), and suffers from a narrowness of perspective.
3 Early on in their course novices commonly gain initial school experience which is then discussed as part of the university-based course. Arguably this helps to intertwine the perspectives from school and university in the novices' professional development. When novices go out on teaching practice, however, the focus tends to be very much on survival in the classroom, with few mechanisms for ongoing reflection with others built into the structure of their work.

What all these practices point to is a conception of ITE which promotes a focus on the individual to the exclusion of collaborative work, and to implement this model is inherently conservative. Unlike medical education and counselling (Remley, Benshoff and Mowbray, 1987; Borders, 1991; Lincoln and McAllister, 1993), there is little in the way of research devoted specifically to the potential that structured peer support offers in teacher education. In theoretical terms, it represents the potential for a more integrated curriculum code (Bernstein, 1971; Furlong *et al.*, 1988). In practical terms, in the context of moves towards school-based work it takes on a potentially important supportive role. Clearly there are limitations to what peer support can be expected to achieve since novices do not have the experience that mentors and tutors bring to the task. Given the pressures that mentors work under, however, when novice teachers are not being directly supervised in school, it represents a supplementary approach which might help in their professional development.

RESEARCH QUESTIONS AND DATA COLLECTION

Within this conceptual framework of peer support and drawing on the research literature into teachers' professional development, the research project had two broad questions: What is the nature of peer post-lesson interaction? Do novices contribute to the professional development of their peers during the PGCE course?

The research was carried out at Exeter University during the 1992–3 course. It focused on novice teachers taking history as a main or subsidiary subject on a PGCE course which was substantially school based. During the autumn term, three pairs of novice teachers watched each other teaching and discussed the lesson afterwards. Analysis of the taped conversations led to a refining of the research in the second phase. During the spring term, two pairs of PGCE novice teachers recorded all post-lesson discussions carried out with each other during the one-term block teaching practice. Participation in the project was voluntary, and novices selected the partner they wished to work with.

Observer's communication style

The findings from the autumn term pilot suggested that although novice teachers felt the need to express their emotions and to run over the details of the lesson (Tickle, 1991), they also moved beyond this to constructive forward planning. The very presence of a second novice, keen to support his or her peer, seemed to help the discussion to 'move on'. In my analysis of the spring-term taped conversations, I therefore decided to focus on the observer's communication style in giving feedback in order to evaluate how far this contributed to the other novice's reflections.

Arguably a questioning approach is most likely to promote reflection and may indicate the degree to which novice teachers feel comfortable with opening up to a range of uncertainties. By contrast, a style of giving general support only, while certainly functional, may suggest a hesitation with opening up to a wider range of considerations. A style of offering advice may indicate a confidence in either one's own knowledge, or confidence in identifying a particular characteristic in the other novice teacher. It may indicate a reluctance to engage in critical discussion, preferring safe certainties instead. While it is valuable to examine the overall balance between styles of communication used by the observers, the categories remain very broad, so that the communication must be looked at in context in order to gain an understanding of the speaker's intention.

Criteria for lesson evaluation

Another feature of the discussions during the autumn term was the extent to which novices cited pupil enjoyment as the main criterion by which to judge the success of a lesson (Griffiths and Tann, 1992). The frequency with which this was mentioned, unsubstantiated with evidence or discussion, could be taken to indicate a concern with survival (Gibson, 1976). In the spring term I therefore decided to focus on how novice teachers evaluated their lessons. By using the categories of class management and subject application, I was not only able to analyse the concerns that novice teachers had but also to examine whether these changed as their teaching practice term progressed. A pre-occupation with class management to the exclusion of subject application issues might indicate a prevailing concern with survival in the classroom rather than with the quality of the learning experiences. Likewise, a concern with pupil enjoyment, unsubstantiated by evidence, could be taken as an indication of concern with survival. A move away from such concerns towards a consideration of what pupils were learning could be taken as an indication of the development of critical reflection.

During the second phase of the research, the taped conversations were analysed in two ways. First, the observer's communication style (as outlined above) was examined and, secondly, the criteria used in lesson evaluation by both the 'teacher' and observer were analysed.

FINDINGS

The most common observer's communication style used by both pairs was that of giving general support to the teacher. Words commonly used were 'impressed', 'not bad', 'fine', 'brilliant', 'excellent', 'wonderful'. The observer rarely substantiated this general support with any evidence.

The questioning style was not used so much, and used rather differently by each pair. Pair 1 (both men) used very general questions, while Pair 2 (both women) were more specific in their questioning as this extract shows: 'Do you find the programme of study useful?' 'What about timing?' 'Do you find the work differentiated enough?' 'Do you recognize who needs most prodding?' (C.G., lesson 1)

Perhaps related to this, Pair 1's conversations were also far less interactive than those of Pair 2. Pair 1 each spoke between once and three times during each conversation with the observer taking more of the lead, while Pair 2 each spoke on average eight times during each conversation. It may be that more specific and, indeed, probing questions emerge from more interactive conversations.

A further explanation for this might focus on the participants' gender. Feminist research with qualified teachers suggests that women tend to be particularly skilled at raising alternative perspectives and possible actions within a supportive atmosphere (Biott and Nias, 1992, p. xviii). Such groups tend to be egalitarian with the lead shifting between participants in response to the task, rather than resting with one member exclusively. With only two pairs participating in this part of the research, this explanation is at best extremely tentative, and should be regarded rather as a hypothesis warranting further research.

Both pairs used a style of giving suggestions, advice and opinions. In one case the observer was able to identify an area which her partner needed to address. Significantly she was confident enough to offer suggestions, while at the same time taking great care to maintain support, sometimes through empathetic understanding, to avoid presenting the advice as criticism.

When it came to lesson evaluations, pupils' enjoyment was frequently cited, although this never led to a discussion of the value of the activity. The enjoyment was always perceived as a global evaluation of the whole class.

Class management, and in particular discipline, was also frequently mentioned as a factor in evaluation, and pupils working 'quietly' was mentioned several times as a measure of success, with no reference made to what they were doing quietly.

Evaluations which focused on subject application were less common. The following extract, however, illustrates the potential value there may be in setting up cross-subject peer work:

> C.F.: I'm sure some of them didn't actually understand why they were doing it and what they were doing it for.
>
> C.G.: But surely you can build on that next lesson when you do the triangular trade, because they'll only understand it when you do the triangular trade, won't they?
>
> C.F.: My aims were to actually tell them about America, and I think they understood . . .
>
> C.G.: How do you, well, do you think you're looking at it from a geographer's perspective a lot?
>
> C.F.: Yes.
>
> C.G.: Because I notice that the stuff they did on America was very much about the country, which is fine. I tended to bring out the native American Indians, and the fact that they died out more, but, then that's because I probably wouldn't look at the other bits, I should have looked at the other resources as well. So I find it really interesting to think of the geography point of view as well.
>
> C.F.: I think I should have put more about the natives there and why they were used, because if I'm going to try to go on to the triangular trade I need to explain the natives had disappeared.
>
> C.G.: Yes, but you'll be able to do that next lesson anyway . . .
>
> (Lesson 1)

Other notable features of the taped conversations illustrate a number of missed opportunities when a concern was introduced but not taken up for discussion by the partner, as the following extract illustrates:

> It disturbs me sometimes this business of going round and talking to pupils. It disturbs me that some are a lot more demanding on your time than others, and consequently you tend to spend a lot of time with a few, some time with a lot, and no time with a few. And, although on the whole you don't spend any time with the ones who can do the task fairly easily, I still feel sometimes that I'm ignoring them and I worry about that.
>
> (P.C., lesson 1)

On this occasion the opportunity for discussion was not taken up, demonstrating the clear need for additional discussion with an experienced supervisor. The extract does, however, demonstrate a readiness to air such concerns with a peer. It may be that within the fairly unthreatening environment of working with another peer novices are more willing to express anxieties than with a tutor or mentor.

The style of observer's communication and the factors used in lesson evaluations did not change in any appreciable way over the period of the taped conversations. It may well be that the term involved was too short a time to be able to establish whether any changes had occurred. The following extract, however, does illustrate possible benefits of peer collaborative work which did develop over the period: 'I was very apprehensive beforehand, however David convinced me to do it and it was a thoroughly enjoyable experience for me. It's the first time I've ever done anything like that and I was probably more nervous than I've been for anything in teaching' (P.C., lesson 5). The extract shows a growing confidence in each other to the point where one novice teacher takes part in a role play in the other's lesson, an activity which he was very nervous about. By their final lesson 'together', sufficient trust had been established to enable one novice teacher to acquire a wider teaching repertoire by actually taking part in the lesson. Moreover, this acquisition took place in a safe and protected environment of a lesson where P.C. didn't carry full responsibility. The interaction suggests that there is benefit in peer collaborative planning and teaching, and also that this may only be 'comfortable' with some novices when it arises out of the more general sharing of experience which peer support work offers.

CONCLUSION

The research here confirms much of the literature relating to the rhythm of how novices learn to teach. Concerns with survival certainly tend to predominate (Gibson, 1976; Griffiths and Tann, 1992). The research also confirms the existing literature relating to the benefits of peer contact as offering much valued support (Booth, Furlong and Wilkin, 1990; Swanwick, 1990), and being largely free from the tensions which are associated with a supervisor in authority (Blumberg, 1976; Boothroyd, 1979; Zimpher, DeVoss and Nott, 1980; Williams, Butt and Soares, 1992).

There remains, however, much work to be done. First, there is a need to know much more about those who choose to get involved in postlesson conferences, their images of self as teacher, their perceptions of how they will learn to teach and their intentions in engaging in peer support work. Secondly, there is a need to find out much more about the significant experiences which novices choose to discuss with their peers rather than with mentors or tutors, and to establish whether there are some areas where they learn more from their peers than from mentors or tutors. Thirdly, there is a need to examine how far peers can, if at all, offer the appropriate challenge, as well as support, which is needed in the development of critical reflection. There are a variety of peer-directed strategies ranging from clinical supervision and peer coaching, to developing the use of teaching metaphors which warrant investigation. There is a need to carry out further research examining the impact that these different intervention strategies have on the professional development of novices.

PART FOUR

Students Learning to Teach

CHAPTER 17

The Importance of 'Bad' Lessons

ROD BRAMALD, FRANK HARDMAN, DAVID LEAT and
ELIZABETH MCMANUS
University of Newcastle upon Tyne

INTRODUCTION

The government's proposals for the reform of secondary teacher education (DES, 1992) led to the 'competencies expected of newly qualified teachers'. Edwards (1992) criticized them because of their mechanical view in which it is assumed that a set of technical operations can be assessed against closely specified criteria drawn from detailed analysis of the demands of the job. While there was a reference in the DES's main text to the difficult task of 'defining competencies that are precise and capable of assessment without being excessively detailed and over-prescriptive', there is no reference to the professional knowledge that often underpins such competencies (for example, looking at ways of how children learn) nor to the process of how student-teachers learn to teach.

Research (e.g. Zeichner and Liston, 1987; Leinhardt, 1988; Calderhead and Robson, 1991; Knowles, 1992), however, has often focused on student-teachers' thinking and suggests they begin their training with definite views about teaching and learning which have developed from their own educational experiences; it also suggests these views shape their perceptions of teaching and developing practice and seem resistant to change. More recent research (e.g. Kagan, 1992; Powell, 1992; Bird, Anderson and Swindler, 1993; Guillaume and Rudney, 1993; Wubbels, 1993) has started to look at how these belief systems, which are often unrealistic or inappropriate in the classroom, can be influenced by more effective teacher training courses so that the student-teachers are helped to develop a more sophisticated understanding of how pupils learn. The research suggests that, without the opportunity to identify and examine their beliefs and practice through critical reflection, student-teachers are likely to adopt practices they remember experiencing as pupils and thus merely reinforce the status quo.

This chapter will argue that 'bad' lessons can be an important source of learning about teaching for some students. As part of a continuing process of critical self-reflection on practice, they may offer a means by which more sophisticated thinking about teaching and learning can be developed and from which some reshaping of subsequent practice may emerge.

CONTEXT

Throughout the period 1991–3, a mixed-methods study (Bramald, Hardman and Leat, 1994), using both qualitative and quantitative data, had been undertaken with secondary student-teachers who had been following one-year training courses (PGCE) in various subjects. In contrast to many other studies into student-teachers' thinking, this study made use of a large sample size using the whole cohort of students each year (typically around 170). The data-gathering was done at three different stages in the course: at the very beginning (September), in the middle (December) and at the end (June).

A questionnaire was used to measure, among other things, the student-teachers' views on teaching and learning. The resulting bipolar scale allowed for the identification of subgroups whose views had moved either in a more student-centred direction, characterized by a constructivist view of learning, or in a more teacher-centred direction, characterized by a transmissional view of learning. Subsequent analysis showed that, at the macro-level, the majority of student-teachers did not substantially change their mean score throughout the course, but at an individual level there were significant changes, reflecting the findings of a study at Exeter University with primary PGCE students (Bennett and Carré, 1992). From these much smaller and relatively homogeneous subgroups, individual students were identified and interviewed in depth to explore the reasons behind the changes in their thinking. The interviews revealed different levels of reflection, as suggested by McIntyre (1992). Those students who showed a more critical level of thinking and changes in personal theory, as measured by this scale, were also the ones who had moved in a more student-centred direction. Their changes in opinion appeared to be rooted in strong emotions which seemed to be triggered by surprising experiences, usually, but not always, during lessons that could be characterized as 'bad'. This led the writers to hypothosize about the importance of dissonant experiences, commonly found in 'bad' lessons, in challenging student-teachers' thinking and providing an important source of learning for some students.

ECOLOGICAL ANALYSES

In order to test the hypothesis about the importance of 'bad' lessons in stimulating student-teachers' reflective thinking, a self-reporting technique called ecological analysis – inspired by the work of Doyle (1977) – was used. Three different curriculum groups (English – $n = 24$, geography – $n = 24$, mathematics – $n = 30$), were targeted to explore in greater depth the hypothesis about the effect of experiences in lessons. The students were given some guidelines on producing ecological analyses of their lessons and, during their first teaching practice, were encouraged to prepare accounts of at least one 'good' and one 'bad' lesson (see Figure 17.1 for an example). Deliberately, no guidance was given on how to make judgements about what made 'good' or 'bad' experiences; the decisions about these categories were, therefore, personal to each student-teacher. They were asked to describe the thinking behind their lesson planning, their feelings about the class and its characteristics, any environmental factors they thought pertinent and a synopsis of their actual lesson plan. The visual effect of the account of a specific lesson is that of a flow diagram. Boxes are used to identify particular events and connecting lines, often accompanied by notes, to provide an explanation of the causal linkage between

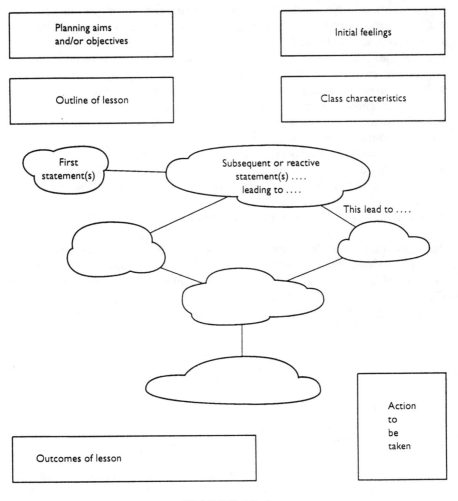

FIGURE 17.1

events. The most specific of the guidance given was that they were expected to make reference to their thoughts and feelings as the lesson unfolded.

METHOD OF ANALYSIS

A categorization system had been developed during the pilot study and this was employed in the analysis of the analyses in this study. Doyle's system was refined so that it was a more precise instrument that allowed the patterns existing in this particular data-set to emerge more clearly and coherently. The categories used to classify the statements are shown below together with illustrative examples:

- *Environment* – the weather, room temperature, the pupils' prior lesson, etc.
- *Class characteristics* – the class's typical behaviour, or likes and dislikes.
- *Preparation* – by the student-teacher.
- *Pupil consonant behaviour* – i.e. that which fitted what the student-teacher expected and considered desirable.
- *Pupil neutral behaviour* – i.e. not explicitly expected or unexpected and with no attached judgement as to the desirability.
- *Pupil dissonant behaviour* – i.e. that which did not fit the student-teacher's expectations and/or was undesirable.
- *Teacher planned behaviour.*
- *Teacher emotion.*
- *Teacher reactive behaviour* – which occurred as a response to some event in the classroom during the lesson.
- *Teacher thought* – during and/or after the lesson.

The statements from the analyses were categorized by one of the researchers. In order to eliminate as far as possible the effects of any biasing, and to ensure an acceptable level of reliability, random examples of the categorizations were examined and discussed by the writing team. The end result was that the categorization of the data had been standardized against that of the other researchers.

RESULTS

Only the data from students who supplied both a 'good' and a 'bad' analysis were used. Once the data were collected, various frequency analyses were performed upon them, the results of which are presented in Tables 17.1 and 17.2.

As can be seen, there are some surprisingly large differences between the numbers of statements for each category. With the exception of 'pupil neutral behaviour', all those referring to behaviour, whether it is that of teachers or

TABLE 17.1
Global results of 'good' and 'bad' lessons (n = 43)

CATEGORIES USED TO ANALYSE THE STUDENTS' LESSON ANALYSES

	ENVIRON-MENT	PUPIL CHARAC-TERISTICS	PREPARA-TION	PUPIL CONSON-ANT BEHAV-IOUR	PUPIL NEUTRAL BEHAV-IOUR	PUPIL DISSON-ANT BEHAV-IOUR	TEACHER PLANNED BEHAV-IOUR	TEACHER FEELING	TEACHER REACTIVE BEHAV-IOUR	TEACHER THOUGHT	TOTALS
Good											
Raw no. of statements	37	15	5	284	37	114	360	90	153	244	1,339
Mean no. of statements per analysis	0.9	0.3	0.1	6.6	0.9	2.6	8.4	2.1	3.6	5.7	31.1
% of total	2.8	1.1	0.4	21.2	2.8	8.5	26.9	6.7	11.4	18.2	
Bad											
Raw no. of statements	41	22	5	151	21	291	247	152	250	310	1,490
Mean no. of statements per analysis	0.9	0.5	0.1	3.5	0.5	6.8	5.7	3.5	5.8	7.2	34.6
% of total	2.8	1.5	0.3	10.1	1.4	19.5	16.6	10.2	16.8	20.8	

TABLE 17.2
Behaviour-related statements in 'good' and 'bad' lessons (%)

	'GOOD'	'BAD'
Pupil dissonant behaviour	12	30
Teacher reactive behaviour	16	26
	28	56
Pupil neutral behaviour	4	2
Pupil consonant behaviour	30	16
Teacher planned behaviour	38	26

pupils, are very large and significantly larger than the others. The only other categories which even approach the size of these behaviour-related ones are 'teacher feeling' and 'teacher thought' and these too could be considered to be behaviour related for they may well be thought of as consequential. The first three categories, not surprisingly, play only a minor role in the overall picture of the data, as does the data relating to 'neutral' behaviour.

For the students of this study, 'bad' lessons were found to be a richer vein of dissonant experiences than 'good' ones. This is clearly illustrated in Table 17.2, which looks only at the students' recorded statements about behaviour, whether it is their own or their pupils'. As can be seen, consonant behaviours (i.e. pupil consonant and planned teacher behaviour) are reported in both types of lesson but they are far more common in 'good' lessons.

The dissonant experiences (i.e. pupil dissonant behaviour and teacher reactive behaviour) account for only 28 per cent of reported statements concerning behaviour in so-called 'good' lessons but for 56 per cent in 'bad' lessons. In more specific terms:

1 'Bad' lessons generate more elaborate accounts than 'good' lessons – a mean of 34.6 statements for each 'bad' lesson account compared to a mean of 31.1 per 'good' account. Although this difference was not found to be statistically significant, a number of students commented that it was easier to write accounts of 'bad' lessons because 'they give you more to think about'.

2 In 'bad' lessons, there were significantly fewer references to consonant pupil behaviour than in 'good' lessons – means of 3.5 and 6.6 respectively ($t = -4.25$, $p < 0.0001$, one-tailed). In contrast, 'bad' lessons have over twice as many references to dissonant behaviour as 'good' lessons, means 6.8 and 2.6 respectively ($t = 5.96$, $p < 0.0001$, one-tailed).

3 'Bad' lessons have significantly fewer references to planned teacher behaviour than 'good' ones – means 5.7 and 8.4 ($t = -3.89$, $p < 0.0004$, one-tailed).

4 'Bad' lessons have significantly more references to emotion than 'good' ones – means of 3.5 and 2.1 ($t = 3.34$, $p < 0.002$, one-tailed). Most references to emotion in the 'good' lessons appear to refer to a general sense of relief or euphoria.

5 'Bad' lessons have almost twice as many references to the student-teachers' reactive behaviour. A mean of 5.8 compared to 3.6 – a statistically significant difference ($t = 3.35$, $p < 0.002$, one-tailed).

6 'Bad' lesson accounts contain significantly more references to the student-teachers' reactive thought – a mean of 7.2 compared to 5.7 for 'good' lesson accounts ($t = 2.65$, $p < 0.01$, one-tailed).

In summary, therefore, there appears to be a general pattern to the accounts of 'good' and 'bad' lessons. 'Bad' lessons more commonly contain dissonant pupil behaviour and possibly as a consequence they also contain more reactive teacher behaviour, thought and reference to emotion. As one would expect, they are more troubling to the respondent.

DISCUSSION

Two important ideas need to be discussed in the context of interpreting this data: cognitive conflict and cognitive theory of emotions. Cognitive conflict is a concept which has been used particularly in science education to accelerate the understanding of new concepts (Driver, 1983). One of the barriers to pupils' understanding in science is thought to be the existence of naive concepts: that is, personal theories based on everyday experience that are either wrong or which contain some misunderstanding. For example, many pupils believe that a bare floor and a carpeted floor in the same room are at different temperatures because one feels colder than the other. This misconception acts as a barrier to learning because science, as taught, makes little sense as incoming information is interpreted through the framework of the existing naive concepts. Where there is a serious mismatch between the existing and the new, no connection may be made and the new information is lost as no sense is made of it. Cognitive conflict occurs when the learner puts his or her existing understanding together with the new information and struggles to make sense of the two apparently contradictory meanings; therefore, it is associated with the formation of new concepts. The ability to process information almost certainly has much bearing on an individual's ability to resolve the conflict. The significance for teacher education is that, as discussed above, student-teachers come to their courses and first encounters with personal theories about or images of teaching which are highly resistant to change. These theories could, therefore, represent a serious barrier to learning by student-teachers.

The cognitive theory of emotion attempts to make connections between thought and feeling (Mandler, 1984; Oatley and Johnson-Laird, 1987). It is suggested that emotions arise following disturbances or interruptions to goals. Plans are strategies employed to achieve goals. These can be conscious or unconscious. There are five basic emotions widely recognized as existing pan-culturally, although debate surrounds the five as a definitive list. The five are all associated with facial expressions; they are happiness, sadness, anxiety, fear and disgust – these latter four being termed dysphoric. Oatley and Johnson-Laird suggest that the function of emotions is an evolutionary adaptation to allow one priority to be exchanged for another in a system of multiple goals. So an emotion which switches some mental routines off invokes others, the whole system being geared towards self-preservation. Clearly, many interruptions to plans are just local difficulties for which small adjustments can be made. The four dysphoric emotions are more likely when there is serious incompatibility between goal and reality. Oatley and Johnson-Laird add that dysphoric emotions are more common for the novice and that most emotions relate to social experiences.

This theory needs some interpretation in the context of novice teachers and the data presented here. Student-teachers have plans, not necessarily their lesson plan but rather a mental plan for the lesson, in which self-preservation in terms of being able to maintain control and purpose is a high priority. Furthermore, their plan is almost certainly highly congruent with their image of teaching. 'Bad' lessons for them are probably those in which pupil behaviour or reaction does not match their plan. This triggers a dysphoric emotion, which sets in train a cognitive sequence which, when translated into action, seeks to redress the balance and thus to re-establish their goals. This interpretation supports the general pattern found in the data extremely well: that is, 'bad' lessons have more interruptions (pupil disonnant behaviour) which trigger dysphoric emotions and subsequently teacher reactive behaviour and thought. In 'good' lessons, and to a lesser extent in some 'bad' lessons, difficulties encountered are regarded as local and are usually absorbed through small adjustments.

The mismatch between what the students expected to happen, their plan, and what actually happened, is a potential source of cognitive conflict. They have personal theories about lessons which predispose them to expect certain outcomes which mostly relate to pupil behaviour. In many lessons, however, their plans are thwarted and the pupils' behaviour (not necessarily mis-behaviour) does not fit expectation. One might expect the student-teachers' learning outcomes from 'bad' lessons to be highly significant for the development of their thinking about teaching and learning. However, this seems to be true in only a small number of instances, as the data from the 1992–3 cohort suggested that only a small proportion of students moved significantly in their thinking.

If some students are highly stimulated by dissonant experiences, which are most common in 'bad' lessons but which may occur in lessons which have gone surprisingly well, why doesn't this happen to all students? First, there are problems with the data: some students felt that they had not had any lessons that they felt were 'bad', just 'less good'. Perhaps plans had not been interrupted and subsequently that there was no potential conflict, only local difficulties. Secondly, there are certain cultural pressures which operate in schools (Carter and Doyle, 1987) that put a high premium on good, immediate control of classes. In some instances good teaching is defined by good classroom control. Summarizing previous research, they point to smooth management being the most important criterion by which many teachers operate and that learning is not a very visible concept.

Thirdly, what is troublesome to one person may well be unproblematic to another. There are differences in information processing and problem-solving abilities which make the resolution of the cognitive conflict less likely for some; hence the decision to leave the judgement about what constitutes a 'good' or 'bad' lesson to the individual student-teacher each time. Lastly, and in our view very importantly, the ability or willingness to reflect varies, a suggestion strongly verified in Korthagen (1988) and Laboskey (1993) and supported by our own interviews (Bramald, Hardman and Leat, 1994). Instead of the mismatch leading to reappraisal of teaching, there is among some a strong tendency to locate the blame in the pupils, which may or may not be appropriate, and the student-teacher will revert to classroom coping strategies to contain the problem.

These points can be illustrated with material from the students' lesson accounts used in this study. One student-teacher of English, after a complex account of a lesson in which the failure to sustain the pupils' attention with the use of materials was highlighted, concluded simply that the materials needed to be collected in carefully and that several paper-clips had been lost! A mathematics student gave an account of a lesson in which the pupils are described as reluctant to answer questions, failed to show initiative and needed to be told when to go on to the next question; the outcomes of the lesson refer to the need to be more organized, not to deal with individuals at the start of the lesson and to wait to find the right culprit when misbehaviour occurs. There is little reference to the pupils' learning in such accounts. By way of contrast, a geography student concludes after a chaotic lesson that she is not happy with her planning and that she has to know what she wants the pupils to learn and know what they are learning.

To summarize, therefore, dissonant and often threatening experiences that have been characterized here as 'bad' lessons have a great learning potential which seems not to be realized in many instances.

CONCLUSION

Much of the learning that takes place in the early stages of teacher training courses can be described as situated knowledge (Leinhardt, 1988) – that is, learning from context where the main concern is classroom management and keeping pupils gainfully occupied. This is cumulative learning which is easily assimilated into existing knowledge structures. This would correspond to the lowest level of reflection described commonly as the technical level (Zeichner and Liston, 1987; Handal, 1990; McIntyre, 1992). However, more powerful learning which might transform teaching is less common; that is, learning that assumes a form that promises to affect fundamentally that individual's personal theories about teaching and thus to have consequences for their ability to be effective teachers.

There are a number of implications from the findings for the development of partnership courses where mentors have greater responsibility to help student-teachers reflect on their teaching experiences. First, courses aimed at mentor development undertaken by higher education partners need to help these mentors to understand how novice teachers learn. For example, mentors need to avoid hasty judgements about a novice's teaching; judgements that may be made on the basis of how closely the novice follows the template of the mentor. Furthermore, mentors need to understand the importance of early experiences, both in terms of the emotional dimension (Leat, 1993) and the tendency to focus on classroom management to the detriment of a focus on the quality of pupils' learning. Finally, mentors need to be helped to realize the potential of the so-called 'bad' lesson and its wealth of dissonant experiences.

CHAPTER 18

Student Learning Experiences
in Pre- and Post-Reform Courses

ALMA HARRIS
University of Bath

INTRODUCTION

The 1990s have witnessed an increasingly interventionist stance by the government towards reform across the educational spectrum. Policies to control and manage the professional training and development of teachers have been a central part of this process. In particular, the move towards a corporate model of school-based training has had major implications for the way in which initial teacher education is currently conceptualized and delivered (Talbot, 1991). Placing greater training responsibility and control into the hands of schools has had major repercussions for teacher training establishments. Initial training institutions have had to respond to government legislation with some speed and have restructured their training programmes quite drastically to meet the new requirements. A spectator to these recent government and allied pronouncements could be forgiven for imagining why such moves have met with widespread criticism from the teaching profession. However, it is clear that how teachers acquire, or develop, professional knowledge is at the very centre of this debate.

Plainly, what school-based training most readily provides is the opportunity for learning through practice and through observation of practice – in other words, experiential learning. Developing the capacity to optimize learning from experience is of central importance in initial teacher education (ITE) and for ongoing professional development. The ideas of 'teacher as researcher' (Stenhouse, 1975), 'action research' (Carr and Kemmis, 1983), the reflective practitioner (Schon, 1983) and experiential learning (Kolb, 1984) have gained a currency across initial teacher education reflecting a commitment to fostering high-quality professional performance. However, the question currently under debate is whether the new training arrangements will provide the range of quality experiences necessary and appropriate for professional development.

While it is somewhat premature to make definitive judgements about this issue, some preliminary evidence is available concerning the school experiences of students participating in the new course. This has resulted from a research project funded by the University Funding Council (UFC) which was designed to explore experiential learning in higher education. This three-year research programme systematically collected evidence about the ways in which experiential learning was both conceptualized and realized within the context of teacher education. It aimed to provide information about the experience component of ITE programmes and to draw conclusions about the ways in which learning from experience could be best facilitated and supported. Students were interviewed at three stages during their postgraduate certificate year, prior to, during and following their school-based experience. All students were training to teach in the secondary phase and were specialists in either science or arts subjects. Overall, 40 novice teachers were interviewed during the life of the project about their experiences during school-based time.

During the course of the project the new regulatory framework in Circular 9/92 (DFE, 1992d) and the subsequent note of guidance from CATE significantly redefined both the process and practice of teacher education. In consequence, during the latter part of 1992 a new 'partnership PGCE' model was designed to meet the new requirements. This made the provision for students to be placed in schools for a larger proportion of their course time and dramatically altered the balance of the course towards much greater school responsibility for training. Consequently, it was clear that the UFC research project provided a unique opportunity to compare and contrast the previous and the current PGCE course. The systematic collecting of information about the nature and type of student experiences on both courses allowed for some preliminary comparative judgements to be made. These judgements focus on the quality and range of students' learning experience as evidenced in the different course structures.

THE RESEARCH FINDINGS

The comparison of student experiences proved to be illuminating and some interesting contrasts emerged. For example, in the previous PGCE course the learning experiences which students described were far more varied than those described by students involved in the current course. The experiences students described differed considerably between the courses in their content, range and depth. One typical account from a student on the previous course demonstrated this range:

> It's difficult to pinpoint one significant experience as there has been so much I've learnt. This week I've been working with my own tutor group on PSE (Personal and Social Education) issues, I've been out on a visit to the museum with them. I've taught history across years 7 to 9 and have run a lunchtime history club. I've been involved in departmental meetings where we've talked about assessment and

have contributed to a parents' evening. I feel like a real teacher because I've been teaching but I've done so much more than just that.

In direct contrast, a typical account from a student on the current PGCE course described the school experience in far more limited terms:

We've done most of the activities prescribed in the course booklets. I've taught several lessons with the classes allocated to me but I've only really been involved with those two groups on a regular basis. I've sat in on tutorial lessons but not taken any. I'd like to get involved more but our mentor seems restricted by the course programme, there seems to be little flexibility to do anything different or extra.

Many other student accounts demonstrated the same contrast between the content, range and depth of experiences on the two courses. An English student on the current course noted, 'There's more I'd like to experience but there isn't time or opportunity. A lot of time is taken up with course activities which we complete while in school.' Similarly, a maths student commented: 'We spend more time in school but we are not gaining more experience. We just stay there for longer, often just sitting in the staffroom or empty classrooms.' In the previous course, the school-based time had been largely free of coursework constraints and thus time had been more available for students to involve themselves in a wider range of activities. One student on the previous course summed up the distinction neatly in the statement: 'When we are at school, we are at school. There is little thought of university. I just want to experience as many aspects of teaching as possible. When I go back to university, then I'll think about assignments.'

This demonstrated that, for some students, the additional time spent in school on the current PGCE course had not led directly to additional, or richer, learning experiences. This extra time for them had been spent on completing course activities which previously would have been undertaken at the university or college. As a result, students on the current course presented a diffuse and disparate account of their experiences which often lacked depth or variety.

There was also evidence which showed that students on the current course were less sure about their role in school than students on previous courses. The fact that students spent more time in schools did not lead to a greater clarification of their role, as might be expected. In the previous course, when students were in school their main function was to practise classroom teaching and as such they generally viewed their role as 'student-teacher' or 'novice teacher'. In contrast, on the current course students felt that this was not the role they could adopt with any conviction because, for periods of time, they were in the school but not teaching. One student summed this up by saying:

We spend a lot of time in schools which seems rather pointless. We sit in the staffroom doing assignments and when I am teaching I'm always thinking about my next piece of work. Because staff have a responsibility for assessing you and coaching you, I'm never quite sure if I am a teacher or a student. I'd really like the time in school to be focused on teaching, not just a convenient base where I spend more time in the staffroom than the classroom.

This raises some fundamental questions about the amount of school-based time on the current course and, more importantly, how that time is being interpreted and used by students. The comparative findings showed that placing students in school for a greater length of time did not necessarily lead to a greater number of teaching experiences and that for some students it resulted in confusion over roles and responsibilities. These findings would seem to suggest that the whole issue of school-based time in the current course needs careful reconsideration and possible restructuring.

Another feature the course comparison highlighted was the fact that the range and type of schools available on the current course was far more limited than on the previous course. The findings showed that in the previous course students had been exposed to a diverse set of schools and had experienced many different types of school. One student described this in the following way:

> I have been in so many schools this year which have all been very different. I don't mean in the obvious way but in context, catchment, climate and location. This has helped me to get a hold of the range and has showed me the types of schools I would like to work in and those I would not.

In the current course, students did not refer to such diversity and most of the experiences they described reflected their experience in only two schools. For example, one student commented: 'I guess the two schools are not so different. I'd really like to experience an inner-city school.' Similarly, another student noted: 'I know I could teach in the types of schools I've been teaching in on this course, nice middle-class schools. But what about the others? I have no experience of those to fall back on.'

Consequently, the examples of professional learning which current students described largely reflected their experience in only one or two schools. In contrast, students on the previous course provided examples from a much wider range of schools. Also, in the previous course, individual tutors were more able to exercise their professional judgement in selecting schools and allocating students. In contrast, only 'partner' schools were able to be considered on the current course, which automatically limited the range of schools for selection. The research findings suggested that students on the previous course had been exposed to different types of schools. As one student concluded at the end of the previous course:

> I am exhausted but exhilarated. I've experienced so much on this course. I've taught in a rural school, an inner-city school, visited a special school, been into lots of different schools on the theatre-in-education programme and have taught primary and secondary classes. I feel prepared to teach now, I feel I have enough experience behind me. I feel a well rounded and well grounded teacher.

In contrast, a student on the current course commented:

I don't feel I'm getting anywhere. I'm teaching the same three groups who are always the same, well behaved, easy to teach. I want other experiences but the school cannot offer them. They have ten students and don't want pupils to experience student overkill. Consequently, I'm repeating my experience but not building upon it, or reflecting upon it in any way. I'm frustrated, but what can you do?

The feeling that students were not 'building upon' or 'reflecting upon' their experiences adequately was not an uncommon view from participants on the current course. Several students had voiced frustration about not being able to consolidate their learning in any structured way and readily commented on 'the lack of opportunity and time for structured reflection'. On the previous course students had been able to articulate more readily about their ability to reflect. For example, one student noted: 'I know that we are told to reflect on experience, but I found that quite hard initially. With the help of my tutor, however, I have made progress and can now reflect in quite a structured way.' While another student commented: 'I was fed up of reflecting back all the time but now I see the value of it.'

Two explanations can be offered for this difference. First, in the previous course there was a course emphasis upon reflection which was reinforced through structured recording in a record of student experience (Harris and Russ, 1994) which was not retained in the current course. Secondly, in the previous course tutors had more time available to work with students to develop the techniques of critical reflection. Student evidence suggested that the mentors, who now have this responsibility, vary quite significantly in their capacity to undertake this crucial role.

The student accounts of their experiences on the current course revealed that in some cases they were not being given the support and critical engagement needed for learning to take place. In the previous course with greater tutor time allocated and a greater responsibility for assessing teaching practice, students had described how tutors' intervention had aided their learning. For example, one student noted: 'You need outside help to learn, you need someone to challenge you and criticize you. I find the time with my tutor invaluable. After a lesson I learn so much from that discussion.' Similarly, many other students reinforced the importance of tutor support and interaction and generally welcomed the opportunity for structured reflection. From the research findings, it was evident that both the quality and quantity of these interactions varied significantly. While there were examples from students of mentoring of a high quality, there were also incidences where students had not been in receipt of any kind of quality structured feedback. The evidence from students on the current PGCE course does little to suggest that poor-quality mentoring is only in evidence in some schools. What students' descriptions revealed was a lack of time available for mentors to undertake the debriefing process and a lack of skill in the rudiments of the feedback process itself. For example, one student commented:

I teach a lesson but I have no idea why it didn't go too well, I need some feedback but the mentor does not seem able to give it. At the other extreme, I seem to be doing OK, the class get on with their work but I could not tell you why this is working. I need someone else with expertise to tell me why.

In summary, the findings from the comparative data provided some clear messages about the nature and quality of students' experiences on the current course. First, in the current 'school-based' model, the range and quality of student experience was highly variable and was often not geared to the specific learning needs of the student. Secondly, the changes to the way in which the university or college tutors were able to operate in the 'school-based' model severely curtailed the opportunities for students to reflect on and to learn from experience. Thirdly, there was evidence to suggest that student experiences were frequently limited and restricted to the context of their two 'partnership' schools. Finally, student learning from experience was highly dependent on the quality of mentor interaction, which varied quite significantly across the current course.

CONCLUSION

These research findings collectively reinforce other research work which has demonstrated that, by and large, schools are not places where novice teachers learn to become most effective (Goodlad, 1988). Much research documentation exists which shows the individualistic, isolated cultures of schools can inhibit innovation and teacher improvement (Lortie, 1975; Rosenholt and Kyle, 1984; Fullan and Stiegelbauer, 1991). This is not to suggest that the school experience component of ITE does not have a significant part to play in the professional development of teachers. Instead, it argues that this experience in itself is insufficient for professional development to occur and that the epistemological basis of the 'school-based' model is both reductionist and mechanistic.

The emerging framework of regulatory, legislative and structural changes demonstrates this mechanistic view of the role of the teacher. It is essentially this ideological framework which is the driving force to what has been termed a 'social market' view of teacher education and development (Elliott, 1993). The main features of this model of professional learning is that it views trained teachers as products which may be valued by consumers (school managers, governors and parents) and is premissed on the notion that required outcomes can be prespecified in performance terms. The aspiration of the competency-based 'social market' model is, it has been suggested, for improved standards and improved quality of teaching (DES, 1972). Yet it is largely debatable whether the demands of professional training can be defined in terms of narrow, prescribed, behaviourally construed skills.

This research evidence has demonstrated the consequences of moving down the 'social market' route. It has shown how the range and quality of students' learning experiences have been affected, and how the opportunities for students to reflect upon experience have been curtailed. It has demonstrated the narrowing of experience and opportunities for professional development and growth implicit in the new model. In essence, it has highlighted that quality learning experiences are not automatically provided when students spend more time in school and that professional development requires specialist intervention. Essentially, it has demonstrated the importance of grounding teacher education within the highest tenets of professional development rather than reducing it to the lowest common denominator of market forces.

CHAPTER 19

Student-Teachers' Thinking

CHRIS KYRIACOU and MEI LIN
University of York

Over the last ten years, increasing interest has been paid to how student-teachers develop their ideas about effective teaching in the classroom (e.g. Cruickshank, 1990; Kyriacou, 1993). Particular attention has been paid to

1 the development of their understanding of how and why certain learning activities may be effective in generating the desired learning outcomes in pupils;
2 the development of the skills required to put their understanding into practice; and
3 the key factors and features operating during an initial teacher training (ITT) course which influence such development.

In the 1980s, a number of authors (such as Shulman, 1987) began to outline the key areas of knowledge, understanding and skills that student-teachers need to develop, and these writings have shaped much subsequent research. For example, a series of studies by Calderhead (e.g. Calderhead and Robson, 1991) is typical. He has pointed to how primary school student-teachers appear to build up 'schema' (or mental plans) for classroom teaching. At the beginning of an initial training course such schema for classroom teaching are very crude and in some areas totally absent, and this makes it difficult for them to make sensible decisions about lesson structure, choice of learning activities, timing of lesson sequence, matching the level of work to pupils and the monitoring of the lesson while it is in progress. As the training experience progresses, however, they build up schema which constitute their knowledge, understanding and skills and through these their decision-making and classroom teaching improves. As a result of such research, teacher training courses have now focused much more on developing student-teachers' practical competencies by an appropriate mix of experiences which explicitly help them develop these schema for teaching. Such training experiences typically include lectures, seminars, guided reading and simulations running in parallel with, and/or before and after, periods of classroom teaching practice in schools. The key features of these activities, in contrast to typical courses in the past, is their much greater emphasis on helping student-teachers to make sense of what is happening in a way which helps improve their own thinking and performance (see Wallace, 1991).

While numerous research studies have been published dealing with primary school and secondary school student-teachers, either as a whole or with respect to particular topic or subject areas (e.g. teaching of reading in primary schools; or teaching of mathematics in secondary schools), few studies have focused on student-teachers of modern languages in secondary schools.

This relative neglect in focusing on foreign languages (FL) student-teachers is perplexing, since there has been a strong tradition of research and writing concerning FL pedagogy (Swarbrick, 1994). It may in part, however, be explained by the strong interest in relating curriculum delivery to matters of course design and materials in the context of linguistically based theories of language learning rather than by exploring how 'expert' classroom practitioners teach. Nevertheless, there have been over the years a number of important studies dealing with the latter (see, for example, Sanderson, 1983; Peck, 1988; Brumfit and Mitchell, 1990).

This study thus sought to explore student-teachers' ideas about effective learning activities by focusing on a sample of student-teachers of FL. The focus of this chapter is on the impact of aspects of the PGCE course on the development of their thinking rather than detailing the nature of their views about FL learning activities themselves.

THE STUDY

The main aim of the study was to explore how student-teachers' ideas about effective learning activities in the FL classroom developed over the course of a one-year postgraduate course of ITT. The study was conducted at the University of York. The PGCE course at York at the time of the study essentially comprised a campus-based course in terms 1 and 3 (with some limited school experience in term 1), together with a block practice in term 2. The main data for the study comprised semi-structured interviews with a sample of 15 PGCE student-teachers in each of terms 1, 2 and 3. These interviews focused on their ideas about effective learning activities in the FL classroom, and how these ideas had been developed and influenced by their experiences. All interviews were tape-recorded and transcribed. In addition, in order to contextualize this interview data, four FL course tutors and five heads of the FL department in the term-2 schools were interviewed concerning their views on how student-teachers' ideas develop over the course of the PGCE year. A sample of PGCE course activities were also observed over the year, including a sample of the student-teachers' lessons in terms 1 and 2.

RESULTS AND DISCUSSION

The interviews in term 1 revealed that the students had few expectations of the PGCE course before starting it. In general, they simply hoped that by the end of the course they would be able to teach. The students felt that the term-1 sessions had been successful in giving them clear ideas about how the teaching of FL had changed since they had been pupils and about the different types of learning activities and approaches they would typically find being used in schools nowadays and would be expected to adopt in their own classroom practice. At the start of the course, the students did an intensive course in Russian for one week. Students felt this had been very successful in reminding them of what it was like to begin learning a new language, and it had also usefully demonstrated to them the approach to teaching being advocated, and how such learning activities could be employed in their own teaching.

Of particular interest is that, despite sessions on the key tasks of classroom teaching, such as planning lessons, students felt towards the end of term 1 that they still did not know how to plan and prepare lessons. In effect, this reflects a distinction between knowing something in theory and knowing it in practice; a distinction which will be picked up later.

As well as the curriculum area course in term 1, the FL students also attended a common course alongside the PGCE students from other curriculum areas dealing with issues of importance to all students (for example, classroom management and discipline, special educational needs, pastoral care and crosscurricular themes and issues). The students felt these sessions provided them with some general ideas concerning their wider role and what they could expect to find in schools, but in terms of having an impact on their ideas about effective learning activities in the FL classroom, only the sessions on classroom management and discipline were felt to have been particularly influential.

The students generally felt that visits to schools and the short experiences of teaching in term 1 were helpful in giving them a clearer idea of how modern languages are typically taught. They also felt the tutorials on campus were helpful in this respect. In addition, role play and simulations of classroom teaching on campus also helped develop students' thinking about how to use different types of activities, but the point was made by some students that, since the audience comprised other linguists, these activities could not adequately highlight how pupils might react.

Students felt that the term-2 block-practice experience clearly had the greatest impact on their development. They often made the point that teaching practice made all the difference between thinking about a learning activity in a vacuum as against the reality of its use in a classroom. Classroom practice highlighted what factors and features enhance and hinder the effective use of a learning activity. In addition, the students felt that observing pupils' reactions to what they did was the single most important influence on their learning to teach.

Students felt that an initial period at the start of term 2 spent observing lessons by the normal class teacher was helpful in giving them a feel for the class, its social environment and the teacher's general approach and routines, and a feel for the practical application of some of their ideas about learning activities. The students felt they were going to be 'borrowing' the class from its normal teacher and consequently felt they should not introduce radical changes, but neither did they feel this meant they should attempt to simply copy the teacher's style or approach.

The visits from the college tutors were felt to be helpful, but were dominated by the feeling that they were being assessed rather than having an opportunity for further support and help. Students felt such visits were successful in giving general feedback on progress, but they also felt more detailed feedback and discussion would have better shaped the development of their thinking. Comments from staff at the school were generally regarded as very helpful, but some students felt they were trapped in a more traditional department that did not allow them to try out some activities they would have liked to. Feedback from other student-teachers in the evening on campus allowed a useful sharing of ideas. Those students who were placed at a school with another FL student found sharing ideas in the school with the other student was particularly helpful. Some students also said that pupils occasionally made useful comments about particular lessons and activities.

In general, term 3 was felt to be useful but somewhat an anti-climax. By the start of term 3 many students had already got jobs fixed for the following September, and this partly coloured their enthusiasm for the third term. However, the students did feel the term had been useful in allowing them to collect further ideas, particularly by looking at examples of each other's curriculum materials produced and used during term 2. While students felt term 3 provided an opportunity to take stock and further reflect on their ideas about teaching, most students said that the most important reflection about classroom practice had already occurred in term 2 and during the vacation before term 3. They felt term 3 did not contain enough structured activity which explicitly encouraged reflection. Some made the point that it was assumed students knew how to reflect and evaluate their teaching to best effect, but this was not always the case, and more ideas about how to reflect effectively would have been useful throughout the course.

Interestingly, most students felt it was only after term 2 that they properly appreciated some of the inputs and activities which occurred in term 1, and in retrospect they felt term 1 had provided a very useful and important preparation, even though they did not always see the purpose and value of some activities at the time.

In thinking about the role of the school in influencing their thinking, students expressed a number of concerns about the nature of the impact of school experience. Notably, they felt that in schools there was little time to stand back and think about what you were doing; you are also very much constrained by the approach to teaching adopted in that particular FL department; and for about half of the schools where the students were placed, the students felt there were only somewhat limited and often very dated curriculum materials available in that school. In addition, and particularly interesting, was their feeling that during term 2 they were gradually moving in how they saw themselves and were seen by others, from being a student-teacher towards being a practitioner. This meant that as the term-2 block practice progressed, they felt less willing to ask for help and advice from the school staff, as this was not consistent with trying to establish themselves in their new role as a practitioner. The college-based experiences were felt to be of immense value in redressing these areas of concern.

SOME IMPLICATIONS FOR CURRENT REFORMS

It is clear from this study that the student-teachers felt that the greatest impact by far on the development of their ideas was the block teaching-practice experience. It was here that they made frequent reference to being able to understand the nature of teaching only by actually doing it. However, it is also clear from the interviews that the term-1 college-based input had been successful in providing them with a framework and vocabulary of ideas and principles that helped them to develop a set of 'proto-schema' which they were able to utilize in making sense of their experience of the block practice. In one sense, student-teachers felt that during the practice term they had learnt largely 'by their own efforts'. However, further probing revealed that what was taking place here was a sense in which what they felt they knew 'in theory' was gradually being made meaningful and more sophisticated. In effect, for example in the use of flashcards, it was a move between knowing how flashcards can be used effectively (viz., at the level of knowing what flashcards were and the procedures and techniques that can be used), to knowing what it feels like to be using them effectively. The latter has an emotional and interactive quality to it that the former lacks. In other words, one might know that 'in theory' one should stand centre-stage and distribute the questions well, but 'in practice' doing this successfully involves looking around to decide whom to direct the question to, sounding enthusiastic and deciding what type of response is correct or good enough. All these qualities led to an enrichment of the proto-schema for the use of flashcards in ways that built upon the college-based inputs. At a time when the school-based experience has increased as a proportion of the PGCE year, there is a real danger that these proto-schema are not adequately developed as part of the preparation for or support during the classroom practice. There is a real issue here concerning whether school mentors on a wholly or almost wholly school-based PGCE can provide these important proto-schema for supporting the student-teachers.

Another important influence for student-teachers' thinking was being able to share experiences with other student-teachers and tutors both about teaching and about learning to teach. As most students live on campus and travelled to their practice schools, it meant that the sharing of experiences drew on experiences in different schools. This was a great strength as they were able to reflect on the different styles and approaches adopted in different school FL departments. Again, there is a danger here that wholly or almost wholly school-based courses will severely limit such sharing of experiences across schools, and possibly even allow some student-teachers to assume that a weak department's practice was actually good practice.

In addition, the third term's experience allowed students to reflect further on their experiences, to assess their progress and need for further development at a critical distance from the school, and to share ideas, for example, by having a display of curriculum materials produced by students in term 2. Again, it is hard to see how this can occur easily and so richly in a wholly or almost wholly school-based course.

Finally, looking overall at the students' comments about the impact of the PGCE course on their thinking, they felt that the course would have been of greater benefit if more coherent and well planned cycles of college input, followed by school practice followed by reflection, could have been built into the course on a more regular basis over the year. There is thus clearly a need to consider how different models of course structure for a PGCE course can deliver such cycles to best effect.

CONCLUSIONS

This study has provided some insight into the impact of a PGCE course on how student-teachers' ideas concerning effective learning activities in the FL classroom develop over the course of a PGCE year. It is clear that the student-teachers actively accumulate ideas which they then test out and modify over the course of the year. While the student-teachers themselves report experiencing much of this as a personal endeavour, particularly in relation to teaching lessons during block practice, it is clear that the training experiences provided before and after their block practice, and the support they receive from school and college staff during the block practice, all feed into the development of their thinking in a way that is crucial for a quick and effective transition towards becoming a successful practitioner, and supports the view that such structured support for student-teachers makes a major contribution to the development of their classroom teaching expertise.

CHAPTER 20

Withdrawals from PGCE *Courses*[*]

MARGARET SANDS and PAM BISHOP
University of Nottingham

One of the largest secondary PGCE courses in England is at the University of Nottingham. Most students stay the whole year, are successful, leave with a qualification and go straight into teaching in State schools. A few fail. However, more fall during the year than fail at the end, as students who sense their own dissatisfaction with or inadequacy in the classroom withdraw from the course.

This chapter examines the pattern of student withdrawal over six years, 1988–94, at different times of the year, and in relation to subject specialism and earlier qualifications, together with students' stated reasons for withdrawal. It also examines student response to the rigours of the course in the light of Circular 9/92 (DFE, 1992d) on teacher education.

Over the first years of this research, Nottingham PGCE students had spent at least 21 of the 36 weeks in schools. For 1993–4 it was increased to the statutory 24 weeks: a marginal increase, with a similar pattern of school experience over the year. It has been during the period of school-based work that the withdrawal rate has been highest.

The move to a more school-based course requires funding to be transferred to schools. In addition, the roles and responsibilities of both partners need to be more carefully defined. Enhanced communication and collaboration between the partners have been followed by in-service events for school mentors and co-ordinators. It remains to be seen if the professional support mechanisms now more developed in schools will be enough to alleviate the difficulties faced by those students who, in this survey, withdrew from the course during their time in school.

Circular 9/92 further defines the successful beginning teacher as someone who is able to show that he or she has acquired teaching competences. Newly trained teachers are expected to have a good academic background in their subject specialism, understand its place in the school curriculum and be able to

[*]This chapter is based substantially on an article previously published in *New Era*, Vol. 74, no. 2, pp. 58–64, August 1993: 'Student withdrawals from Teacher Training', by Margaret Sands.

plan suitable content for the full age and ability range of pupils. This has always been the case. However, subject knowledge is now the first on the list of Circular 9/92 teaching competences which perhaps gives it a new emphasis. None of the Nottingham PGCE students identified inadequacies in this area as the cause of drop-out from the course. In fact, as one remarked, she was leaving largely because she was prevented from pursuing an interest in the subject due to the many other demands of the job. It is too simplistic to expect that it is subject expertise which primarily determines teacher effectiveness. The student-teachers in this survey were very well qualified, confident and enthusiastic about their subject but deterred by the intensity and complexity of the school and classroom environments.

WITHDRAWALS OVER SIX YEARS

Table 20.1 shows the number of students who withdrew between 1988 and 1994. The drop-out rate of 1988–9 was unusually high and, in the reasons given by students for leaving, showed how issues of pay, low morale among school staff and poor working conditions greatly lessened their desire to continue. Teacher morale was low as a result of the teachers' industrial action and unrest of previous years, and was further reduced by the phenomenal pace of change in schools, immediately affecting classroom teachers through the National Curriculum. Student-teachers were exposed in schools to a profession reeling from external intervention and change, and suffering from a public image denigrated by the media, one which placed heavy burdens on its shoulders. It was not surprising that some students, faced with a barrage of comment and advice, decided to leave before they invested further time and effort.

TABLE 20.1
Withdrawals from the PGCE *course over six years*

YEAR	STUDENTS STARTING ONE-YEAR PGCE COURSE	WITHDRAWALS	WITHDRAWALS (%)
1988–9	204	25	12.3
1989–90	219	21	9.6
1990–1	224	13	5.8
1991–2	275	12	4.4
1992–3	267	16	6.0
1993–4	301	19	6.3

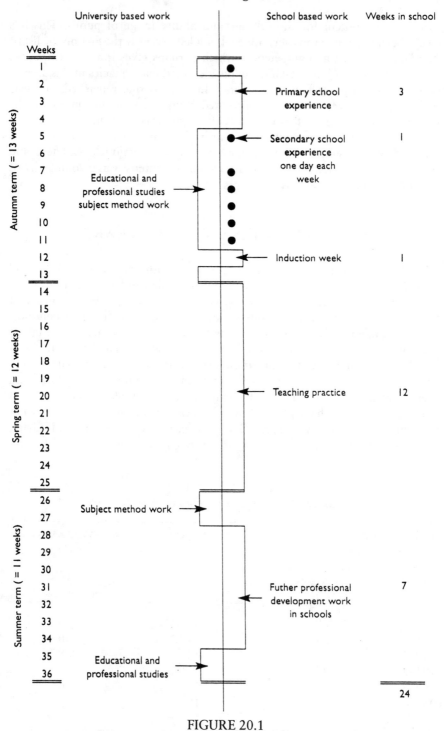

FIGURE 20.1

By the recession the situation had changed. In 1991–2 the withdrawal rate dropped to 4.4 per cent, only one-third of that of four years before. Students thought more than twice before voluntarily going into a job market which they knew was very tight.

WITHDRAWALS OVER THE ACADEMIC YEAR

The Nottingham University PGCE course contains four periods of time in schools (see Figure 20.1). In the three-week supervised primary school experience which starts the course, students are thrown into the thick of children, schools and teachers and – with few exceptions – delight in the experience. They learn that teaching is about children as well as subjects. And they discover that enthusiasm, commitment, initiative, preparation, good time-keeping, stamina and the ability to get on with colleagues count a great deal.

Through the rest of the autumn term in one day a week in a secondary school students follow a closely supervised sequence of activities, including some class teaching. Their main practice occupies the whole of the school's spring term, when students teach half to two-thirds of a full teaching timetable and, as far as possible, behave and are treated like members of staff. The summer term contains further school experience: a seven-week period in different schools based on the requirements of Circular 9/92 and negotiated to take account of each individual's needs and interests. Students' further needs may include A-level teaching, experience of inner-city schools or special needs, or other ways of consolidating and extending their experience. For example, a group taught prisoners at Norwich Prison. Others accompany pupils on field-trips, camps or outdoor pursuits, help with curriculum development, theatre sessions or have other attachments to schools or educational establishments.

Table 20.2 gives the number of students withdrawing during each term of the year. It can be seen that, by the summer term, most students intend to stay the course. Almost all have a successful teaching practice behind them. Very few withdraw at this stage, and only for personal reasons. A recent example was a physicist with a PhD determined to teach and settle in this country after many years abroad in petrochemical engineering. All approaches to him by firms had been rejected, but on the first day of the summer term his LEA announced a cut of 200 teaching posts. The next day he accepted a £30,000 job in an oil company and was gone.

It is during the teaching practice in the spring term that the greatest number (62 per cent) of the year's withdrawals occur. Students leave at a fairly steady rate through the term, with an increase before the external examiners visit. Those who were doubtful earlier in the year but who, by dint of careful placement, have continued until January, show that staying on was just a temporary period of endurance, and confirm their previous inclinations by withdrawing.

TABLE 20.2
Withdrawals from the PGCE course per term

YEAR	AUTUMN	SPRING	SUMMER	TOTAL
1988–9	9	14	2	25
1989–90	7	13	1	21
1990–1	8	5	0	13
1991–2	2	10	0	12
1992–3	4	8	4	16
1993–4	1	16	2	19
Total	31	66	9	105

REASONS FOR WITHDRAWAL

The greatest number of withdrawals, then, are during school-based work. The reasons given by students for voluntary withdrawal from the classroom, from a course in which they have invested many months work and loss of earnings, are almost entirely related to the world of teaching: students question their ability for or commitment to teaching.

Of those who question their ability, some feel that they are not 'cut out to be a teacher' and that teaching isn't for them: 'I no longer wish to teach.' 'I simply do not want to be a teacher.' And those who are more explicit feel that they will never win through:

> . . . lost confidence, can't cope . . . unsuited and having difficulties with most aspects . . . classroom performance not as good as I would wish, particularly in assertiveness, and I haven't the commitment to overcome it . . . lacking in confidence after eight years out of employment looking after my parents, and can't get on top of my classes . . . I enjoy one-to-one relationships but find numbers and discipline beyond me; back to accountancy . . . lack of commitment and enthusiasm . . . my enthusiasm and motivation have all but evaporated . . . I find preparation difficult and assessment frightening . . . happier working with adults . . . my character isn't strong enough, too soft on homework and in class, I'm going with relief.

For these students, tutors and teachers are usually in agreement, having spent time helping and encouraging, but finally reaching the same conclusion. Probing may put the reason given by some into a different perspective. One who spoke at length about 'lacking the dedication for teaching' was described by a friend as needing less work and more pay.

Those who find a waning commitment to the job comment on the amount of work, the conditions in schools, the pay, and the image and morale of teachers:

> The volume of work was higher than I expected . . . The amount of preparation, after a full day, kept me up to the early hours, and I'm just not prepared to do that any longer . . . Disillusioned with the conditions in schools, the amount of paperwork, and the amount of out-of-school work . . . I find it far more demanding than I had imagined . . . My interest is in my subject, not all the extra work teachers have to do . . . Low morale in schools, and the low pay compared with others who graduated with me . . . I am quite exhausted . . . I want to cut my losses . . . Facilities are poor: no lab techs, have to set up and clear own practicals as well as do own typing and worksheet production, kids have no books, only one computer and overhead projector for the whole department . . . I have to travel between two schools every day and can't miss the transport, so urgent jobs don't get done at either building.

Many of this group of students find leaving a difficult decision to take. They may be quite good at teaching. They are good at their subject. They enjoy working with children and may come out of lessons elated with the interactions and with the work they have done. They get on well with their colleagues in school. But the total lifestyle indicated above, of working facilities in school, of excess work out of school coupled with the low rewards, finally defeats them. It is, however, good to note that, as they go, tribute is often paid to the new and useful skills they have learnt during their PGCE year. They find it intensive and recognize their own development as it proceeds.

In the first term of the year, as one would expect, the reasons for withdrawal are not all because of teaching. Indeed, the hearts and minds of most are captured by the three weeks of primary school experience. None the less, for a few, even after such a brief exposure, it is already clear to them that this is a world into which they should not have ventured. About half the first term's withdrawals are the result of difficulties experienced in the classroom or a dawning understanding of the demands teaching makes.

Reports from primary heads which comment penetratingly on lack of ideas or enthusiasm, poor time-keeping, inability to listen to advice, need for reminders, inadequate preparation or lack of commitment, combine with tutors' own understanding of the situation and point to the need for help to adapt to school life or counselling out of the profession. Such students are usually not long before they go on their way.

The remainder of the first term's withdrawals leave for personal reasons: pregnancy, illness or death in the family, no time to complete a PhD thesis, absence of a loved one, return to previous job, delayed job offer, poverty, homesickness. A very few leave very early: a physics graduate left at the end of the first day saying that he'd 'given it a whirl'.

All other students stay the course and most of them retain their commitment to and joy in teaching. But running through the six years of this inquiry are the constant stresses which cause some to go, are commented on by many, but which cannot really be appreciated until trainees move into full time teaching and experience the job in all its aspects. Withdrawals during training are a loss, but arguably less of a loss than the same person leaving later, suffering personal trauma and contributing little to a school. For some, in the first years of a full-time post the exhaustion, the preparation and marking during evenings and weekends, the other jobs and additional duties they are called upon to do, reinforce earlier feelings and their departure contributes to teacher turnover.

About 88 per cent of Nottingham students are teaching in the UK shortly after obtaining their PGCE. Some 4 per cent choose to teach abroad first. A further 3 per cent go into other jobs, some waiting for a suitable teaching vacancy, and a few proceed to further full-time study. Of the 88 per cent, how many stay in teaching, and for how long? And are the reasons which finally cause retreat from the profession to be found in those given above?

WITHDRAWALS BY SUBJECT

The inquiry looked at the pattern of drop-out within each subject area into which students are recruited. Table 20.3 shows the figures over six years. It is the shortage subjects of physics, mathematics and modern languages which lose the most students. Physics tops the list with a 14 per cent withdrawal of those who started, mathematics loses 10.3 per cent and modern languages 8.4 per cent. It is also these same shortage subjects which have a much higher withdrawal rate in the teaching practice term, especially when compared with other subjects. The reasons for going are those given above.

Students make it clear that they have a good idea of the job market outside teaching and are not prepared to put up with a job where they have difficulties in coping or the working conditions are not as good as elsewhere. It may be that those in shortage subjects are in part encouraged to leave because of the job opportunities open to them. Certainly, for such well qualified people, particularly in sought-after subject areas, with their skills and experience extended by participation in a teacher training course, finding employment seems to be no problem.

SELECTION AND QUALIFICATIONS

The degree and A-level qualifications of the Nottingham PGCE students are good. An analysis of the A-level grades of all students reveals that classics and mathematics head the list, with physics second and modern languages sixth. The average A-level score is 24.7 for classics and mathematics, 24.2 for physics, 19.6 for modern languages. With A = 10 a score of 24 is thus equal to, say, ABC.

With regard to degree classifications, over these six years between 81 and 90 per cent of the entry have first or second-class honours degrees. The break-

TABLE 20.3
Withdrawals from the PGCE course by subject and term

	E	D	ML	C	H	G	B	P	CH	M	Total
Autumn											
1988–9	3	0	1	1	0	0	1	0	1	2	9
1989–90	0	0	0	3	1	1	1	0	0	1	7
1990–1	2	0	0	1	2	1	1	1	0	0	8
1991–2	0	0	0	0	0	0	0	0	1	1	2
1992–3	1	0	1	0	0	0	1	1	0	0	4
1993–4	0	0	1	0	0	0	0	0	0	0	1
Total	6	0	3	5	3	2	4	2	2	4	31
Spring											
1988–9	2	0	0	0	0	1	2	3	1	5	14
1989–90	1	0	7	0	2	0	1	0	0	2	13
1990–1	1	0	0	1	0	0	0	0	0	3	5
1991–2	0	0	2	0	1	1	0	2	1	3	10
1992–3	3	0	1	0	0	0	0	1	0	3	8
1993–4	4	0	2	1	3	1	2	1	2	0	16
Total	11	0	12	2	6	3	5	7	4	16	66
Summer											
1988–9	0	0	1	0	0	0	0	0	0	1	2
1989–90	0	0	0	0	0	0	0	1	0	0	1
1990–1	0	0	0	0	0	0	0	0	0	0	0
1991–2	0	0	0	0	0	0	0	0	0	0	0
1992–3	1	0	0	0	0	0	0	1	0	2	4
1993–4	1	0	0	0	0	0	0	0	0	2	16
Total	2	0	1	0	0	0	0	2	0	4	9
Total											
1988–9	5	0	2	1	0	1	3	3	2	8	25
1989–90	1	0	7	3	3	1	2	1	0	3	21
1990–1	3	0	0	2	2	1	1	1	0	3	13
1991–2	0	0	2	0	1	1	0	2	2	4	12
1992–3	5	0	2	0	0	0	1	3	0	5	16
1993–4	3	0	3	0	2	1	1	1	2	0	13
											1
Total	17	0	16	6	8	5	8	11	6	23	100
% withdrawn	5.9	0	8.4	12.8	5	3.5	5.8	14.1	5.6	10.3	

KEY: E – English, D – Drama, ML – Modern languages, C – Classics, H – History, G – Geography, B – Biology, P – Physics, CH – Chemistry, M – Maths down for 1993 is 6.4 per cent with first-class degrees, 45.4 per cent with 2.1 degrees and 36.1 per cent with 2.2. The remaining 12 per cent had third-class honours or unclassified degrees or degree equivalent, some from abroad. In addition, 10.2 per cent had a higher degree.

Of the 13 students who withdrew in 1993–4, two had first-class degrees, five had 2.1 and five had 2.2 degrees, and one had a third. Their mean A-level score was 21.4. Four had higher degrees. Of the 16 students of the 1992 entry who withdrew, two had firsts, nine had 2.1 or 2.2 degrees, two had thirds and three had unclassified or foreign degree equivalents. Their mean A-level score was 22. One had a PhD and two had masters degrees.

With backgrounds such as these it is difficult to argue that the students who withdraw are ill-qualified academically, and one cannot point to a relationship between withdrawal and poor degree or A-level results.

GENDER AND AGE

In numbers the drop-out students are almost equally divided between men and women but with a higher percentage figure for men (8.2) than for women (5.1). With regard to age, the drop-out is low for those under 25 years (2.8 per cent), rising to 8 per cent of students aged 25–39, and to 22 per cent of those over 40. Those who have already had employment other than teaching find the prospect of returning to something similar more attractive than staying in schools.

FAILURES

Over the last five years, of those who have presented themselves for examination, 23 students have failed. They are from all subject areas and no pattern has emerged. Table 20.4 shows the data. The mean A-level score for those failing is 13.5 compared with a course mean of 21.4. Their degree results, however, are in line with those of other students: 19 have good honours degrees, four a pass degree and one has an MA, again suggesting that academic excellence does not necessarily correlate with teaching ability. Contrary to the general trend, however, there are more men, and more students under 24, in the failed group than one would expect: 16 men and 7 women, with 13 under 24 and 3 over 40.

CONCLUSION

The evidence here indicates that students who withdraw from a PGCE course do so largely because, one way or another, their experience in schools convinces them that teaching is a job they no longer wish to do. It is not because they are poorly qualified in their own subject, and probably not because of gender or age.

TABLE 20.4
Number of failures in the PGCE course

YEAR	THEORY	PRACTICE	BOTH	TOTAL
1988–9	0	2	0	2
1989–90	3	3	1	7
1990–1	2	3	1	6
1991–2	2	2	0	4
1992–3	0	4	0	4
1993–4	2	8	0	10
Total	9	22	2	33

Lawlor (1990) has criticized PGCE courses because the method courses seem to be based not on mastering the subject and on subject content but on other activities, work which is related to teaching skills and an understanding of how to adapt one's subject to children and the classroom. She also comments that '. . . assessment does not set out to measure whether the student has mastered the subject sufficiently to teach it confidently' (*ibid.*, p. 46).

Students must have a degree in the relevant subject area of their proposed teaching specialism before being accepted on to a postgraduate training course. With degree and A-level qualifications such as those discussed above, one might expect students to have mastered their subject content and not to need further teaching or assessment in it during the training year.

Lawlor's conclusion is that, '. . . instead of putting mastery of the subject at the heart of the [PGCE] course, as the essential foundation for good teaching, the training course demeans the subject to being little more than a peg on which to hang modish educational theory', and that '. . . one of the principal causes of the shortage of highly qualified able teachers is the present system of training. It deters good graduate specialists from entering the profession' (*ibid.*, p. 42).

It is clear from the details given here that postgraduate trainee teachers are very well qualified in their teaching subject area and could be said to have mastered it after A-levels, an honours degree and (for 10 per cent of the 1993–4 intake) a higher degree. The shortage of highly qualified teachers on the evidence produced here is not related to academic qualifications or lack of subject knowledge but far more to an inability or lack of desire to cope with the classroom, children of all abilities and the working conditions in schools. Rather than being deterred by the training year from entering the profession, it is regarded as an essential staging post. During the year student-teachers discover whether or not they have the ability and commitment to teach: by working in different schools, at different levels, and with different emphases; with supported time away from the classroom to practise skills, to prepare, discuss, read and think; with pastoral care and counselling; and with opportunities to share anxieties, ideas and triumphs with other beginners during a very stressful time. Those who withdraw during the year, regardless of their good previous academic attainment, feel unable to enter the profession. Academic excellence seems not to be related to teaching ability.

Given that involvement in schools and with children in classrooms is a major cause of withdrawal from training, students clearly need to experience work in schools before they can know if they wish to continue. Students are asked at interview to do all they can to see that they have secondary school experience before they come on the course, and all are expected to spend a week in a primary school before the start of the course. Potential students do not have the time or the facilities to engage in anything longer before they join the course, and neither could the schools cope with them. Some drop-out is therefore probably inevitable.

Without time in schools there seems to be little way of ensuring that students know if they wish to continue in teaching. And during the training year, substantial experience in schools is essential and valued, giving a range of rich and diverse experiences which enable the beginning teacher to enter with greater confidence and commitment what he or she has come to realize is a demanding profession.

CHAPTER 21

Agendas in Conflict?

LINDA FURSLAND
Bath College of Higher Education

The first priority for schools is to teach pupils.

(DES, 1991, p. 33)

How does the increased presence of student-teachers in schools affect teachers' primary responsibilities to their pupils? What do schools perceive as the advantages and disadvantages of having student-teachers around the school? Do the student-teachers feel they are getting a good deal from their additional time spent in school? Is there a conflict for the school and its teachers between their work in teaching pupils and the needs and priorities of student-teachers? This chapter seeks to answer these questions in relation to a school-based programme for developing student-teachers' professional skills and understandings.

The costs and benefits of a particular model of school-based initial teacher education (ITE), which places a group of 10 PGCE secondary students in partner schools for 17 days across the year to undertake professional perspectives (PP) involving the study of whole-school issues, is evaluated in this chapter. The 17 days in question were part of 120 days spent in school by 76 PGCE students on a pilot course which took place in 1992–3, fulfilling the requirements of Circular 9/92. Of the 120 days, in addition to the 17 days of PP, 12 of these were spent in serial school experience (SSE) during which student groups under the guidance of a subject specialist learn rudimentary teaching skills by working with groups of pupils; 82 of these were on block school experience (BSE) where students have the opportunity to take on the role of the teacher in the classroom, and nine of these involved primary school experience. Because of the concern by course planners to utilize 'good practice' specialist departments, students may have experienced as many as four different schools for these three types of secondary placement.

The PP course required students to spend 17 days on the school site looking in some depth at a variety of whole-school issues including the role of the teacher, the National Curriculum and assessment, equal opportunities, special educational needs, class management, pastoral care and the work of the form tutor, crosscurricular themes, etc. Students were briefed at the beginning of the day in a lecture session given by a teacher or college tutor and then moved into school-based activities which had been planned in advance by the senior teacher in charge of the programme and which centred upon the particular theme explored in the lecture. Students would already have been expected to do some advance preparation based on a handbook of readings prepared by college tutors. The aims of PP were to enhance students' professionalism by enabling them to develop critical understanding of whole-school issues and competence in the professional skills which are needed by all teachers regardless of subject area.

Assumptions about teaching and learning underlying this course development were based on the notion of students using the school as a resource, as a context in which to explore educational issues through action research methods, which would then lead to critical discussion with teachers and tutors. One of the difficulties faced by course planners was the need to expose students to issues which have emerged from recent educational research, for instance concerning equal opportunities, which would formerly have been studied in college. It was assumed that students spending more time in school would be able to use the school as a field-study base in which to gain experience at first hand of the findings of educational research relevant to the beginning teacher. Students would be engaged in the following means of action research:

1 General observation of, and involvement with the ethos of school (for example, through analysis of the school environment within and outside the classroom, and of expectations of pupils and staff).
2 Structured observation of teachers and pupils in the classroom (for example, through carrying out observation schedules of gender interaction, class management, etc.).
3 Working with or talking to pupils in the classroom, under the guidance of the teacher (for example, children with special educational needs).
4 Interviewing a group of pupils withdrawn from/outside the classroom (for example, to explore and analyse pupils' language development).
5 Interviewing school senior managers and other personnel, as well as teachers outside the classroom context.
6 Analysis of school policy documents, etc.
7 Evaluation, together with school staff and college tutors, of developments within the school in relation to the topics covered.

The research data reported in this chapter is from a project carried out during the academic year 1992–3 investigating students' and teachers' perspectives on the school-based pilot scheme, of which the PP was a part. The points made by students below, specifically about PP, should be set against the background of the positive nature of their comments overall about the whole course, its structure and the amount of time spent in school, as revealed in the broader findings of the research project.

The research methodology for this project involved a new member of staff who was not at that stage a member of the course team, conducting semi-structured interviews with the following:

1 The member of school staff, usually a senior management team member, in charge of the school-based PP programme at each of the partnership schools (seven interviews).
2 An additional member of the school staff at all but one of the partnership schools; all of these staff had been involved with the course in some capacity – e.g. as affiliated tutors (six interviews).
3 Two students who had been placed in each of the partnership schools, or in the case of one school one student only; these were chosen to give a balance between the genders and the student numbers within the different subject areas (13 interviews).
4 Additional data was obtained from student evaluations of the course and from presentations made by partner teachers at a conference at the institution on school-based teacher education.

Feedback from teachers in the seven schools involved with this scheme in its pilot year is significant because this was the first time that whole schools, as distinct from specialist subject departments, had been involved in ITE. What did it feel like for teachers? The perspectives of teachers from partnership schools involved in the delivery of the course tended to be positive overall about the school's involvement in the programme, perhaps because at least half of the people interviewed were the senior teachers in charge of the programme who had made a considerable investment in the planning and delivery of the course; all the other teachers interviewed had some involvement with the PP programme or with other aspects of school placement, SSE or BSE, and therefore again could be said to have vested interests in the success of the programme. Offsetting this, however, is the fact that for many of the student group their sole time in the school was spent pursuing the PP programme while carrying out subject specialist placements in another school setting. This could have been argued to reduce the satisfaction of the school with the programme because the traditional benefits of having students within the subject specialism were not always available to these departments.

The teachers interviewed could see a number of distinct benefits to the school, to the individual teachers, to the pupils and to the student-teachers themselves of being involved with this particular programme only, regardless of their involvement in other partnership school-based activities such as BSE or SSE. The reasons for this are given below.

For the school as a whole, involvement in this programme was said to have challenged the insularity of the school, the narrowness of existing policies, and encouraged the reformulation of these policies. One particular school, as a direct result of the project, set down in writing an explicit policy on bullying and was challenged to look again at its multicultural policy. Involvement in the programme was also described as good training for potential middle managers, who had been able to put new skills into operation including those of 'chairing, interview techniques and group dynamics.' Overall awareness of ITE and higher education was strengthened in schools and many of the staff appreciated the 'invigorating contact with young people' and with mature and interesting people who have given 'a little something' to the school.

For the individual teachers actually involved in the programme, as those being observed or interviewed by students or as leading sessions with the group of students, the gains were, in the judgement of senior teachers, quite considerable. Such teachers were exposed to new ideas, motivated to keep abreast of current trends and to reflect upon and question their own procedures and practices. This approach fits well with the continuous professional development model to which some schools now aspire, and to the philosophy underlying systems of appraisal. As one senior teacher put it: 'If you've got a student with you, you are training the student but you are also training yourself.' In addition the programme was said to have provided a 'showcase' for particular staff responsibilities and enthusiasms which was especially useful as a means of valuing staff whose expertise may have been overlooked in the daily routines of school life; such personnel included the school bursar, caretaker, etc.

In addition to the above benefits, it was felt that, if used properly by teachers, the potential of students in the classroom was considerable even in terms of being able to feed back usefully on their observations. It is harder to make this point in relation to the PP programme, however, than to subject specialist work where the student actually represents an additional pair of hands.

For the students themselves teachers felt it was valuable for them to be able to test out the reality of the theory they had received in the lecture less than one hour later in the classroom, since the '. . . topics that were being investigated lent themselves to immediate feedback from the school'. Additionally, the professional aspect of student-teachers' development, often neglected in the past, had begun to 'come into its own in the school setting'. In opposition to the above point, though, teachers noticed how difficult it was to motivate students outside their subject area before the start of BSE, for instance.

Overall the schools were positive about the benefits of the PP course although decisions about other over-riding priorities in their development plans led four out of the seven schools to pull out of the programme at the end of the year. One school explained that the degree of exposure arising from involvement in this project, while undoubtedly challenging and stimulating change, had also forced the school to '. . . retreat temporarily into a more isolationist position in order to clarify' their position and future goals. Two of the schools felt that their involvement in planning the course had given them expectations about the level of staff development to be provided by the college which had not been matched in reality. These two schools decided to work with another institution whose PGCE partnership course was coming on stream the following year.

Other drawbacks of involvement in this programme expressed by teachers were concerning the time-consuming nature of the preparation involved, which was particularly heavy for the senior staff member in charge of the programme who was, by definition, a person with many other commitments, and who needed to be 'someone with clout' in order to be able to negotiate the programme with other staff. The above point also raised resourcing issues which there is not space to discuss here. It was also felt that overexposure of particular classes to students could be dangerous for both the teachers and the pupils concerned, although at no point in the programme were students used to release teachers from their classes. A criticism of one school in particular was that the returns from this project were less satisfying than in a more traditional model where all the students would be making a contribution to subject specialist departments and schools would benefit from the deepening experience of the students as the year progressed. This may well be the major disadvantage of a model in which student placements are spread over three or four different schools.

Assumptions by course planners about how much of the former college course could be carried out in schools and the means by which this could be achieved, particularly in the case of some of the action research methods, needed reconsideration. In the event the methods of data collection most often used were observation and interviewing of teachers, the latter mostly 'on the hoof'. Interviewing pupils out of lessons was, in the words of one of the senior schoolteachers involved, 'the most disruptive bit'. The pressures of the National Curriculum and assessment and the tight time schedule within which teachers now feel themselves to be operating make it difficult to organize such activities, although one school got round this by withdrawing pupils from the lessons of absent staff being covered by colleagues. Other activities which were formerly part of the PGCE curriculum in higher education, commented the same senior teacher, '. . . didn't naturally lend themselves to school student involvement' and '. . . can't readily be translated into work which can be done in school'. An example of this was an exercise which asked the students to interview pupils about their experiences of bullying; some schools felt able to facilitate this while others felt it might represent an intrusion into the pupils' personal space. The tendency of many student-teachers to want to negotiate their school-based programme also presented some difficulties in some schools with their need to organize well in advance, a point made by the senior teacher quoted above whose words '. . . students have to fit in with the school as an institution that is running with a different agenda' provided the title for this chapter.

Comments by students in the research findings specifically focused on the school-based PP programme suggest that this programme was seen as helpful and relevant to professional development by many. The students were asked if they considered the work undertaken during the PP element of the course to be beneficial. Of the comments by the students about all aspects of PP, approximately a third (22) were positive and most of the rest (45) were constructively critical.

Students valued greatly the opportunity to experience school organization from the inside, to familiarize themselves with its internal workings and relationships, to prepare themselves for the role of the form tutor through the discussion of a wide range of issues, and to have had their consciousness raised in areas such as equal opportunities.

One student summed up the value expressed by a number of students of the practical experience over and above the 'theory' in the words '. . . [we were] not just in college reading about [issues] and then had a lecture, you have gone and followed them up in schools with staff and pupils'.

Many of the students referred to the quality of the senior teacher who arranged the programme for them and tutored them on the school-based activities, in answer to a question about the role of the senior teacher in charge of the programme. In the words of a student: 'The school was very good and the staff at the school, particularly the person in charge of us, was very good. She put a lot of work in . . .' Students recognized that the workload under which such tutors were operating, and were the more impressed and appreciative on account of this. Another student comments that the tutor '. . . was incredibly organized, really did do everything thoroughly . . . she suffered for it . . . she was racing around like a mad thing' but '. . . she was incredibly professional and was very, very helpful.'

Of the 45 critical comments made by students, mostly of a constructively critical nature, a number of them concerned the mental effort required to get to grips with issues outside the subject specialist area. Other comments showed the students making the perennial comments about the links between theory and practice, so familiar to teacher educators, for instance in relation to the relevance of equal opportunities.

However, some of the critical comments made by the students about the PP programme indicate some very real difficulties in its implementation and question some of the underlying assumptions of course planners. One of the difficulties as perceived by students centres around the use of time on the school-based day. Some students were frustrated by the need to be subservient to the agenda of the school and the amount of time when 'we were not doing anything constructive.'

One student puts this strongly: we '. . . sat around twiddling our thumbs and actually on a couple of occasions doing some coursework' but it was '. . . very, very stressful when we could have spent more time in college':

> We found a lot of the activities we were asked to do were completed usually fairly quickly and obviously the school can't accommodate us straight away. So as soon as we leave a lecture we can't immediately go into the classroom and interview children or write up SPE (Social and Personal Education) diaries or whatever. We found that a lot of the time we were sitting around. Although most of us were talking to other members of staff we found that there was quite a waste of time.

There was criticism of some of the school-based activities, raising questions about some of the assumptions about action research held by course planners. As two students commented: 'Dragging children out of classes just wasn't feasible and all these great long lists of questions to ask staff and pupils we just didn't have time to do it.' 'There were ten or so of us in that school, so obviously child observation was quite hard. They had to really do a lot of work to get us into classroom observation, and I think it was a lot of work for the school.'

Another student's comments indicate how schools and teachers operating to a different agenda can be perceived as lack of planning by the student-teacher:

> The day just wasn't planned at all . . . I found I would arrive at lessons where the teacher wasn't expecting me there. Or the lesson wasn't going on. That could have been a complication within the school which we weren't told about, or it could have been they weren't clear on what we were supposed to be doing there. But we found that all of us had that happen to us.

The pressures on tutors in charge of the programme go some way to explaining some of these difficulties, as a student indicated of one tutor, after setting up the programme, '. . . he had to fly back and catch up with his year-10 work'.

The assumptions made by course planners about the nature and modes of data collection available to students in the school context turned out to be overambitious, particularly in the light of pressures on teachers from their National Curriculum and assessment commitments. School-based sessions were able to include some opportunities for action-research type methods including interviews of students and staff, but the difficulties of organizing such sessions meant that there was more time spent on policy analysis or with one teacher who was released to 'teach' the group, and the question must be asked whether the school does lend itself to systematic use as a base for action research and evaluation, without distorting its original mission. It must also be asked whether the amazing contortions of the senior staff, without whose help the scheme could never have operated, were justified in the light of their commitments within the school and the time taken away from these.

The issues raised above could be just the teething troubles of a new mode of working, and there is certainly evidence to suggest that the 1993–4 cohort are more satisfied with the PP programme than their predecessors, or these could be fundamental to aspects of school-based teacher education, particularly those which are concerned with the investigation and development of general professional rather than subject specialist work. Certainly not all areas of study to which PGCE students would have been introduced on college-based courses translate readily into school-based activities and hours of classroom observation may yield only limited data for analysis.

There will be times when school-based teacher education will inevitably involve the conflicting agenda of pupil and student-teacher education and teachers would be right to prioritize pupils in such circumstances. Learning from experience on the job will enable student-teachers to enjoy many valuable experiences and, in particular, to develop their confidence as teachers in the school setting, but it will also, at times, involve frustration and time wasting because the life of the school cannot and should not revolve around the needs of the students or the agenda represented by ITE.

CHAPTER 22

New Teachers Reflecting on Their Training

LYNN D. NEWTON
University of Newcastle upon Tyne

INTRODUCTION

It has been alleged that initial teacher training (ITT) lacks quality and adequate school involvement:

> If there is one thing in the education debate about which most people are agreed it is that success depends on the quality of the teaching profession. A central plank in the policy to improve the supply of teachers is reform of teacher training and even the training institutions agree that it should be more school-based. There is much less consensus about how this should be brought about.
>
> (Anthony, 1993, p. 19)

The move towards apprenticeship, reflected in the school-based training models currently being developed (DES, 1992; DFE, 1993b), is based on the premiss that student-teachers find current training courses inadequate, particularly the institution-based elements. It is seen as better to give students more classroom experience, under the control of practising teachers and with less exposure to the so-called theory-based components in HEIs.

Yet, HMI's evaluation of the school-based training provided by the two-year articled teacher scheme throws doubts on its worth (*The Times Educational Supplement*, 1993). It has led HMI to conclude that despite twice the length of time for training, the articled teachers were no more competent than their colleagues who had followed a much cheaper and shorter one-year PGCE course. Although articled teachers valued their high level of involvement in school, they felt they missed the curriculum training provided in HEIs. They also identified the need for time away from the classroom and school to reflect on their training and development. Edwards (1992), in a National Commission on Education report, argued that chalkface learning must be complemented with theory and wider understanding. He pointed to the necessity to integrate the academic and practical dimensions of teaching and learning. Right-wing assertions that current teacher training practices are too progressive have, according to Edwards, no basis in fact. In discussing the major thrusts in recent government policy on initial teacher education (ITE), Hill (1992, p. 11) concluded that

> ITE should be questioned. Its objectives (whether or not expressed as competences), its content, its pedagogy, and its structuring and siting should be questioned. But they should be questioned on the basis of research findings and consultation – not hare-brained and brain washing schemes flying on the wings of zany, untested, divisive, radical Right ideological social engineering.

Describing the Modes of Teacher Education Research Project, Thompson (1992) noted that over three-quarters of the 207 responding HEIs identified their training models as that of the reflective practitioner or 'theory-into-practice' models.

What of the newly qualified teachers themselves? How do they feel about the balance of their training, the mix of theory and practice? Criticisms seldom seem to have been based on research evidence which reflects their views. Indeed, HMI (DES, 1988, para. 1.18) found 'Two-thirds of the new teachers were well or reasonably well satisfied with their training and over half considered that appropriate emphasis has been given to the various components of their course.' The New Teacher Project at the University of Newcastle upon Tyne has led to conclusions like those of HMI (Newton, 1991a).

A longitudinal study over the last five years has produced information about the needs and views of newly qualified teachers. It will also guide the nature and form of the evolving partnerships between schools and HEIs to meet the training needs of those who are the most important and yet often least consulted elements in this partnership, the student-teachers themselves. This study elicited the views of 118 past primary students who had all followed the CATE-approved one-year PGCE course at the university.

The original aims of the study were connected with course evaluation, to allow tutors to determine how useful exstudents considered their training to be. The intention was to use the data to fine tune the course, building on strengths and eliminating weaknesses in provision, and thus providing a course which meets the long-term and changing demands of primary education as schools move into the twenty-first century.

The course has two components: a school-based element involving the students in school and classroom activities and teaching practices (about 50 per cent of the course time); and an institution-based element which covers curriculum studies (about 35 per cent) and professional studies (about 15 per cent). Students complete an evaluation of the course at the end of the year, but their comments tend to focus on course organization, delivery and personalities rather than the longer-term value of their training. This is to be expected since they have little experience on which to base judgements. Analysis of their views at the end of their first year of teaching reflects more realistically the value they place on the different elements of their training. This is well illustrated by the comment of one student with reference to the emphasis on planning for learning: 'I thought it unnecessary at first but now essential' (1992). Questions asked included: What did past students consider were the essential aspects of the course? Which elements were judged not essential at this stage and could have been omitted? Were they satisfied with the balance of school-based and university-based elements? What were their needs as new teachers during their first year?

THE SURVEY

The study began in June 1989, at the end of the first year of teaching for the 1987–8 cohort of students, and has continued each year through to the present. This period represents the time elapsed between accreditation inspections by HMI (1988 and 1993) and during this period, other than to respond to changes in the National Curriculum and other requirements, the broad structure and main components have not changed significantly.

All students who could be contacted were asked to complete a three-page questionnaire which focused on the different components of the training course: curriculum studies, professional studies (generic skills, educational issues and professional practice) and school-based work. In all cases the students were asked to indicate how well they considered the course had prepared them. Table 22.1 shows the percentage of students contacted each year, the percentage returns and the split between infant and junior teaching. It can be seen that although the percentage of those who responded has fallen over the five years the numbers have remained fairly constant. About 5 per cent of respondents included letters with their returns, some indicating their feelings about the survey. For example:

TABLE 22.1
Respondents to the questionnaire

YEAR	PGCE YEAR	NO. IN YEAR	NO. CON-TACTED	NO. RE-TURNED	TEACH-ING INFANTS	TEACH-ING JUNIORS
1989	1987–8	52	34 (65%)	21 (62%)	13 (62%)	8 (38%)
1990	1988–9	67	43 (64%)	26 (60%)	16 (62%)	10 (38%)
1991	1989–90	68	53 (78%)	23 (44%)	12 (52%)	11 (48%)
1992	1990–1	86	65 (76%)	24 (37%)	15 (63%)	9 (37%)
1993	1991–2	93	56 (60%)	24 (43%)	15 (63%)	9 (37%)
Total		366	251 (69%)	118 (47%)	71 (60%)	47 (40%)

It's nice to know your opinion is still sought after and appreciated.

(1990)

Thank you for sending me this form as it has helped me evaluate my own teaching.

(1992)

THE FINDINGS

Pyke (1993a: 1993b) comments on the National Curriculum Council document which suggests that trainees do not have an adequate knowledge of all the subjects of the National Curriculum or follow courses that focus sharply enough on teaching skills. The New Teacher Project provides evidence to the contrary, challenging assumptions discussed earlier. Overall, the majority of respondents expressed satisfaction with their training, considering most elements to have been of value to them (over 80 per cent) and indicating that many of them use their notes and handouts regularly to support their planning and teaching. Looking for changes in these perceptions over time, it was found that their views tended to be consistent, with little significant change from the beginning of the project to the present. Typical comments included:

I have used experiences gained from all areas of the course.

(1989)

I find my PGCE notes a very good 'reference book' and am referring to it more and more as the year goes by, as an *aide-mémoire* and for ideas.

(1990)

Which aspects were particularly valuable? – Everything!

(1991)

The whole course was extremely valuable.

(1992)

I use my notes as a resource file.

(1993)

. . . have been used for reference again and again.

(1993)

. . . still referring to all notes.

(1993)

Very few areas of the course were seen by the new teachers as not needed and those identified were seldom identified as such by more than one or two individuals.

CURRICULUM PREPARATION

As graduates, the students often begin with expertise in only one or two areas of the curriculum. As primary teachers their confidence and competence must be developed across the full curriculum range, along with the ability to relate this to knowledge and understanding of teaching and learning processes. It was within this curriculum studies element that the greatest satisfaction was expressed. For example:

> The science and environmental studies was an outstanding part of the course . . . It has formed an excellent base for my work in schools.
>
> (1989)
>
> A 'wide' view of music – inspiring.
>
> (1989)
>
> . . . made maths exciting.
>
> (1990)
>
> Art – enjoyed it all; PE – superb preparation for school; technology – well prepared.
>
> (1990)
>
> All [areas] needed.
>
> (1990)
>
> The whole [curriculum] course was valuable.
>
> (1991)
>
> . . . good starting points . . . a good overview.
>
> (1991)

It was not only what was taught which was commented upon but also how:

> Practical ideas adaptable to any classroom.
>
> (1989)
>
> Working together in groups to carry out activities.
>
> (1989)
>
> Progression linked to child development.
>
> (1989)
>
> From an infant viewpoint history and geography were well integrated into topic work.
>
> (1989)
>
> I have used experience gained from all areas of the [science] course, including problem-solving.
>
> (1990)
>
> . . . a good mix of lectures and hands on.
>
> (1991)
>
> . . . the lectures followed by workshops with relevant handouts worked extremely well.
>
> (1992)

For many of these new teachers, the breadth and balance of curricular experiences provided them with confidence to try things with the children:

> Confidence given to 'have a go' with children.
>
> (1989)

. . . part of my confidence and commitment must come from the influences of the PGCE.

(1991)

I have felt comfortable and confident all year in [the] majority of lessons.

(1993)

Such confidence came from having had opportunities in the university to experience a wide range of materials, approaches and equipment. Through practical activities they were able to try things for themselves and share their ideas and understandings. The enthusiasm, expertise and varied experiences of the tutors was also commented on. Also, in the university students have access to a range of specialist expertise and resources, including a range of schemes for the full curriculum, journals and professional periodicals and often very well equipped, specialist facilities. The resource support in schools tends to be much more restricted.

This point was also identified by a few exstudents in another way, in their suggestions of elements which should be included in the PGCE year. Most of the things identified are already included in the course. However, they were not being further developed in schools in any way and so the new teachers felt they needed to be given even more time in the university. A particular example in this context is information technology (8 per cent).

Inevitably, when dealing with responses from over 100 students there were some critical comments on some components of the training programme, but overall these were minor.

The existence and popularity of in-service courses, such as the Grant 11 courses in science and mathematics for experienced teachers, is evidence that such expertise cannot be learnt on the job. It is often the same tutors who deliver PGCE and Grant 11 courses.

PROFESSIONAL STUDIES PREPARATION

For all three components (generic skills, educational issues and professional practice) the majority of the exstudents considered them to have been of value and felt well prepared. Again, the expertise and support of the tutor was noted: 'I feel that I benefited a great deal from input on these issues from my tutor' (1992). Each year, a few exstudents suggested new areas for inclusion – for example, aspects of bilingualism. These seem to reflect individual needs specific to their current teaching situations. Almost 10 per cent suggested the need for more theory to support practice in certain areas. For example, comments on the need for more theory of child development (6 per cent) included the following:

Essential to gain a good base in child development to understand 'how children learn'.

(1991)

... more of this [child development] would be useful background knowledge.

(1991)

Much more time should be given over to the theory of child development – I'm only just discovering what makes them tick!

(1991)

A lot more work on child development is needed.

(1992)

The responses indicated that the exstudents felt these elements, which were covered during the PGCE year, should be more fully covered in the university, rather than left to be developed further in schools. As with curriculum studies, it appears such in-school development does not take place.

SCHOOL-BASED TIME

The majority of the respondents indicated satisfaction with the school-based elements of the course. Comments reflected that the nature of the school-based work and the balance between the school and university elements were generally satisfactory. Suggestions for change tended to focus on organizational matters. Only 8 per cent of the exstudents felt a need for more time in school. Referring to the supervision of student-teachers in schools, the tutor was identified as important by a number of students. For example: 'I would say that the contact with the university and tutors is a vital part of the course' (1993). The school-based time gives students an 'in-depth' experience of at least three schools, through serial visits and block teaching practices. In the university the students gain access to a broader perspective on practice, since staff are involved with a large number of schools in a variety of ways, from in-service work to research studies as well as initial training. This enables the students to be more outward looking by drawing on this breadth of experience (Furlong, 1993).

INDUCTION AND IN-SERVICE NEEDS

Earley (1992) expressed considerable unease about the abolition of the probationary period. He identified the potential for a lack of comparability and inequity in the treatment and support of newly qualified teachers during their induction year, both within and between LEAs. A similar unease was identified in the report of the National Commission on Education (1993). Again, the New Teacher Project provided justification for this unease. Of the 118 respondents, over 93 per cent completed the open section about induction and in-service needs.

Progression and continuity across the transfer period from student-teacher to experienced teacher seems to be an aspect of professional development which is being ignored. Lack of support during this period was specifically identified as a problem by a small number of them. For example: 'Probationary year – should definitely get more support from authority, especially in first term. I was in desperate need of "time out" to breathe, self-evaluate, communicate with other probationers and advisers and observe other classes and schools' (1990). There was an obvious stress factor – the need to balance their enthusiasm and commitment with realism. The use made of the induction period – the old probationary year – seems to be very important for these newly qualified teachers. They had moved from the relatively supportive environment of the HEI to the often isolated world of the classroom:

> During my probationary year I have been released for half a day a week to visit other schools, spend time in other classes, etc. It would have been useful to me if time such as this could be spent in university on a sort of follow-up forum course where problems which arose in school could be discussed. This would have been especially useful during the first term in school.
>
> (1991)

One suggested, 'A long week in Newcastle to meet exstudents and tutors to discuss problems being experienced – a shared experience and advice/support' (1992). Some suggested that the PGCE course should be linked to the subsequent induction year in school, with some type of assessment at the end of that year.

The new teachers were also aware of the gaps in their own expertise. There were over 30 different areas identified as needing support, the majority by only one or two people. However, some elements occurred more frequently as a focus for in-service support as the new teachers felt ready to develop further in these areas. These included the following:

• Working with pupils with special needs	6.8%
• Managing pupil behaviour/class control	7.6%
• 'Whole curriculum' planning	9.3%
• Curriculum leadership skills	11.1%
• Assessment and record-keeping	14.4%
• Information technology	16.9%
• Management of classrooms/time/resources	17.8%
• Language development/reading	19.1%

Some of the exstudents suggested that these needs could be met through more structured support involving HEIs as well as LEAs, again emphasizing the role of the HEI.

CONCLUSION

Furlong (1993, p. 14) argues that there is an assumption that '. . . a well-structured school experience is all the students need' to become effective teachers. The data from the New Teacher Project challenges the assumptions which underpin arguments for apprenticeship training of primary teachers and also supports HMI's 1987 findings. In reality, newly qualified teachers need a lot of other things, too. The majority of our past students were happy with their PGCE training and considered that it had been of value to them as new teachers. While some would have appreciated more time in school it was not at the expense of the institution-based side of the course. Both were thought to be of value to them as new teachers in the uncertain world of education, and especially so where they found themselves teaching in schools and LEAs where little support was provided for new teachers in their first year. Many expressed the need for continued support in this first year, support of the kind they had been given during their PGCE training:

> Training teachers, however professionally valuable and rewarding, must always be a secondary activity for schools. But don't students deserve to be supported, at least in part, by professionals for whom they are the first priority?
>
> (Furlong, 1993, p. 14)

> Of course school teachers are capable of delivering all aspects of initial teacher training just as college tutors are capable of teaching school pupils; it does not follow that because we can, therefore we ought. Our concern should be to organize the components of the courses in such a way as to secure the best possible training for students.
>
> (McManus, 1993, p. 16)

Macdonald (in Thompson, 1992, p. 7) discusses what is to be gained by insisting that teaching is an uncertain craft:

> . . . if we could rout the idea that teaching is only about skill and method, if we could foster a public perception of its moral complexity, if we could honour the role played in teaching by the teacher's productively ambivalent self, then I think we would have the chance to build the kind of schools our children and grand-children will need in the twenty-first century.

I believe that newly qualified teachers are, on the whole, satisfied with their PGCE training as a starting-point for their professional careers. This survey would seem to support the evidence of HMI and reiterated by Edwards (1992), that the present fifty:fifty training model is a more satisfactory model than its critics will admit. It is a training which, as MacDonald puts it, routs the idea that teaching is only about skill and method. I believe it to be a training based on a sound working relationship between schools and institutions which can begin to stimulate the reflective, analytical, inquiring and creative teacher. It is this sort of teacher who will have the independence of judgement, critical self-awareness and will to succeed in the schools of the next century.

PART FIVE

Headteachers' and Others' Views of the Changes

CHAPTER 23

Headteachers', Parents', Students' and Tutors' Responses to the Reform of Primary Initial Teacher Education

ANDREW HANNAN
University of Plymouth

INTRODUCTION

The research reported here was launched immediately after the DFE published their consultation document/draft circular with the title, *The Initial Training of Primary School Teachers: New Criteria for Course Approval*, dated 9 June 1993 (DFE, 1993a). Questionnaires were sent to the headteachers of all the county and voluntary-aided primary sector schools in Devon, to parents of pupils at seven of those schools and to students and tutors at the Rolle Faculty of Education of the University of Plymouth. The project was intended to serve a dual purpose in that it aimed to provide immediate feedback to the DFE (by 31 July 1993) from all these groups as part of the consultation exercise and to provide valuable research evidence about the perspectives of those who would be directly affected by the reform of primary initial teacher education (ITE).

SURVEY POPULATIONS AND RESPONSE RATES

This research is unusual in its range in that other surveys have tended to draw only on the views of headteachers (Carrington and Tymms, 1993b; Standing Conference of Principals, 1994) or students and teachers (Hannan and Newby, 1993; Hodgkinson, 1992). Here we have an account which reports the reactions of four categories of those who would be affected by the proposed reforms, i.e. headteachers, parents, students and tutors. The respondents were all drawn from Devon, one of England's largest counties. The samples and response rates are given in summary form below (for further details, see Hannan, 1993).

Headteachers' survey

All 433 primary schools in Devon were sent copies of the questionnaire; 264 replied, giving a response rate of 61 per cent, which is very impressive for a postal survey under such circumstances. The nature of the sample in terms of size of school was as follows: 77 schools with less than 100 pupils (29.1 per cent); 128 with 100 to 299 pupils (48.5 per cent); 41 with 300 or over pupils (15.5 per cent); and 18 schools (6.8 per cent) which did not provide this information.

Parents' survey

1,040 copies of the questionnaire were distributed to parents at seven primary sector schools: 267 were returned, a response rate of 26 per cent. These seven represented an 'opportunity sample' with a reasonable degree of representativeness for Devon county schools, i.e. in terms of pupil age ranges, location (rural, small town, large town) and pupil numbers.

Students' survey

The survey took place at the very end of term, when many students were without lecture commitments, so it was not possible to reach them all. None of the fourth-year BEd students were available as they had finished their exams and had dispersed. All students who took part in the survey were undertaking courses of ITE in order to work in primary schools. Those taking the BEd were engaged in a four-year honours degree. Those graduates (with BA and BSc or equivalent) taking the primary PGCE could take either a one-year course or spend two years as articled teachers. Overall, whereas 769 students (not counting those who had just finished the fourth year of their BEd) were eligible to take part, it was only possible to distribute 593 copies of the questionnaire. Of these, 242 were returned, a response rate of 41 per cent.

Tutors' survey

In all, 53 full-time tutors and 18 part-time tutors of Rolle Faculty of Education were sent the questionnaire, a total of 71. Of these, 50 were returned, 41 from full-timers and 9 from part-timers, giving response rates of 77 and 50 per cent respectively and 70 per cent overall.

THE QUESTIONNAIRES

The survey instrument had four varieties, one for each of the target groups. These were piloted with small subsamples of each category, the final versions owing much to the advice of the Devon Association of Primary Headteachers (DAPH), which acted as sponsor of the headteacher and parent surveys. The link with DAPH was of value to them in that the researcher provided a convenient means by which they could respond to the DFE. The research itself was greatly enhanced by the access they gave and their contribution ensured that the surveys were the work of a partnership between schools and a higher education institution (HEI), rather than merely reflecting the definition of the situation provided by the HEI.

All the items were derived from the DFE document and were put in the form of proposals to which respondents were asked to indicate their degree of support or opposition (using a five-point Likert scale with an invitation to provide further comment). The parents were given three such items, the first two of which were the same as those put to the headteachers, students and tutors, while the third was the same apart from the inclusion of a phrase which attempted to clarify what was meant by 'HE' in that context (using the explanation, 'i.e. old teacher training colleges or departments'). The headteachers, students and tutors were asked to respond to seven identical proposals (including the three which they shared with the parents).

The questionnaire began with a preamble which described the government's proposals in the following manner:

> The proposed reforms are intended to ensure that newly qualified teachers are fully equipped to contribute to high quality teaching and improved standards of achievement in primary schools. This is to be achieved by:
>
> - requiring all teacher training courses to meet 'tough' new criteria (HE institutions, the old teacher training colleges or departments, will have to be accredited and they must be able to demonstrate that their courses enable students to develop certain specified competences);
> - giving schools a greater role in such training;
> - continuing to allow for study in HE of the subject knowledge necessary for teaching the National Curriculum (HE institutions will also work alongside their partner schools in developing student competences in terms of their teaching and professional roles);
> - providing a greater diversity of courses.
>
> The items below highlight a number of aspects of these proposals and ask for your reactions.

RESPONSES FROM EACH SURVEY

The reactions given to the three proposals which were put to all four categories of respondent are summarized below. Each table is preceded by the question posed. The figures given are valid percentage (which leaves missing responses out of account) and frequency.

Thus, headteachers (96.6 per cent), students (89.3 per cent) and tutors (96 per cent) were overwhelmingly opposed to the proposal for a one-year training course for non-graduates (often known as the 'Mums' Army' route) to qualify them to teach children up to 7 years of age (Table 23.1). The extent of opposition from headteachers was similar regardless of the size of school. It is perhaps significant that none of the ten articled teachers (who were undertaking a two-year school-based PGCE) favoured the establishment of such a route to qualified teacher status. Although more parents were against (48.1 per cent) than were in favour (42.5 per cent, with 9.4 per cent neutral), the extent of opposition was significantly less than for the other groups.

In response to 'More time in schools' (Table 23.2), all four categories of respondent had sizeable majorities (71.6 per cent of headteachers, 77.3 per cent of parents, 71.4 per cent of students and 62.5 per cent of tutors) in favour

TABLE 23.1

One-year courses of training should be established for parents and other mature students with considerable previous experience of working with young children who have the necessary academic qualifications (such as two A-levels and English and maths at GCSE grade C or above), to train them to teach nursery and infant pupils only. What is your view of such a proposal?

	HEADTEACHERS		PARENTS		STUDENTS		TUTORS	
	VALID (%)	FREQ.	VALID (%)	FREQ.	VALID (%)	FREQ.	VALID (%)	FREQ.
Strongly support	0.0	0	6.4	17	0.8	2	2.0	1
Support	2.7	7	36.1	96	6.6	16	0.0	0
Neutral/ don't know	0.8	2	9.4	25	3.3	8	2.0	1
Oppose	12.9	34	18.0	48	28.1	68	10.0	5
Strongly oppose	83.7	220	30.1	80	61.2	148	86.0	43
Not answered		1		1				
Total		264		267		242		50

of increasing the period of time student teachers spend in schools (by the amounts proposed by the DFE). The amount of support from headteachers was not affected by size of school. None of the eight PGCE students or ten articled teachers opposed such increases, whereas 29 (13.2 per cent) of the 219 BEd students did so.

TABLE 23.2

The minimum time to be spent in schools by student-teachers should increase – from 20 to 32 weeks in four-year, and from 15 to 24 weeks in three-year BEd and equivalent courses; and from 15 to 18 weeks in one-year primary PGCE and two-year BEd and equivalent courses. What is your view of such a proposal?

	HEADTEACHERS		PARENTS		STUDENTS		TUTORS	
	VALID (%)	FREQ.	VALID (%)	FREQ.	VALID (%)	FREQ.	VALID (%)	FREQ.
Strongly support	17.6	46	22.7	60	24.9	60	6.3	3
Support	54.0	141	54.5	144	46.5	112	56.3	27
Neutral/ don't know	10.3	27	14.0	37	16.6	40	12.5	6
Oppose	13.4	35	5.7	15	10.8	26	18.8	9
Strongly oppose	4.6	12	3.0	8	1.2	3	6.3	3
Not answered		3		3		1		2
Total		264		267		242		50

Opposition to groups of schools taking the lead in setting up their own training arrangements was strongest among the tutors (94 per cent) but was also high among both headteachers (69.9 per cent) and students (76 per cent) (Table 23.3). Size of school again does not seem to have been a significant influence on headteacher response, although those with less than 100 pupils had the lowest overall level of support, 9.2 per cent, compared to 16.5 per cent of schools with 100 to 299 pupils and 17.1 per cent for schools with 300 and over. None of the articled teachers who replied were in favour of the proposal, which may be worthy of note given that they were taking part in a programme in which schools played a strong, if not leading, role. Although more parents opposed the proposal (48.3 per cent) than supported it (32.8 per cent, with 18.9 per cent neutral), the extent of opposition was again significantly less strong than for the other groups.

TABLE 23.3

Groups of schools wishing to take the lead in designing and running their own course of training for primary schoolteachers should be able to obtain direct government funding for this purpose – without necessarily having to involve HEIs. What is your view of such a proposal?

	HEADTEACHERS		PARENTS		STUDENTS		TUTORS	
	VALID (%)	FREQ.	VALID (%)	FREQ.	VALID (%)	FREQ.	VALID (%)	FREQ.
Strongly support	5.7	15	10.6	28	1.2	3	0.0	0
Support	9.9	26	22.3	59	5.8	14	0.0	0
Neutral/ don't know	14.5	38	18.9	50	17.0	41	6.0	3
Oppose	32.1	84	26.0	69	34.9	84	22.0	11
Strongly oppose	37.8	99	22.3	59	41.1	99	72.0	36
Not answered		2		2		1		
Total		264		267		242		50

Responses to the other four items (proposals put to headteachers, students and tutors but not parents) may be summarized as follows:

● In all three of the groups asked, more opposed than supported the idea of moving towards three-year BEd courses (rather than the currently dominant four-year mode), with 70 per cent of tutors against (20 per cent in favour and 10 per cent neutral) compared to 40.9 per cent of headteachers (39.7 per cent in favour and 19.5 per cent neutral) and 42.1 per cent of students (37.9 per cent in favour and 20 per cent neutral).

- A majority of each of the three groups opposed the introduction of two-year BEd courses for students with one year's experience of HE.
- Both headteacher (63.7 per cent) and tutor (57.1 per cent) responses favoured moves to establish partnerships where schools would play a more significant role in teacher training.
- Of headteachers, 61.8 per cent favoured the transfer of resources to schools to reflect their increased role in such partnerships, whereas only 26.5 per cent of tutors did so, with 46.9 per cent against and 26.5 per cent neutral.

DISCUSSION

The consultation process of which this research was a part did not appear to count for much as, on 7 September 1993, a 'green paper' entitled *The Government's Proposals for the Reform of Initial Teacher Training* (DFE, 1993b) was issued without any reference to the results of the earlier exercise. However, the final version of the circular, which detailed the new criteria for initial teacher training (ITT) for primary schools (DFE, 1993c), did take some account of the sort of feedback which is detailed above by dropping the proposal for one-year trained non-graduate nursery and infant teachers (known as the 'Mums' Army'). General opposition to this scheme had been very strong indeed, with the work of Carrington and Tymms (1993b) on headteacher responses being often quoted. The overwhelming opposition of headteachers, students and tutors demonstrated in the research reported here is perhaps unsurprising in the light of their shared interest in maintaining the professional status of the teachers of 'early years children'. The lower level of opposition from parents, however, needs some explanation (although it must be remembered here that 128 parents were against the 'Mums' Army' proposal whereas only 113 were in favour). An understanding of the reasons for favouring such a reform is perhaps best afforded by looking at the views of those parents who indicated that they were its supporters and who took up the option to provide 'further comments'. However, only 17 of the parents who favoured the proposal decided to do so. Of those the following identified reasons for their support:

Parent 41
I think that mature students and parents often have a lot of useful experience that they can bring to the job.

Parent 54
I would only support this proposal if it meant increased teaching staff in individual schools, thus reducing numbers of pupils in the classroom or to enhance teaching for pupils with learning difficulties.

Parent 119
Real-time 'experience' with young children and an understanding of their needs and expectations is more than a substitute for over-qualified people.

Parent 129
Mature students will already have good communication skills with young children, which will create a relaxed but confident approach to the learning environment from which the child will benefit.

None the less, there is an absence here of strongly worded attacks on the teacher training establishment – with the exception of Parent 119. The extent of support from parents for the proposal, however, indicates that HEIs and schools themselves have not succeeded in persuading a significant minority of parents that what infant and nursery schoolteachers do is sufficiently demanding to require professional training and study beyond the one-year programme envisaged in the 'Mums' Army' proposal.

Whereas that idea was eventually dropped (to be replaced by more emphasis on the accreditation of prior learning and training for classroom assistants), the move towards more school-based teacher 'training' continues apace. Those aspects of the draft circular which referred to significant increases in the amounts of time student-teachers would have to spend in schools remained unamended in the final version published as Circular 14/93 (DFE, 1993c). The research reported here demonstrated across-the-board support by majorities of heads, parents, students and tutors for such measures. The following 'further comments', all from those who indicated 'strong support', illustrate the sort of arguments advanced in their favour:

Headteacher 134
We strongly support the proposal to increase time spent in schools. This time is valuable for students, as real experience allows them many opportunities, it consolidates college work, allows students chances to experiment with teaching styles and gives practical experience. The value of in-school experience must not be underestimated.

Headteacher 135
Student-teachers need to gain far greater understanding of classroom management, teaching styles and strategies for discipline – I believe more time in class would help this.

Parent 6
The only way to learn the job is in the classroom – only that way will you find out if you are suited to it.

Parent 17
The more time spent in schools by student-teachers can only be for the better to provide hands-on experience working with the children.

Parent 23
More practical experience is a lot more beneficial than all theory.

Student 88
The more time spent in school, obviously the better – putting theory into practice and gaining as much experience of children as possible. Particularly important for young students without a family and younger siblings, etc.

Student 208
Many of the learning experiences come from being in school and working with the children. Although theory and knowledge are important, it is necessary not to forget that it is the children we want to teach and therefore we need to spend time learning from them and with them. I strongly feel there should be more time spent in schools.

Tutor 44
Current time certainly too brief for sustained practice as basis for reflection – further action.

Many other generally supportive statements contained reservations about proper resourcing for schools and defended the part played by the HEI – several wanted the increased time in schools to be added to the total number of weeks rather than subtracted from the time previously spent in the HEI. It is apparent, however, that the seductive logic of 'learning by doing' has a strong hold on the minds of headteachers, parents, students and tutors alike. Although this is not necessarily to imply that HEIs are not concerned with such matters nor that the time spent in HE is not well used, the respondents are none the less willing, as they indicate with their responses in Table 23.2, to shift the balance of time spent increasingly in favour of the schools. Majorities of heads and tutors also favoured moves to establish school–college partnerships where schools would play a more significant role in teacher training, although all the groups had majorities against schools establishing their own training schemes which they could run independently of HEIs (see Table 23.3).

CONCLUSION

It remains to be seen just how radical the reforms to primary ITE are. The 'Mums' Army' proposal was withdrawn, but many argued that it was always intended as a sacrificial offering designed to draw attention away from the other measures. The shift towards school-based 'training' is undoubtedly under way and, according to this research, increasing the time students would spend in schools has considerable support from all quarters. However, the amount of the increase is not so dramatic as to endanger the survival of the primary BEd or the primary PGCE in broadly similar forms to those already in existence. It seems that the biggest impact will be felt from the likely change from four-year to three-year BEds, which will significantly reduce the time available to HEIs to open up broader issues previously addressed in time given to teaching or education studies elements. It appears that the school-led schemes are not likely to make a significant impact on the primary sector (only two such arrangements had gained outline approval by March 1994) but it may be significant that 41 Devon headteachers in this research indicated their support in principle for such schemes. None the less, the small size of primary schools and their relatively underdeveloped departmental structures seem to provide natural limits to the expansion of their role in teacher education. The immediate effect, however, of the new criteria (DFE, 1993c) is the battle over the scarce resources available now that HEIs are obliged to pay schools in some way for their increased role in teacher training and the discussions about the roles to be played by each in the new 'partnerships'. The outcome of negotiations over such matters will do much to decide the future of primary ITE.

CHAPTER 24

Headteachers' Perspectives on Primary Education Policy

BRUCE CARRINGTON and PETER TYMMS

University of Newcastle upon Tyne

INTRODUCTION

Since the passing of the Education Reform Act in 1988 and the introduction of the National Curriculum, primary schools in England and Wales have been placed under increasing pressure by government to review aspects of their curriculum organization, teaching methods and classroom practice. Concerned about the nature and pace of the government's reforms in primary education and the apparent low state of staff morale in this sector, we undertook a postal survey of primary headteachers' opinions in the north of England in February 1993 (Carrington and Tymms, 1993a). This was refined and extended to include a nationally representative sample in the summer of the same year.

THE NATIONAL SURVEY

During June 1993, the extended version of the questionnaire was sent to 970 primary heads – a 5 per cent random sample in England and Wales. The questionnaire was completed by 541 individuals: the majority were heads of primary or junior schools (73 per cent); the remainder of the sample were either first or infant school heads (23 per cent) or the heads of middle schools (4 per cent). Their schools varied in size and location, as well as in type: 34 per cent had urban locations, 38 per cent were suburban and 28 per cent were rural. While three-fifths of the schools had between 100 and 300 pupils, a quarter had over 300 pupils on their rolls and the remainder had fewer than 100 pupils.

THE QUESTIONNAIRE

The questionnaire allowed the heads both to outline their school's current practice in relation to curriculum organization, teaching methods and differentiation by ability and describe their own attitudes towards the government's policies on teaching and learning at Key Stage 2. The headteachers were also invited to express their opinions about the feasibility of the policies. Additionally, the questionnaire attempted to gauge the heads' views on various matters relating to initial teacher education (ITE) and training at primary level and to staff morale and job satisfaction in their schools.

THE USE OF 'SPECIALISTS' AND 'SEMI-SPECIALISTS' AT KEY STAGE 2

In the clear majority (87 per cent) of the schools teaching pupils at Key Stage 2 'subject specialists' or 'semi-specialists' were employed as curriculum co-ordinators advising class teachers. The data do not allow us to consider changes in practice and comment on the government's claim that '. . . a growing number [of schools] are deploying "specialist" teachers' (DFE 1993c, para 3.14), but they do suggest that such practices tend to be the exception rather than the rule. Intriguingly, we found very significant differences in the use of specialists in relation to the size of the school.

TABLE 24.1

Current use of 'specialists' or 'semi-specialists' at Key Stage 2 (%)

| | NO. ON ROLL | | |
	0–100	100–300	300+
As curriculum co-ordinators advising class teachers	64	92	93
As teachers working alongside class teachers	13	2	3
As teachers in specific areas of the curriculum	24	6	5

Note:
$p < .003$: chi-square test.

Table 24.1 indicates that the employment of 'specialists or semi-specialists' as teachers *per se* is much more likely to occur in small schools. Nearly a quarter of such specialists were employed to teach specific subjects in schools with less than 100 on the roll as opposed to just 5 per cent in schools with more than 300 on the roll. The head of a rural school (comprising just three full-time teachers) made the following observations about the use of 'specialists':

We do swap classes so that we can use our various expertises with different age ranges. But with only three of us, this can only be on a limited basis. I think that teachers can become 'specialists' in most subject areas if given the time, training and support. We are never given time.

It would seem that where there is greater freedom to choose – in larger schools – the predominant practice has been to employ 'specialists or semi-specialists' as subject co-ordinators.

Further responses indicated that where specialist teaching existed it tended to be concentrated in particular areas of the curriculum. For many subjects it was very rare, and even for science, technology and maths the proportion of respondents who indicated that their schools did employ specialist teaching never exceeded 5 per cent, even in year 6. Music was very different, however, with 15 per cent of schools employing specialists throughout the junior range.

The vast majority of primary and junior school heads (81 per cent) also reported that their schools lacked specialist facilities, or indicated that their present staffing structures gave little scope for further change in practice (86 per cent). Similarly, there was widespread agreement among our respondents that the Education Secretary's proposals have major implications for INSET (86 per cent). Despite the many constraints upon subject specialist teaching at Key Stage 2, the heads appeared to be divided in their views about its value. Table 24.2 gives results for the statement: 'I believe that specialist or semi-specialist teaching is desirable for older children.'

In contrast to our respondents, The National Association of Headteachers (1993) was far less equivocal in its response to the government's policy on specialist teaching at Key Stage 2. Replying to the draft circular on initial training, the association stated (p. 4):

> It is no part of his [the Education Secretary's] role to tell heads how to deploy staff. It is as well to be clear about the role of the specialist in the primary school. Primary heads would expect such a teacher to be first and foremost a skilled teacher with a thorough understanding of teaching and learning appropriate to children at primary school age. . . . It is, and indeed likely to remain, very rare for a primary teacher to teach only one or two specialist subjects for the whole of the timetable.

'HAMPERED BY THE INFLUENCE OF HIGHLY QUESTIONABLE DOGMAS'?

Contrary to the popular stereotype, very few of the heads came across as 'unreconstructed Plowdenites'. When asked to describe their school's overall approach to the curriculum at Key Stage 2, about two-thirds of the headteachers said that this was varied, combining both project work and subject-based teaching. A sixth indicated that they made extensive use of crosscurricular projects and less than a tenth of the heads indicated that their schools made 'extensive use of subject-focused projects' with 7–11-year-olds.

TABLE 24.2
Headteacher responses to policy change (%)

	STRONGLY DISAGREE	DIS-AGREE	NOT SURE	AGREE	STRONGLY AGREE
I believe that specialist or semi-specialist teaching is desirable for older children	5	24	20	43	8
Teachers at my school are unlikely to make any principled objection to setting	17	31	17	29	6
Greater use should be made of specific subject teaching for older children	6	28	21	38	8
More use should be made of whole-class teaching	8	35	17	35	5
I would encourage a young person to take up a career in teaching	23	22	28	23	4

GROUPING BY ABILITY AND SETTING

Grouping by ability was prevalent throughout Key Stage 2 in maths and English and, to a lesser degree, in science (Table 24.3). By contrast, setting was far less widespread and practised in just 7 per cent of schools in maths and only 4 per cent in English (Table 24.4). These differences in practice were mirrored by differences in attitude. Consequently, while most heads (91 per cent) accepted the view that 'Grouping by ability in "mixed ability" classrooms is essential in some areas of the curriculum', attitudes towards setting were far less clear-cut. For example, under half of the heads (43 per cent) agreed with the proposition: 'Teachers at my school are unlikely to make any principled objection to setting' (Table 24.2).

TABLE 24.3
The use of grouping by ability within mixed-ability classrooms (%)

	YEAR 6	YEAR 5
Maths	58	57
English	41	40
Science	11	11
Geography	6	6
History	5	5
Music	4	4
Technology	4	4

TABLE 24.4
The use of setting (%)

	YEAR 6	YEAR 5
Maths	9	7
English	4	4
Science	1	1
Music	1	0

TEACHING METHODS AND CLASSROOM PRACTICE

The heads' attitudes to some of the Education Secretary's proposals relating to teaching methods at Key Stage 2 also revealed that opinions were divided. Similar numbers of the heads agreed with the following statements as disagreed: 'Greater use should be made of specific teaching for older children.' 'More use should be made of whole-class teaching' (Table 24.2). But there was far greater consensus on other issues. For example, more than seven out of ten respondents agreed that 'Decisions about teaching methods and classroom organization should be taken on a "whole-school" basis' and 'Limitations should be placed on the number of activities going on in a classroom at any one time'.

ITE

Respondents were very critical of the government's stance towards primary ITE. Less than 2 per cent concurred with the view – implicit in draft circular 14/93 – that teaching nursery and Key Stage 1 children demands lower teaching skills than teaching older children. Heads were also in accord in claiming that any move to reduce the qualifications of teachers in this sector would have a detrimental effect on educational standards (90 per cent). Not surprisingly, 96 per cent felt that the public standing of such teachers would be lowered if the government had continued with its plans to introduce shortened training courses for non-graduates. One first school head referred to '. . . the threat of a licensed one-year trained "Mums' Army" and the consequent devaluation of the role of early years educators'. In a similar vein, an infant head remarked: 'Key Stage 1 teachers have borne the brunt of educational reform since 1988 . . . and feel demoralized that it is now considered possible for a one-year trained "Mums' Army" to do the job.'

Our respondents tended to echo the views expressed by HMI in their recent survey of newly qualified teachers, *The New Teacher in School* (OFSTED, 1993c). The inspectors reported that over 90 per cent of the headteachers in their sample considered that 'initial teacher education was responding well to the new demands of the Education Reform Act of 1988 and subsequent legislation' and that a similar proportion thought that new teachers were 'adequately prepared for their first teaching post' (*ibid.*, p. 3). The heads in our survey were also generally satisfied with the quality of the intake to the profession. In fact, 65 per cent agreed with the statement: 'The quality of newly qualified teachers entering schools during the past few years has been high.' The head of an urban junior school told us:

> The quality and training of trainee teachers over the last ten years have produced emergent teachers who are a credit to themselves and the institutes of higher education. This is based on 20 years of headship and ten years' involvement with the CNAA as an external examiner and a member of course evaluation teams.

Although most respondents (96 per cent) believed that the education and training of new primary teachers should be based on '. . . a real partnership between schools and institutions of higher education', they were nevertheless critical of other facets of government thinking on this issue. For example, 95 per cent thought that the total responsibility for such training should not be passed to schools. In fact, 93 per cent of the heads felt that higher education institutions (HEIs) should retain '. . . overall responsibility for the welfare, development and assessment of trainee teachers'. Most accepted the need for the school-based element of initial training to be as varied as is practicable: more than three-quarters of the heads thought that trainee teachers should spend sustained periods of time in at least three schools.

MORALE AND JOB SATISFACTION

Nearly four out of five heads said that they enjoyed their work, although more than a third said that they would take a 'job with comparable pay outside teaching' if they could get it. About a quarter (28 per cent) thought that their own morale was not as high now as it was five years ago and a similar proportion (29 per cent) agreed with the statement: 'The morale of staff in my school is high.' This corresponds to the heads' consensus (97 per cent agreed) that 'The existing workload of staff in my school is too high' and to the worrying finding that only a quarter of heads (27 per cent) concurred with the statement: 'I would encourage a young person to take up a career in teaching.' As one urban primary school head wrote at the end of her questionnaire: 'Although I love my job, I would not press any student to train.' Table 24.2 gives results for the statement: 'I would encourage a young person to take up a career in teaching.'

The data from the open-ended questions on morale and job satisfaction were equally revealing. As Tables 24.5 and 6 show, the heads were far more likely to highlight issues and events having a negative influence on staff morale and job satisfaction. The most common response to the question 'What recent events or issues have had a positive impact on the morale of teachers at your school?' was in fact 'None'!

As Table 24.5 indicates, the pace of change and increase in administrative load was of particular concern to our respondents. There was a feeling among those surveyed that the government had pressed ahead with its reforms regardless of professional opinion as to their desirability or viability. One head of a

TABLE 24.5
'What recent events or issues have had a negative impact on the morale of teachers at your school?'

	NO. OF MENTIONS	%
Pace of change	229	42
Increased administration	205	38
SATs	139	26
John Patten/the government	136	25
Media responses to education	121	22
Changes in teacher training	119	22
Cuts	98	18
1993–4 pay award	98	18
National Curriculum	93	17

TABLE 24.6

'What recent events or issues have had a positive impact on the morale of teachers at your school?'

	NO. OF MENTIONS	%
'None'	90	17
Teamwork/whole-school planning	78	14
Campaign against SATs	63	12
Parental support	48	9
Internal changes	47	9
LMS	45	8

suburban first school wrote of '. . . the constant change in government dogma with a total disregard for chalkface opinions', while the head of a Church of England primary school complained of '. . . rapid changes which have often been ill-conceived' and the government's 'total lack of understanding of education'. Many of our respondents made reference to the increase in workloads – both their own and teachers' – which had accompanied the implementation of the National Curriculum and its attendant assessment procedures. The stance taken by some sections of the media towards teachers, the government's handling of its programme of national testing and changes in teacher training were also major sources of disaffection. And Mr Patten himself was frequently singled out for admonition! Thus, a middle school head complained of '. . . the hail of directives from the Secretary of State' and 'the continuous barrage of poor press coverage which depicts teachers in a poor light', while the head of a suburban junior opined: 'I have always willingly accepted student-teachers on teaching practices and enjoyed having them in my schools. But we're not a training institution; we are here to teach children and not to provide initial training for teachers.' The mood of many of our respondents and the reasons for their apparently low morale is perhaps best encapsulated by the head of a large urban primary school, who wrote:

> The pace of change . . . has been much too fast, consultation with practising teachers negligible and too much credence has been given to media coverage of bad practice, stereotypical images and anecdotal information.
>
> If the National Curriculum had been introduced following consultation with primary teachers, then a greater sense of ownership would have developed, together with a sense of commitment to the proposed changes. The arrogance and insensitivity of recent education ministers (except John MacGregor) is appalling and we are now suffering the effects of totally inept and politically dogmatic leadership.

As we have already noted, the heads had far less to say about the positive influences on teachers' morale. For example, the head of a rural primary school told us: 'I can't think of any positive events which have taken place during the last three years – the profession in general is constantly criticized, debased and undermined by both the government and the media.' Despite this, 14 per cent of our respondents said that the advent of whole-school planning had served to stimulate the development of greater collaboration among staff in their schools. Thus the head of a suburban school told us: 'I strongly believe that increasingly schools will need to initiate their own internal support mechanisms to improve morale and well-being.' And another suburban head stated: 'Many external influences have had a detrimental impact but morale is kept reasonably high by staff working together [and providing] mutual support and encouragement.' While a similar proportion of our respondents (12 per cent) mentioned the positive effect which the 1993 boycott of the SATs had had on staff morale (e.g. 'recent union action and unity' – urban primary head), others spoke enthusiastically about the level of parental support in their schools (9 per cent), the benefits of having greater financial autonomy with LMS (8 per cent), or brought our attention to various internal changes which had taken place within their schools (9 per cent).

CONCLUSION

Primary schools have, unwittingly, found themselves at the centre of a national educational debate in which the main protagonists play the game according to different rules. Everybody agrees that we need 'good schools', and few would disagree about the particular importance of the primary sector. But in the absence of good evidence, rumours can flourish and consensus rapidly disappear. Reports in the media castigating '. . . the hair-brained, sentimental concept of child-centred teaching' or teachers 'specifically trained not to exercise constraint or to instil learning by anything smacking of "didactic" methods' (*The Daily Telegraph*, 7 November 1991) do much to dramatize the untypical and foster public disquiet.

But this 'discourse of derision', to use Stephen Ball's (1990) phrase, is not simply confined to the media. The aggressively right-wing stance taken by the government, coupled with their ownership of legislation and the accompanying perceived need to manipulate behaviour and attitudes in schools, has meant that pronouncements by ministers must be read increasingly not for their overt content but for their subtext. The mismatch between governmental edict and research evidence is often so stark as to mean that any real engagement is unlikely to be productive. The period of stability for schools envisaged in Sir Ron Dearing's report (1994) should help to ease the tension between teachers and the government by taking education away from the glare of the media spotlight. And for its part, the government must now ensure that any further policy shifts in the primary sector are based on hard evidence – rather than hearsay or 'Chinese whispers'.

ACKNOWLEDGEMENT

We are grateful to the National Union of Teachers for funding this research and Professor Andrew Pollard and his co-researchers for allowing us to draw on materials from their forthcoming book, *Changing English Primary Schools? The Impact of the National Curriculum and Assessment at Key Stage One* (1994).

CHAPTER 25

Off Site, in Tune, on Target

MARGARET ALFREY and CARL PARSONS
Canterbury Christ Church College

INTRODUCTION

Quality assurance processes in education need to yield data which help an organization improve its performance and demonstrate to a public that it is performing well (Parsons, 1994). This chapter reports the results of two follow-up surveys conducted at Christ Church College and a survey of primary school headteachers conducted by the Standing Conference of Principals (SCOP). The issue on which all three surveys offer evidence is the extent to which the college or higher education ('off-site') vocational and educational experience provided equips newly qualified teachers (NQTs) for the job. Is the off-site provision on target and is it in tune with the needs of schools and children? Moreover, is it the basis for a professional person's exercise of initiative and continued development? The SCOP survey asks if schools can train teachers and what role they wish to play in the training of teachers. These findings, like other analyses (Alfrey and Sharpe, 1994), suggest that the reforms driving teacher education into the workplace have gone far enough.

THE COURSES

Numbers of primary-trained NQT graduates from the college have grown from 84 in 1988 to 139 in 1992. The first survey was sent to receiving headteachers of ex-students from the college who had been in the 1988 graduating cohort, the first to follow a four-year BEd honours primary course. The questionnaire was sent out in May 1989 when the new teachers had been in post for two terms. The BEd course comprised serial and block practice through the four years with a ten-week final practice in the spring term of the fourth year. Tutors worked with their tutor group in schools on the serial practice and ensured work carried out by students met the needs and abilities of the children and fitted closely with existing school topics/projects. Students covered all curriculum subjects, aspects of pedagogy such as children learning, classroom control, discipline and management, assessment and record-keeping and cross curricular issues. They worked alongside BA/BSc students for half the time in the first three years studying their subject specialism. The fourth year was entirely teacher education.

The second survey was sent to receiving headteachers, and the ex-students on this occasion, in May 1993. This was the first cohort to complete a four-year BA(Ed) joint honours course which had been written to meet the requirements of the DES and CATE (DES, 1989b) following the introduction of the National Curriculum. This course increased the time spent on the core subjects, introduced options in the final year on current educational issues and a 90-hour module in the final year entitled 'Principles and methods of teaching the specialist subject'. School-based work placed a greater emphasis on the development of a professional partnership between college and the schools and again included serial and block practice, culminating in a ten-week block in the spring term of the fourth year. For example, during the serial practice in year 1, each tutor group spends a day in school for ten weeks working with the same headteacher and tutor who works with them in college on professional and theoretical issues. A similar pattern is followed in year 2 when each tutor group works with teachers and their tutor in two schools preparing, implementing and evaluating a cross-phase creative arts project over five days in the spring term and in year 3 when the work in school reflects the core subjects and humanities. In this way work undertaken in schools by students links in with the schools' current schemes of work and is supported by the curriculum courses being followed in college. Serial experience in the fourth year is spent working across the age range on an independent research project related to students' subject specialism.

Overall, the college, through its initial teacher training (ITT) courses, continues as always to aim to:

- train competent, efficient practitioners who are thoughtful and critical members of the profession able to analyse and develop their own skills and make decisions about quality primary practice in class and whole-school settings;
- enable newly qualified teachers to support and enhance effective practice with an understanding of relevant theory;
- provide academic rigour and challenge, at degree level, to meet the needs of reflective professionals; and
- train teachers who understand and can meet the demands of the whole curriculum, while making a specific contribution through their knowledge and understanding of the structure, content and methodology of a specialist subject.

THE SURVEYS

The intention behind the surveys was not to find out how our ex-students were faring in their first appointment but to find out from headteachers in the 'real' workplace whether our courses prepared teachers to meet *their* demands and expectations of a newly qualified teacher. Implicit is the question of whether heads want thinking, reflective teachers (Carr, 1989) capable of action research and development (Elliott, 1991a) in schools.

The follow-up surveys complement each other and use very similar items. The data from the questionnaires has allowed a monitoring of some 'customer satisfaction' over the period. A copy of the second questionnaire is provided in the Appendix. Table 25.1 shows the respective numbers graduating, the numbers of questionnaires sent out and the response rates. The findings, some of which are given below, indicate a large measure of satisfaction by headteachers with the preparation of newly qualified teachers where it counts – in the workplace.

TABLE 25.1
Questionnaire survey response rates

	STUDENTS GRADU- ATING	NO. OF QUESTIONNAIRES SENT OUT		RETURNS	
		HEADS	STUDENTS	HEADS	STUDENTS
1988	84	73	0	61 (73%)	0
1993	139	74	136	45 (61%)	41 (30%)

CURRICULUM PLANNING, IMPLEMENTATION AND ASSESSMENT

Headteachers in 1993 found their NQTs from Christ Church very well prepared, well prepared or adequately prepared in the core subjects – 89 per cent (93 per cent) in mathematics, 91 per cent (90 per cent) in science and 86 per cent (95 per cent) in English (figures in brackets refer to 1989 results). The NQTs tended to be a bit harder in their judgements of themselves but still recorded over 80 per cent satisfaction. The foundation subjects were judged to be well catered for also, with headteachers recording over 80 per cent satisfaction in all seven other areas, including religious education. NQTs were recording over 90 per cent satisfaction in art, history, music, PE and technology. Heads and NQTs also registered high levels of satisfaction with the preparation received in the crosscurricular dimensions and themes – equal opportunities, education for a multicultural society, economic and industrial understanding and environmental education.

Typical comments (from headteachers) were:

> '. . . good and constantly improving' . . . 'excellent in all respects' . . . 'appropriate work is set according to children's needs . . . a most professional person' . . . 'she has been prepared well – particularly in assessment' . . . 'we are well pleased with her management, teaching, preparation and planning.'

The suggestion here is that the college course had enabled students to adapt the procedures and standards for a particular task to the purposes, needs and abilities of the children they teach.

APPLICATION OF THEORY TO PRACTICE

Headteachers commented

> '. . . he is aware of concepts of child development and puts them to good use' . . . 'sets realistic goals . . . a continuous sense of achievement for the pupils' . . . 'shows good understanding of how children learn and ways to meet varied abilities.'

This is best summed up by an ex-student who commented, '. . . the concentration of the college course on relating theory to practice, in retrospect, stood me in good stead'.

PRODUCING COMPETENT TEACHERS

Again headteachers indicated that the training course was meeting its aims and, more importantly, producing confident, newly qualified teachers who were able to make a full contribution to the life of a school. For example:

> '. . . a particularly able, enthusiastic, confident NQT' . . . 'an excellent addition to our staff and to the education service – keep turning them out this way' . . . 'you obviously had good material to work on but . . . is a credit to your college' . . . 'I congratulate the college on consistently producing excellent teachers' . . . 'overall a well trained, receptive and enthusiastic colleague' . . . 'the ability to learn from advice and experience and to work as a member of a team are key qualities which have led to a successful first year' . . . 'I am delighted with . . . he is very teachable and highly motivated' . . . 'the course our NQT followed was obviously comprehensive, giving an excellent basis on which to found her career.'

Our ex-students were, perhaps somewhat late and rather grudging in expressing their appreciation of the course, commenting:

'. . . it's only now you appreciate how much, and the relevance of what, you learnt in college' . . . 'what I learnt in college is coming into its own – encourage other students – it will be valuable when they get into school' . . . 'college has prepared me well' . . . 'having chatted to other NQTs our course definitely covered everything adequately and most things in great detail.'

As well as an extremely encouraging response it does seem that BEd/BA(Ed) courses, through the development of effective partnerships with schools, the extension of school-based work, the close integration of students' experience in schools with their studies in college and helped by the requirement for all tutors to have recent, relevant and successful teaching experience in school *do* produce newly qualified teachers who are well equipped professionals motivated to continue their learning. There is support for this claim across the whole range of higher education teacher training from Ofsted (1993, p. 25): 'The majority of headteachers considered the new teachers to have been adequately prepared for their first teaching post.'

THE SCOP REPORT

The response to the questionnaire sent by the SCOP Teacher Education Group to primary schools was extremely good at 1,202 returns, despite the fact that it had to be circulated after many primary schools had broken up for the Christmas holiday in 1993. Analysis shows how strongly headteachers feel about the government's proposals for the reform of primary ITT and that they are overwhelmingly reluctant to assume a major responsibility for the totality of it (SCOP, 1994). Where schools were prepared to take a major responsibility it was in guiding and supervising students within the school and assessing their professional competences – a role they already largely undertake. It was quite clear that for the vast majority of headteachers effective and efficient ITT is best undertaken through a close partnership between schools and higher education institutions (HEIs). Strong feelings were expressed with many headteachers seeing the government's proposals as a catastrophic retrograde step after decades of struggling to improve the public esteem in which the primary teaching profession is held. They saw the goal of an all-graduate profession being gravely jeopardized by school-centred training and, far from raising standards, as the government contends, denuded of the intellectual challenge, stimulation and resources of HEIs school-centred training would represent institutional confirmation that 'anyone can do the job'. Headteachers pointed out that students are less likely to be attracted to courses that are neither run nor validated by an HEI and this will have an impact not only on their future career prospects but also on recruitment into the profession.

Practical problems were highlighted, such as inadequate provision of space and resources, and headteachers felt primary schools were neither equipped to deliver the higher education core skills aspect of ITT nor were they in a position to help students acquire the subject knowledge they need (at level 1, 2 and 3) to deliver the primary curriculum. They frequently stated '. . . our job is to teach children, not train teachers' and '. . . training teachers would be an unwise use of teaching time, the education of the children would be disrupted and parental objections increase'. One headteacher summed up with the observation that

> We need professionals properly trained to a high intellectual level – the best practice is intellectually informed and responsive to the latest research – we in schools cannot respond to this adequately – especially for early years education we need intelligent and thinking, articulate practitioners who are confident in their teaching skills *not* some partially trained force who see teaching as a 'nice little job'.

The evidence from this college's surveys and the SCOP questionnaire points to the fact that present undergraduate ITT courses, in partnership with schools, *are* providing academic challenge and rigour at degree level to meet the needs of reflective practitioners, *they are* producing teachers who understand and can meet the demands of the whole curriculum while making a specific specialist contribution *and they are* producing NQTs who are efficient, thoughtful, critical members of the profession able to make, and act on, decisions about quality primary practice in schools.

The Lord Bishop of Guildford, debating the Education bill in the House of Lords on 7 December, provides an apposite final comment. He stated: 'We need not just trained teachers but educated people. To separate teacher education from other Higher Education is to deprive student teachers of the opportunity of interaction with people in other disciplines . . . it might even make teaching seem a non-academic profession' (House of Lords, 1993, p. 847).

APPENDIX CANTERBURY CHRIST CHURCH COLLEGE: BA(ED) EVAL-
UATION: FOLLOW-UP STUDY

Section A

This section of the questionnaire asks for your rating and comments on the work of a newly qualified teacher who left Christ Church College in 1992. (*Please circle the appropriate number.*)

	Very well pre-pared	Well pre-pared	Ade-quate	Poorly pre-pared	Very poorly pre-pared	Not appli-cable
Core subjects						
Maths	5	4	3	2	1	0
Science	5	4	3	2	1	0
Language	5	4	3	2	1	0
Foundation subjects						
Art	5	4	3	2	1	0
Geography	5	4	3	2	1	0
History	5	4	3	2	1	0
Music	5	4	3	2	1	0
Physical education	5	4	3	2	1	0
Technology	5	4	3	2	1	0
Religious education	5	4	3	2	1	0
Thematic or topic work	5	4	3	2	1	0
Crosscurricular dimensions and themes						
Equal opportunities (especially in terms of gender and ability)	5	4	3	2	1	0
Education for a multicultural society	5	4	3	2	1	0
Economic and industrial understanding	5	4	3	2	1	0
Health education	5	4	3	2	1	0
Education for citizenship (including a European dimension)	5	4	3	2	1	0
Environmental education	5	4	3	2	1	0

Section B

This section of the questionnaire asks for brief comments on aspects of classroom organization and management. (*Please write in the space below.*)

1. Application of knowledge of child development to planning

2.   Producing and using teaching aids and resources (including displays)

3.   Planning and classroom management

4.   Pupil assessment and record-keeping

5.   (a)   Relationship with children

     (b)   Relationship with staff

Section C

1.   Are there areas of performance or knowledge where you would want a newly appointed teacher to be better prepared by a higher education course of training? *If so, please specify*

2.   Please indicate any special responsibilities the newly appointed teacher has taken on during the year however informally defined (e.g. curriculum area)

3.   Please indicate any in-service or staff development opportunities the newly appointed teacher has been offered

4.   Comments on preparation for:

   •   core subjects

   •   foundation subjects

   •   crosscurricular dimensions and themes

5.   Any other comments

PART SIX

Conclusion

CHAPTER 26

Implementing Change in Teacher Education

HILARY CONSTABLE

The chapters in this book show a range of work seeking to monitor changes in teacher education. The approaches vary in their starting-points and focus of attention as well as in the methods they employ. The themes of developing effective partnership practice, mentoring and supporting student-teachers, students learning to teach and headteachers' and others' views of the changes have been used to organize the book. When deciding upon such a plan, it is always evident that there are numerous other connections between the chapters and new themes emerge. In this closing chapter, some of the connections and themes in different dimensions and directions have been identified.

The cost of teacher education is a recurring subtheme of some of the work in the book and one which will certainly shape future developments: already the way the resource limit shapes teacher education is more than evident. The question of whether, and to what extent, the current changes deliberately, or otherwise, deprofessionalize teachers is another matter of continuing interest. Inevitably these accounts expose the processes of implementing educational change and, in this instance, show participants creating current versions of teacher education. Gaining more information about how students learn is clearly of importance to all those involved in teacher education and provides a firm basis for the rational development of teacher education. How quality and its development relates to this is somewhat problematic. Finally, the chapter closes with the theme of building on experience.

THE COSTS OF TEACHER EDUCATION

The fact that schemes survive and, evidently, beginning teachers have a high-quality learning experience is the result not only of the subsidies made by schools and higher education but also of the personal investment made by teachers and tutors. School-based tutors, commonly short-handed as mentors, mention the large amount of their time taken by work with and for the students. For this to take place at all there is an opportunity cost for institutions and individuals – something else is not getting done. As against this, Haylock (Chapter 8) reports the 'added value' to schools and teachers of having students and that this contributes to the development of the profession.

As the schemes settle down a number of possibilities present themselves. There may reasonably be a reduction in time consumed when school-based tutors are both clearer about what is involved and more experienced and skilled in providing it. Or there may not, and this is not at all clear yet. In addition, institutions and individuals may claw back the time they claim rightfully to be theirs, and needed for other work, irrespective of the time needed for quality work with student-teachers. In the end the training can only be as good as the best use of the time available for it.

It is clear that teacher education has been and continues to be subsidized not only by schools but also by higher education institutions (HEIs). The finances show sign of strain to breaking-point on all sides and it seems likely that a critical feature in the ultimate success or failure of the new schemes will be resources or their shortage. Certainly the investment is unacceptably low – a curious phenomenon where investment in education is talked of as a high priority for national economic regeneration.

DEPROFESSIONALIZING TEACHERS

There are fears that the new schemes are part of an overt attempt to deprofessionalize teachers – to reduce entry qualifications and training – opening the door to cost cutting primarily through pay. Teacher educators as well as teachers have been criticized for their work, and one view is that the radical reforms to teacher education have been introduced on the presumption that if all the ills of the social and economic state of the nation cannot be laid on teachers then it must be teacher educators who are to blame. If little else this provides a solution to the puzzle that if schools have failed pupils then it seems perverse to base the training of teachers there. There is little to refute a gloomy view but there is a surprise coming from these chapters – the goodwill of teacher educators.

Not only are teacher educators involved in detailed and systematic evaluation of the new courses but this is also carried out from the stance of making the new forms of teacher education work. Indeed, the dominating goodwill of teacher educators in making the changes work is a feature of many of the contributions, almost come what may. Much of the work is close focused – reflecting a combination of researchers' need to get hold of some aspect to provide a basis for systematic inquiry, and teacher educators' needs to inform practical decisions quickly. Whether or not in this process a critical appraisal of the context has been lost or limited is debatable. And whether such limitation, if there is one, is part of a permanent self-censorship (perhaps the least attractive explanation for academics to contemplate), the result of control through overload (not too attractive) or a research succession (plausible, but not especially well supported) also remains to be seen. More optimistically, however it is the questions asked have been shaped, the questions raised are less controlled.

It is interesting to note in this respect that all the mentors questioned by Campbell and Horbury (Chapter 10) '. . . voiced a concern that the articled teacher might actively try to replicate or inadvertently acquire a mentor's own particular teaching style or idiosyncratic traits and become "mentor clones" ', although the evidence from Drake and Dart (Chapter 12) is more equivocal.

IMPLEMENTING EDUCATIONAL CHANGE

Whatever else is going on, it is clear that change is taking place. In the air, at least, there are alterations in materials, procedures and beliefs: the components of educational, as opposed to other sorts of change, identified by Fullan (1982). The style of the introduction of the changes has presented its own effects with some advantages and some disadvantages. These effects need to be taken account of. There is strong central control over the changes with opportunity for local interpretations. Unlike the curriculum developments of the early Schools Council which were, so to speak, front-end loaded with a high proportion of effort involved in conceptualizing and planning the change, and with correspondingly less attention to implementation and even less to institutionalization, the scale of the changes to teacher education, together with the administrative context of higher education and of schools, has left little time for meaningful education planning in the current circumstances. This may not be altogether a bad thing. It is as well to be reminded that it is not possible for pre-implementation planning to solve all the problems of innovation. Loucks-Horsley and Hergert (1985, p. ix) go so far as to say that 'Help and support given teachers *after* planning and initial training is much more critical for success than the best (pre-implementation) training money can buy'. It is not a foregone conclusion that there will be change: for instance, Galvin (Chapter 7) found that, where teachers were most needed, schools were least able to provide the support they needed. Here the preconditions for change were not sufficiently present.

What then needs to be done in terms of implementing an educational change is to realize that teacher education is being created in what is implemented and, more lastingly, in what is institutionalized, not in what is legislated or in what is planned. The first attempts to put the changes into practice, what is learnt from them, and the adjustments that are made are therefore crucial in developing the actual educational change, including its subjective and objective meanings. The chapters show the meaning of the changes being created.

CREATING TEACHER EDUCATION

A recurrent theme in these chapters is of the importance of clear and unambiguous communication and perhaps, at the same time, the impossibility of ever achieving it. Foskett, Ratcliffe and Brunner (Chapter 4) report specifically on the importance of communication. Their three areas (administration, interpersonal relationships and shared understanding) are a signal that communication is a term to be unpacked and in their term 'shared understanding' a significant nail is hit on the head.

Clear communication in terms of written materials or mentor training does not automatically produce a shared meaning. This takes time to develop and elaborate. Rothwell, Nardi and McIntyre (Chapter 3) found that 'Other variations in practice, however, have occurred despite very clear conceptualization of role responsibilities, and detailed guidance about how those responsibilities can be met'. Foskett, Ratcliffe and Brunner (Chapter 4) found '. . . a large number of mentors (17; 18.2 per cent) expressed the view that they did not know what tutors in the university were doing with students on university-based days. This is despite the fact that the handbooks and mentor training produced agreed programmes for each element of the course'. Communication in educational, perhaps for that matter any, innovation goes beyond the transfer of information involved in, say, a press release or a course document. Eventually a shared understanding must be created or, without it, apparently clear communication remains ambiguous. This shared understanding is not in lumps waiting to be passed from one person to another like marbles changing hands in a game, but needs to be created in the minds of the people involved. Neither is it the case that there is a pre-existing understanding which has only to be revealed to be shared. In these changes to teacher education the meaning is being created collectively by the participants as they implement the changes and as the implementation creates learning experiences.

The school-based tutors did not at first conceptualize their role as fully as the university tutors and *apparently* clear communication was not by itself sufficient to produce a predictable shared meaning. They quickly took up the importance of working with trainee teachers but a fuller and sufficiently elaborate version of what the role entailed was harder to come by. Campbell and Horbury (Chapter 10) bring this into sharp focus:

> Initially he [the mentor] considered that an articled teacher would learn simply by observing teaching. He later changed his practice as he realized it was insufficient just to observe teaching. It was necessary 'to spell it out'. He reported that '. . . it wasn't really enough to let them watch. They might get some sense that this is a good lesson but the mechanics of its achievement can be tacit'.

Mentors took time to come to terms with aspects of the role beyond immediate contact with students: 'Meetings and administrative activities involving staff tended to receive low ratings, and were the focus of questioning comments, especially from mentors' (Rothwell, Nardi and McIntyre, Chapter 3).

'[The] course needed, according to mentors, "an awful lot of administration" ' (Campbell and Horbury, Chapter 10). It is interesting to note the mentors having much the same experience with their colleagues: 'Mentors reported that, initially, their colleagues were neither as committed to the articled teacher course as they were nor did they have much understanding of how it was to work' (Campbell and Horbury, Chapter 10). Much the same consequences ensue: '. . . *despite their efforts at the start of the academic year*, mentors had to brief staff on the course, explain their expected contribution and outline the potential benefits. They also had to provide INSET sessions on working with articled teachers and monitor how well staff did this' (*ibid.*, my emphasis).

There is no failure involved in changes that do not work out exactly as intended, for it is only by putting into operation a change that participants can get a picture of what is involved in that change, in that place, at that time. Put another way, the possible shape of the innovation emerges only as the participants act. The key to success or improvement lies in the next stage.

It is as well to be clear here about the extent to which the change is mutually adaptive and where fidelity is required (see Fullan, 1982). In some ways the local interpretation in context suggests a mutually adaptive model in which participants using some guiding structure and principles bring their own contributions to the realization of the innovation. This is to miss out the fact that there may be important elements of the change where fidelity is required, at least in the first stages of implementation – for instance, in creating a shared understanding of what is involved in the various roles. It is by sticking faithfully to a relatively rigidly defined version of the change that participants can get the best chance of experiencing and seeing what was intended by those who planned the innovation (see Constable and Long, 1991).

Against this background, lists of good practice points make sense. Where the points may seem to be rather obvious it is worth bearing in mind the discussion about creating shared meaning. The facets of practice identified in the lists may be ones where communication has been rather less than straightforward and certainly more tricky than was imagined before implementation (see, for instance, Rothwell, Nardi and McIntyre, Chapter 3; Foskett, Ratcliffe and Brunner, Chapter 4; Aspinwall, Garrett and Owen-Jackson, Chapter 11). These lists set a baseline for discussion and draw attention to the areas where there are likely to be matters to be made yet clearer.

STUDENTS LEARNING

Busher and King (Chapter 5) report students as preferring a more structured approach to the further professional studies element of their course. One interpretation of this is that the students cannot be expected to have a sufficient grasp of the cognitive map of what is intended by further professional studies to initiate learning activities confidently.

Bramald *et al.* (Chapter 17) argue for the importance of dissonant experiences – there is a lot to be learnt from a bad lesson: a familiar idea to teachers and teacher educators but a painful one for students. Brooks, Fitch and Robinson in Chapter 13 point out the importance of harnessing students' existing experience partly as a resource for the school but also as a channel of meaningful communication. They note that this can have a good effect on students' self-esteem. The collusion of teachers and students in avoiding the transformational and in sticking with support and guidance in Collison and Edwards' chapter (15) and the similar practice between students in Hawkey's chapter (16) is an indication of the vulnerability of participants and the power behind the need to maintain self-esteem.

The work of Drake and Dart (Chapter 12), together with Constable and Norton (Chapter 14) and Fursland (Chapter 21), raises the question of subject knowledge and expertise. Drake and Dart point to differences between maths and English teachers in their views of being a good teacher and suggest there is a need to consider whether or not there should be specific variations in competence profiles. Constable and Norton (Chapter 14) raise the question of the extent to which the training arrangements are geared to help the development of subject knowledge needed in moving from being a student to being a teacher.

DEVELOPMENT OF QUALITY

It is relatively straightforward to collect views on the quality of initial training but rather more difficult to give these their correct weight. It is difficult, perhaps impossible, to establish cause and effect and, furthermore, all the actors – teachers, higher education tutors, students – have interests. What opinion is worth paying attention to and what should be considered significant enough to alter decisions? Responses that are reasonable negative reactions to parts of the training which are poor and need improvement should be discriminated from responses that merely indicate that some element of the training has been undersold or the significance of which cannot be expected to emerge until some later date.

In innovation the initial steer is given by the planners and a strong pull comes from the quality-control mechanisms with the actors finding their way between the two. The chapters address a number of issues concerning quality. In teacher training quality is hard to police – timescales are a problem as are changing views of what counts as quality. The divisions of responsibility and high stakes in the new system could disintegrate into a culture of blame – the last thing that is needed when the changes will still take time to implement fully.

When is the appropriate time to look back from a teacher to their training and make wise comments about how initial and continuing teacher education should proceed? Is it after 20 years by which time the teacher can be considered established but by when many other factors beside initial training will have entered the frame, or after five years when the teacher is still relatively new but when career variation may be great and colour the responses? The easiest time to obtain opinion from students is when they are still in training, but their responses are exactly that – those of students in training. Such opinions are a pertinent and immediate source of information on 'how things were for them' but this is not the same as a balanced view of what is required to become a teacher. Indeed, the very notion of professional training suggests that the trainee is not expected to have a clear picture of what is required – that is what the training is for. In this respect, Newton's chapter (22) is instructive. Students in their PGCE year reported that they valued both the parts of the course based in the university *and* the part in school, rather than one *or* the other. But in their first year of teaching they had more to say about the university-based parts of the course. In this year they came to rely on the work they had done in the university as an important source of material and speculated that, if they had not had such information from the university, they didn't know whence they would have got it.

Consistency of treatment is commonly regarded as a facet of quality. Drake and Dart (Chapter 12) note, for instance, that it is easy for criteria of performance to '. . . evolve implicitly and differentially from mentor to mentor', and Rothwell, Nardi and McIntyre (Chapter 3) in the comment quoted earlier noted unintended variations in practice in spite of best efforts to produce consistency. Consistency is one of the more easily detectable aspects of practice but it needs to be defined rather than taken for granted. There are some aspects of practice that not only do but should vary, perhaps greatly. The support needed by this student in this school with this class may be enormous and a high demand on all parts of the system, whereas for another student such support would be intrusive and overwhelming. Rather than coming at the issue from the research question of consistency, perhaps the response is better framed in terms of student entitlement. In any case consistency of procedure, while valuable, should not be allowed, without question, to colonize practice.

BUILDING ON EXPERIENCE

Building on experience happens whether or not it is planned for; participants must, of necessity, use their own current experience as a basis for their future development. An interesting feature of the work was the evolution of school-based tutors' capacities and skills to deal with students. There is no doubt that, in general, school-based tutors put in a considerable amount of effort and this was with good intentions. The work took time and was generally given time (see Constable and Norton, Chapter 14; Campbell and Horbury, Chapter 10). The picture of what the time and effort added up to was rather more mixed (see Wright and Moore, Chapter 6; Collison and Edwards, Chapter 15; Harris, Chapter 18; Fursland, Chapter 21). School-based tutors developed skills in dealing directly with students and supporting as carers and sometimes as guides. They were less confident as challengers of practice (see Collison and Edwards, Chapter 15).

The most striking finding was the rapid way in which mentors' views of their role evolved. In some circumstances mentors were able to offer fully articulated views of their subject pedagogy (see Drake and Dart, Chapter 12). There is further interesting work to be done in relation to mentors' theories of teaching and, separately, of teacher education. The fact that mentors were concerned about the possibility of cloning (Campbell and Horbury, Chapter 10) reveals an underlying view of teaching as intellectual activity in which there is a demand for teachers to frame the situation and to make decisions beyond the application of known techniques. One feature of professionality is the ability and requirement to frame situations as well as produce solutions, and to ask significant questions about worthwhileness and education. It was less clear whether teaching was seen as a moral activity in which decisions were to be made about the way teachers might respond to their social and economic context.

It is not out of place to end by recalling Fullan and Stiegelbauers's (1991, p. 27) comment: 'Politically motivated change . . . produces over-load, unrealistic timelines, uncoordinated demands, simplistic solutions, misdirected efforts, inconsistencies, and underestimation of what it takes to bring about reform. If one is on the receiving end, as nearly all of us are, the main piece of advice is *caveat implementer*.'

References

ALEXANDER, R. (1990) Partnership in initial teacher training: confronting the issues, in M. Booth, J. Furlong and M. Wilkin (eds), *op. cit.*.

ALEXANDER, R.J., ROSE, J. and WOODHEAD, C. (1992) *Curriculum Organization and Classroom Practice in Primary Schools: A Discussion Paper*, Department of Education and Science, London.

ALFREY, M. and SHARPE, K. (1994) A reform too far: off site, off target, *Junior Education*, May.

ANTHONY, V. (1993) Tensions in training reform, *The Times Educational Supplement*, 22 January, p. 19.

BALL, S. (1990) *Politics and Policy Making in Education: Explorations in Political Sociology*, Routledge, London.

BALL, S. (1993) Education, Majorism and 'the curriculum of the dead', *Curriculum Studies*, Vol. 1, no. 2, pp. 95–213.

BARBER, M. (1993) The truth about partnership, *Journal of Education for Teaching*, Vol. 19, no. 3, pp. 255–62.

BARNES, D. (1992) The significance of teachers' frames for teaching, in T. Russell and H. Munby (eds), *op. cit.*

BARRETT, E., BARTON, L., FURLONG, J., GALVIN, C., MILES, S. and WHITTY, G. (1992) *Initial Teacher Education in England and Wales – A Topography*, Goldsmith's College/University of London, London.

BARRETT, E. and GALVIN, C. (1993) *The Licensed Teacher Scheme: A Modes of Teacher Education Project Survey*, University of London Institute of Education, London.

BARROW, R. (1990) Teacher education: theory and practice, *British Journal of Educational Studies*, Vol. 38, no. 4, pp. 308–18.

BARTON, L., POLLARD, A. and WHITTY, G. (1992) Experiencing CATE: the impact of accreditation upon initial teacher training institutions in England, *Journal of Education for Teaching*, Vol. 18, no. 1, pp. 41–57.

BENNETT, N. (1978) *Teaching Styles and Pupil Progress*, Open Books, London.

BENNETT, N. and CARRÉ, C. (eds) (1992) *Learning to Teach*, Routledge, London.

BENTON, P. (ed.) (1990a) *The Oxford Internship Scheme: Integration and Partnership in Initial Teacher Education*, Calouste Gulbenkian Foundation, London.

BENTON, P. (1990b) The internship model, in P. Benton (ed.), *op. cit.*

BERNSTEIN, B. (1971) On the classification and framing of educational knowledge, in M.F.D. Young (ed.), *op. cit.*

BIOTT, C. and NIAS, J. (eds) (1992) *Working and Learning Together for Change*, Open University Press, Milton Keynes.

BIRD, T., ANDERSON, L.M. and SWINDLER, S.A. (1993) Pedagogical balancing acts: attempts to influence prospective teachers' beliefs, *Teaching and Teacher Education*, Vol. 9, pp. 253–67.

BLUMBERG, A. (1976) Supervision: what is and what might be, *Theory into Practice*, Vol. 15, pp. 284–92.

BOOTH, M. (1993) The effectiveness and role of the mentor in school: the students' view, *Cambridge Journal of Education*, Vol. 23, no. 2, pp. 185–97.

BOOTH, M., FURLONG, J. and WILKIN, M. (1990) *Partnership in Initial Teacher Training*, Cassell, London.

BOOTHROYD, W. (1979) Teaching practice supervision – a research report, *British Journal of Teacher Education*, Vol. 5, no. 3, pp. 243–50.

BORDERS, L.D. (1991) A systematic approach to peer group supervision, *Journal of Counselling and Development*, Vol. 69, January/February, pp. 248–52.

BOYD, R. and RICHERSON, P.J. (1985) *Culture and the Evolutionary Process*, University of Chicago Press, Chicago, Ill.

BRAMALD, R., HARDMAN, F. and LEAT, D. (1994) Initial teacher trainees and their views of teaching and language, *Teaching and Teacher Education*, Vol. 10, no. 6.

BRUMFIT, C.J. and MITCHELL, R.F. (eds) (1990) *Research in the Language Classroom*, ELT and British Council, London.

BUSHER, H., CLARKE, S. and TAGGART, L. (1988) Beginning teachers' learning, in J. Calderhead (ed.), *op. cit.*

BUSHER, H. and SIMMONS, C. (1992) Living with CATE: the case of reflective student teachers, *Educational Studies*, Vol. 18, no. 1, pp. 37–48.

BUSHER, H. and SMITH, M. (eds) (1993) *Managing Educational Institutions: Reviewing Development and Learning. Sheffield Papers in Education Management 5.* Centre for Education Management and Administration, Sheffield Hallam University.

BUTLER, J. (1992) Teacher professional development: an Australian case study, *Journal of Education for Teaching*, Vol. 18, no. 3, pp. 221–38.

CALDERHEAD, J. (ed.) (1987) *Exploring Teachers' Thinking*, Falmer, London.

CALDERHEAD, J. (ed.) (1988) *Teachers' Professional Learning*, Falmer, Lewes.

CALDERHEAD, J. (1989) Reflective teaching and teacher education, *Teacher Education*, Vol. 5, no. 1, pp. 43–51.

CALDERHEAD, J. and GATES, P. (eds) (1993) *Conceptualizing Reflection in Teacher Development*, Falmer, Lewes.

CALDERHEAD, J. and ROBSON, M. (1991) Images of teaching: student teachers' early conceptions of classroom practice, *Teaching and Teacher Education*, Vol. 7, no. 1, pp. 1–8.

CARR, W. (1989) *Quality in Teaching: Arguments for a Reflective Profession*, Falmer, Lewes.

CARR, W. and KEMMIS, S. (1983) *Becoming Critical, Knowing through Action Research*, Deakin University Press, Geelong.

CARRINGTON, B. and TYMMS, P. (1993a) Not in Plowden's camp, or Patten's, *The Times Educational Supplement*, 5 March.

CARRINGTON, B. and TYMMS, P. (1993b) *For Primary Heads, Mum's Not The Word!* National Union of Teachers, London.

CARTER, K. and DOYLE, W. (1987) Teachers' knowledge structures and comprehension processes, in J. Calderhead (ed.), *op. cit.*

CHITTY, C. (1992) *The Education System Transformed*, Baseline Books, Manchester.

CLARKE, K. (1991) Primary education (a statement issued by the Secretary of State for Education and Science on 3 December), DES, London.

CLIFT, R.T., HOUSTON, W.R. and PUGACH, M.C. (eds) (1990) *Encouraging Reflective Practice in Education: An Analysis of Issues and Programs*, Teachers College Press, New York.

COCKCROFT, W.H. (1982) *Mathematics Counts, Report of the Committee of Inquiry into the Teaching and Learning of School Mathematics*, HMSO, London.

COMINO FOUNDATION (1991) Note: Getting Results and Solving Problems.

CONSTABLE, H. and LONG, A. (1991) Changing science teaching: lessons for a long-term evaluation of in-service education for teachers, *International Journal of Science Education*, Vol. 13, no. 4, pp. 405–19.

COOPER, B. (1990) PGCE students and investigational approaches in secondary maths, *Research Papers in Education*, Vol. 5, no. 2, pp. 127–51.

COULBY, D. and BASH, L. (1991) *Contradiction and Conflict: The 1988 Education Act in Action*, Cassell, London.

CRUICKSHANK, D.R. (1990) *Research that Informs Teachers and Teacher Education*, Phi Delta Kappa, Bloomington, Ind.

DART, L. and DRAKE, P. (1993) School-based training: a conservative practice?, *Journal of Education for Teaching*, Vol. 19, no. 2, pp. 173–89.

DAVIES, I. (1994) Initial teacher education in the new Europe, *Journal of Further and Higher Education*, Vol. 18, no. 1, pp. 14–20.

DAY, C. (1993) Reflection: a necessary but not sufficient condition for professional development, *British Educational Research Journal*, Vol. 19, no. 1, pp. 83–93.

DEARING, SIR R. (1994) *The Final Report*, School Curriculum and Assessment Authority, London.

DEMAINE, J. (forthcoming) Radical approaches to the reform of teacher education.

DEPARTMENT OF EDUCATION (1992a) *The Accreditation of Initial Teacher Training*, Circular 9/92, CATE, HMSO, London.

DEPARTMENT OF EDUCATION (1992b) *Initial Teacher Training (Secondary Phase)*, Circular 9/92, HMSO, London.

DEPARTMENT OF EDUCATION AND SCIENCE (1992c) *Initial Teacher Training of Secondary School Teachers*, Circular 9/92, HMSO, London.

DEPARTMENT FOR EDUCATION (1992d) *The New Requirements for Initial Teacher Training*, Circular 9/92, HMSO, London.

DEPARTMENT FOR EDUCATION (1992e) *The New Requirements for the Initial Training of Teachers*, HMSO, London.

DEPARTMENT FOR EDUCATION (1992f) *Choice and Diversity: A New Framework for Schools*, HMSO, London.

DEPARTMENT FOR EDUCATION (1993a) *The Initial Training of Primary School Teachers: New Criteria for Course Approval*, Draft Circular, 9 June, HMSO, London.

DEPARTMENT FOR EDUCATION (1993b) *The Government's Proposals for the Reform of Initial Teacher Training*, HMSO, London.

DEPARTMENT FOR EDUCATION (1993c) *The Initial Training of Primary School Teachers: New Criteria for Courses*, Circular 14/93, HMSO, London.

DEPARTMENT FOR EDUCATION (1994) Analytical Services Branch, Mowden Hall, Staindrop Road, Darlington, Co. Durham, DL3 9BG.

DEPARTMENT OF EDUCATION AND SCIENCE (1972) *Teacher Education and Training (James Report)*, HMSO, London.

DEPARTMENT OF EDUCATION AND SCIENCE (1982) *The New Teachers in School*, HMSO, London.

DEPARTMENT OF EDUCATION AND SCIENCE (1983) *The Treatment and Assessment of Probationary Teachers*, Administrative Memorandum 1/83, HMSO, London.

DEPARTMENT OF EDUCATION AND SCIENCE (1984) *Initial Teacher Training: Approval of Courses*, Circular 3/84, HMSO, London.

DEPARTMENT OF EDUCATION AND SCIENCE (1985) *Better Schools*, HMSO, London.

DEPARTMENT OF EDUCATION AND SCIENCE (1988) *The New Teacher in School: A Survey by HM Inspectors in England and Wales 1987*, HMSO, London.

DEPARTMENT OF EDUCATION AND SCIENCE (1989a) *Qualified Teacher Status: A Consultation Document*, HMSO, London.

DEPARTMENT OF EDUCATION AND SCIENCE (1989b) *Initial Teacher Training: Approval of Courses*, Circular 24/89, HMSO, London.

DEPARTMENT OF EDUCATION AND SCIENCE (1989c) *The Professional Training of Primary School Teachers*, HMSO, London.

DEPARTMENT OF EDUCATION AND SCIENCE (1989d) *The Education (Teachers) Regulations 1989*, Circular 18/89, HMSO, London.

DEPARTMENT OF EDUCATION AND SCIENCE (1990) *Report of the School Management Task Force*, HMSO, London.

DEPARTMENT OF EDUCATION AND SCIENCE (1991) *School-Based Initial Teacher Training in England and Wales*, HMSO, London.

DEPARTMENT OF EDUCATION AND SCIENCE (1992) *Reform of Initial Teacher Training: A Consultation Document*, HMSO, London.

DEPARTMENT OF EDUCATION AND SCIENCE (1993) *The New Teacher in School*, HMSO, London.

DOYLE, W.C. (1977) Learning in the classroom environment: an ecological analysis, *Journal of Teacher Education*, Vol. 28, no. 6.

DOYLE, W. (1986) Classroom organization and management, in M.C. Wittrock (ed.), *op. cit.*

DRIVER, R. (1983) *The Pupil as Scientist?*, Open University Press, Milton Keynes.

DUQUETTE, C. (1993) A school-based teacher education program: perceptions and attitudes, *The Alberta Journal of Educational Research*, Vol. 39, no. 4, pp. 419–32.

EARLEY, P. (1992) Getting off to a good start, *The Times Educational Supplement*, 4 December, p. 5.

EDWARDS, A.D. (1992) *Change and Reform in Initial Teacher Training (Report No. 9)* National Commission on Education, London.

EDWARDS, A. (1994) Curricular applications of classroom in groups, in P. Kutnick and C. Rogers (eds), *op. cit.*

EDWARDS, T. (1992) Issues and challenges in initial teacher education, *Cambridge Journal of Education*, Vol. 22, no. 3, pp. 283–91.

ELLIOTT, J. (1991a) *Action Research for Educational Change*, Open University Press, Milton Keynes.

ELLIOTT, J. (1991b) Changing contexts for educational evaluation: the challenge for methodology, *Studies in Educational Evaluation*, Vol. 17, no. 4, pp. 309–18.

ELLIOTT, J. (1991c) A model of professionalism and its implication for teacher education, *British Education Research Journal*, Vol. 17, no. 4, pp. 309–19.

ELLIOTT, J. (1993) Professional Development in a land of choice and diversity, in D. Bridges and T. Kerry (1993) *Developing Teachers Professionally*, Routledge, London.

ELLIOTT, J. (ed.) (1994a) *Reconstructing Teacher Education*, Falmer, Lewes.

ELLIOTT, J. (1994b) Three perspectives on coherence and continuity in teacher education, in J. Elliott (ed.), *op. cit.*

EVANS, C. (1993) *English People: The Experience of Teaching and Learning English in British Universities*, Open University Press, Milton Keynes.

EVERTON, T. and WHITE, S. (1992) Partnership in training: the University of Leicester's new model of school-based teacher education, *Cambridge Journal of Education*, Vol. 22, no. 2, pp. 143–55.

FARRAR, M. (1992) Initial teacher training: a school perspective, *Education Review*, Vol. 6, no. 2, pp. 4–7.

FULLAN, M. (1982) *The Meaning of Educational Change*, Teachers College Press, New York.

FULLAN, M.G. and STIEGELBAUER, S. (1991) *The New Meaning of Educational Change*, Cassell, London.

FURLONG, J. (1993) Why wear blinkers?, *The Times Educational Supplement: Platform*, 29 January, p. 14.

FURLONG, V.J., HIRST, P.H., POCKLINGTON, K. and MILES, S. (1988) *Initial Teacher Training and the Role of the School*, Open University Press, Milton Keynes.

GALTON, M. (1987) Continuity and change in the primary school: the research evidence, *Oxford Review of Education*, Vol. 13, no. 1, pp. 81–94.

GALTON, M., SIMON, B. and CROLL, P. (1980) *Inside the Primary Classroom*, Routledge & Kegan Paul, London.

GALVIN, C. (1992) Licensed teachers and the charge of deprofessionalization of teaching. Paper given at the British Comparative and International Educational Society Annual Conference, 11–13 September, York.

GAMMAGE, P. (1987) Chinese whispers, *Oxford Review of Education*, Vol. 13, no. 1, pp. 95–110.

GIBSON, R. (1976) The effect of school practice: the development of novice teacher perspectives, *British Journal of Teacher Education*, Vol. 2, no. 2, pp. 241–50.

GILROY, D.P. (1992) The political rape of initial teacher education in England and Wales: a *JET* rebuttal, *Journal of Education for Teaching*, Vol. 18, no. 1, pp. 5–22.

GILROY, D.P. (1994) Back to the future: the deprofessionalization of initial teacher education in England and Wales, *Australian Journal of Teacher Education*, Special Edition.

GILROY, P. and SMITH, M. (eds) (1993) *International Analyses of Teacher Education*, Carfax, Abingdon.

GIROUX, H. and MCLAREN, P. (1986) Teacher education as a counterpublic sphere: towards a redefinition, in T.S. Popkewitz (ed.), *op. cit.*

GLASSBERG, S. and SPRINTHALL, N.A. (1980) Novice teacher training: a developmental approach, *Journal of Teacher Education*, Vol. 31, no. 2, pp. 31–8.

GOODLAD, S. (1988) Forms of heresy in higher education: aspects of academic freedom in education for the professions, in M. Tight (ed.), *op. cit.*

GOODSON, I. (ed.) (1992) *Studying Teachers' Lives*, Routledge, London.

GRIFFITHS, M. and TANN, S. (1992) Using reflective practice to link personal and public theories, *Journal of Education for Teaching*, Vol. 18, no. 1, pp. 69–84.

GROSSMAN, P.L., WILSON, S.M. and SHULMAN, L.E. (1989) Teachers of substance: subject matter knowledge for teaching, in M.C. Reynolds (ed.), *op. cit.*

GUILLAUME, A.M. and RUDNEY, G.L. (1993) Student teachers' growth towards independence: an analysis of their changing concerns, *Teaching and Teacher Education*, Vol. 9, pp. 65–80.

HANDAL, G. (1990) Promoting the articulation of tacit knowledge through the counselling of practitioners. Paper given at Amsterdam Pedalogisch Centum Conference, Amsterdam.

HANDS, P. (1986) *The Collins English Dictionary* (2nd edn), Collins, London.

HANNAM, C., SMYTH, P. and STEPHENSON, N. (1976) *The First Year of Teaching*, Penguin Books, Harmondsworth.

HANNAN, A. (1993) *The Initial Training of Primary School Teachers: Response to the DFE (an Interim Report)*, University of Plymouth, Exmouth.

HANNAN, A. and NEWBY, M. (1993) Student teacher and headteacher views on current provision and proposals for the future of initial teacher education for primary schools, *Collected Original Resources in Education*, Vol. 17, no. 1, fiche 1 (also published by the University of Plymouth at Exmouth).

HARGREAVES, D. (1990) Another radical approach to the reform of initial teacher training, *Westminster Studies in Education*, Vol. 13, pp. 5–11.

HARRIS, A. and RUSS, J. (1994, in press) Evaluating records of experience in initial teacher education, *Assessment and Evaluation in Higher Education*, Vol. 18, no. 4.

HARVARD, G. and DUNNE, R. (1992) The role of the mentor in developing teacher competence, *Westminster Studies in Education*, Vol. 15, pp. 34–45.

HEAFORD, M. (1993) School-based teacher training: some French lessons. Paper presented to the UCET conference.

HIGHER EDUCATION FUNDING COUNCIL FOR ENGLAND (1993) *Report R 93/1*, Higher Education Funding Council for England, Bristol.

HILL, D. (1992) What's happened to initial teaching education?, *Education Review*, Vol. 8, no. 2, pp. 8–11.

HILLGATE GROUP (1986) *Whose Schools? A Radical Manifesto*, Hillgate Group, London.

HODGKINSON, K. (1992) Client opinion on the radical reform of initial teacher training for primary schools: a survey of students and teachers, *Educational Studies*, Vol. 18, no. 1, pp. 71–81.

HOGBIN, J. *et al.* (1990) *The New Teacher in School: Interim Report*, Manchester Polytechnic, Didsbury School of Education, Manchester.

HOLYOAKE, J. (1993) Initial teacher training: the French view, *Journal of Education for Teaching*, Vol. 19, no. 2, pp. 215–26.

HOUSE OF LORDS (1993) *Hansard*, London, 7 December.

HOYLE, E. and MEGARRY, J. (eds) (1980) *World Yearbook of Education 1980: Professional Development of Teachers*, Kogan Page, London.

HUBERMAN, A.M. and MILES, M.B. (1984) *Innovation up Close*, Plenum, New York.

JACQUES, K. (1992) Mentoring in initial teacher education, *Cambridge Journal of Education*, Vol. 22, no. 3, pp. 337–50.

JAWORSKI, B. (1993) The professional development of teachers: the potential of critical reflection, *British Journal of In-Service Education*, Vol. 19, no. 3, pp. 37–42.

JAWORSKI, B. and WATSON, A. (1994) *Mentoring in Mathematics Teaching*, Mathematical Association/Falmer, Lewes.

JUDGE, H. (1980) Teaching and professionalization: an essay in ambiguity, in E. Hoyle and J. Megarry (eds), *op. cit.*

KAGAN, D.M. (1992) Professional growth among pre-service and beginning teachers, *Review of Educational Research*, Vol. 62, pp. 129–69.

KNIGHT, C. (1990) *The Making of Tory Education Policy in Post-War Britain 1950–1986*, Falmer, Lewes.

KNIGHT, J., MCWILLIAM, E. and BARTLETT, L. (1995) Reforming teacher education policy under Labour governments in Australia 1983–1993, *British Journal of the Sociology of Education*, Vol. 16, no. 4.

KNOWLES, J.G. (1992) Models for understanding pre-service and beginning teachers' biographies: illustrations from case studies, in I. Goodson (ed.), *op. cit.*

KOLB, D.A. (1984) *Experiential Learning*, Prentice-Hall, Englewood Cliffs, NJ.

KORTHAGEN, F.A. (1988) The influence of learning orientations on the development of reflective teaching, in J. Calderhead (ed.), *op. cit.*

KUTNICK, P. and ROGERS, C. (eds) (1994) *Groups in Schools*, Cassell, London.

KYRIACOU, C. (1993) Research on the development of expertise in classroom teaching during initial training and the first year of teaching, *Educational Review*, Vol. 45, no. 1, pp. 79–87.

LABOSKEY, V.K. (1993) A conceptual framework for reflection in pre-service teacher education in J. Calderhead and P. Gates (eds), *op. cit.*

LACEY, C. and LAMONT, W. (1976) *Partnership with Schools: An Experiment in Teacher Education. University of Sussex Education Area Occasional Paper 5*, University of Sussex, Brighton.

LAWLOR, S. (1990) *Teachers Mistaught: Training in Theories or Education in Subjects*, Centre for Policy Studies, London.

LEAT, C. (1993) Competence, teaching, thinking and feeling, *Oxford Review of Education*, Vol. 19, no. 4, pp. 499–510.

LEINHARDT, G.G. (1988) Situated knowledge and experiences in teaching, in J. Calderhead (ed.), *op. cit.*

LEVITAS, T. (ed.) (1986) *The Ideology of the New Right*, Polity Press, Cambridge.

LINCOLN, M.A. and MCALLISTER, L.L. (1993) Peer learning in clinical education, *Medical Teacher*, Vol. 15, no. 1, pp. 17–25.

LOUCKS-HORSLEY, S. and HERGERT, L. (1985) *An Action Guide to School Improvement*, Association for Supervision and Curriculum Development, Alexandria, Va.

LORTIE, D. (1975) *School Teacher*, University of Chicago Press, Chicago, Ill.

LUCAS, P. (1990) Partnership and reflective practice in the subject training group: some opportunities and obstacles, in M. Booth, J. Furlong and M. Wilkin (eds), *op. cit.*

LUNT, N., MCKENZIE, P. and POWELL, L. (1993) 'The right track'. Teacher training and the new right: change and review, *Educational Studies*, Vol. 19, no. 2, pp. 143–61.

MACLENNAN, S. and SEADON, T. (1988) What price school based work? Reflections on a school sited PGCE method course, *Cambridge Journal of Education*, Vol. 18, no. 3, pp. 387–403.

MANCHESTER POLYTECHNIC (1980) BEd (Honours) (Full-time) Preservice, Manchester Polytechnic Faculty of Community Studies and Education.

MANDLER, G. (1984) *Mind and Emotion: Psychology of Emotion and Stress*, Norton, New York.

MAYNARD, T. and FURLONG, J. (1993) Learning to Teach and Models of Mentoring in D. McIntyre, H. Hagger and M. Wilkin, *op. cit.*

MCDONALD, J. (1992) *Teaching: Making Sense of an Uncertain Craft*, Teachers College Press, New York.

MCCULLOCH, M. (1993) Democratization of teacher education: new forms of part-nership for school-based teacher education, in P. Gilroy and M. Smith (eds.), *op. cit.*

MCINTYRE, D. (1980) The contribution of research to quality in teacher education, in E. Hoyle and J. Megarry (eds), *op. cit.*

MCINTYRE, D. (1988) Designing a teacher education curriculum from research and theory on teacher knowledge, in J. Calderhead (ed.), *op. cit.*

MCINTYRE, D. (1992) Theory, theorizing and reflection in initial teacher education, in J. Calderhead and P. Gates (eds), *op. cit.*

MCINTYRE, D. and HAGGER, H. (1992) Professional development through the Oxford Internship model, *British Journal of Educational Studies*, Vol. 40, no. 3, pp. 264–83.

MCINTYRE, D. and HAGGER, H. (eds) (1993) *Mentoring in Initial Teacher Education: A Report Synthesizing Five Research Studies of Mentoring*, Supported by the Paul Hamlyn Foundation, Oxford.

MCINTYRE, D., HAGGER, H. and WILKIN, M. (eds) (1993) *Mentoring: Perspectives on School-Based Teacher Education*, Kogan Page, London.

MCMANUS, M. (1993) Oh yes, we can work together, *The Times Educational Supplement: Opinion*, 22 January, p. 16.

MCNAMARA, D. (1992) The reform of teacher education in England and Wales: teacher competence; panacea or rhetoric?, *Journal of Education for Teaching*, Vol. 18, no. 2, pp. 273–85.

MITCHELL WALDROP, M. (1992) *Complexity*, Penguin Books, Harmondsworth.

MORTIMORE, P. (1993) Managing teaching and learning: two sides of the same coin: the search for a match, in H. Busher and M. Smith (eds), *op. cit.*

MORTIMORE, P., SAMMONS, P. STOLL, L. LEWIS, D. and ECOB, R.B. (1988) *School Matters: The Junior Years*, Open Books, Wells.

MOUNTFORD, B. (1993) Mentoring and initial teacher education, in P. Smith and J. West-Burnham (eds), *op. cit.*

NATIONAL ASSOCIATION OF HEADTEACHERS (1993) *The Initial Training of Primary School Teachers, NAHT Response to the Draft Circular issued by the Department for Education*, NAHT, London, 6 July.

NATIONAL COMMISSION ON EDUCATION (1993) *Learning to Succeed*, HMSO, London.

NEWTON, L.D. (1991a) Who needs trained relations?, *Primary Teaching Studies*, Vol. 8, no. 1, pp. 62–7.

NEWTON, L.D. (1991b) What comes next? The in-service needs of newly qualified primary teachers, *British Journal of In-Service Education*, Vol. 17, no. 1, pp. 75–80.

NIAS, J. (1989) *Primary Teachers Talking*, Routledge, London.

NICHOL, J. (1993) The Exeter school-based PGCE: an alternative initial teacher training model, *Journal of Education for Teaching*, Vol. 19, no. 3, pp. 303–21.

OATLEY, K. and JOHNSON-LAIRD, P.N. (1987) Towards a cognitive theory of emotions, *Cognition and Emotion*, Vol. 1, pp. 29–50.

OFFICE FOR STANDARDS IN EDUCATION (1993a) *The Articled Teacher Scheme*, HMSO, London.

OFFICE FOR STANDARDS IN EDUCATION (1993b) *The Licensed Teacher Scheme: September 1990–July 1992*, HMSO, London.

OFFICE FOR STANDARDS IN EDUCATION (1993c) *The New Teacher in School: a Survey by HM Inspectors in England and Wales*, London, HMSO.

O'HEAR, A. (1988) *Who Teaches the Teachers? A Contribution to the Public Debate on the DES Green Paper*, Social Affairs Unit, London.

OWEN-JACKSON, G. (1993) Partnership in initial teacher training: a case study. Unpublished MEd dissertation, University of Derby.

PARSONS, C. (ed.) (1994) *Quality Improvement in Education: Case Studies in Schools, Colleges and Universities*, Fulton, London.

PECK, A.J. (1988) *Language Teachers at Work. A Description of Methods*, Prentice-Hall, London.

POLLARD, A., BROADFOOT, P., CROLL, P., OSBORN and ABBOTT (1994, in press) *Changing English Primary Schools? The Impact of the National Curriculum and Assessment at Key Stage One*, Cassell, London.

POLLARD, A. and TANN, S. (1987) *Reflective Teaching in the Primary School: A Handbook for the Classroom*, Cassell, London.

POPKEWITZ, T.S. (ed.) (1986) *Critical Studies in Teacher Education*, Falmer, Lewes.

POWELL, R.R. (1992) The influence of prior experiences on pedagogical constructs of traditional and non-traditional pre-service teachers, *Teaching and Teacher Education*, Vol. 8, pp. 225–38.

PROCTOR, N. (1984) Towards a partnership with schools, *Journal of Education for Teaching*, Vol. 10, no. 3, pp. 219–32.

PYKE, N. (1993a) Training revamp in spring, *The Times Educational Supplement*, 22 January, p. 11.

PYKE, N. (1993b) Intake of student teachers cut back, *The Times Educational Supplement*, 29 January, p. 11.

PYKE, N. (1994a) Harrow hasn't the time for trainees, *The Times Educational Supplement*, 11 February, p. 3.

PYKE, N. (1994b) Heads set to abandon training, *The Times Educational Supplement*, 4 March, p. 5.

RABAN, B., CLARK, V. and MCINTYRE, J. (1993) *Evaluation of the Implementation of English in the National Curriculum at Key Stages 1, 2 and 3 (1991–1993)*, University of Warwick/NCC, Warwick/York.

RANELAGH, J. (1991) *Thatcher's People*, Harper Collins, London.

REID, I. (1986) Hoops, swings and roundabouts in teacher education: a critical review of the CATE criteria, *Journal of Further and Higher Education*, Vol. 10, no. 2, pp. 20–6.

REID, K. and NEWBY, M. (1988) Is the green paper a cheap license to teach?, *Education*, Vol. 172, no. 7, pp. 150–1.

REMLEY, T.P., BENSHOFF, J.M. and MOWBRAY, C.A. (1987) Postgraduate peer supervision: a proposed model for peer supervision, *Counsellor Education and Supervision*, September, pp. 53–60.

REYNOLDS, M.C. (ed.) (1989) *Knowledge Base for the Beginning Teacher*, Pergamon, New York.

ROGERS, E. (1983) *Diffusion of Innovations* (3rd edn), Free Press, New York.

ROGERS, E. and SHOEMAKER, F. (1971) *Communications of Innovations: A Cross-Cultural Approach*, Free Press, New York.

ROSENHOLTZ, S.J. and KYLE, S.J. (1984) Teacher isolation: barrier to professionalism, *American Educator*, Winter, pp. 10–15.

RUDDUCK, J. (1991) The language of consciousness and the landscape of action: tensions in teacher education, *British Educational Research Journal*, Vol. 17, no. 4, pp. 319–31.

RUSSELL, T. and MUNBY, H. (1991) Reframing: the role of experience in developing teachers' professional knowledge, in D. Schon (ed.), *op. cit.*

RUSSELL, T. and MUNBY, H. (1992) *Teachers and Teaching from Classroom to Reflection*, Falmer, Lewes.

RUTHVEN, K. (1993) Pedagogical knowledge and the training of mathematics teachers. Paper presented at the British Congress in Mathematics Education, July, Leeds.

SANDERSON, D. (1983) *Modern Languages Teachers in Action: A Report on Classroom Practice*, Language Materials Development Unit, University of York.

SCHON, D.A. (1983) *The Reflective Practitioner: How Professionals Think in Action*, Basic Books, New York.

SCHON, D.A. (1987) *Educating the Reflective Practitioner*, Basic Books, New York.

SCHON, D.A. (ed.) (1991) *The Reflective Turn*, Teachers College Press, New York.

SHAW, R. (1992) *Teacher Training in Secondary Schools*, Kogan Page, London.

SHULMAN, L.S. (1987) Knowledge and teaching: foundations of the new reform, *Harvard Educational Review*, Vol. 57, no. 1, pp. 1–22.

SIMMONS, C. and WILD, P. (1992) New forms of student teacher learning, *Educational Review*, Vol. 44, no. 1, pp. 31–40.

SMITH, P. and WEST-BURNHAM, J. (eds) (1993) *Mentoring in the Effective School*, Longman, Harlow.

SMITHERS, A. (1989) Licensed teachers – a solution or substitute?, *NUT Education Review*, Vol. 3, no. 2, pp. 59–63.

SOLOMON, J. (1987) New thoughts on teacher education, *Oxford Review of Education*, Vol. 13, no. 3, pp. 267–74.

SPENCE, B.V. (ed.) (1993) *Secondary School Management in the 1990s: Challenge and Change*, Aspects of Education, Hull.

STANDING CONFERENCE OF PRINCIPALS (1994) *Education Bill – Primary ITT Questionnaire: Commentary on Findings*, SCOP, Cheltenham.

STENHOUSE, L. (1975) *An Introduction to Curriculum Research and Development*, Heinemann Educational Books, London.

STONES, E. (1984) *Supervision in Teacher Education: A Counselling and Pedagogical Approach*, Methuen, London.

STONES, E. (1992) *Quality Teaching: A Sample of Cases*, Routledge, London.

SWANWICK, K. (1990) Teacher education and the PGCE, *Educational Research*, Vol. 32, no. 3, pp. 202–9.

SWARBRICK, A. (ed.) (1994) *Teaching Modern Languages*, Routledge, London.

SYLVA, K., ROY, C. and PAINTER, M. (1980) *Child Watching at Playgroup and Nursery School*, Grant McIntyre, London.

TALBOT, C. (1991) Towards school-based teacher training, *School Organization*, Vol. 11, no. 1, pp. 34–45.

TICKLE, L. (1991) New teachers and the emotions of learning teaching, *Cambridge Journal of Education*, Vol. 21, no. 3, pp. 319–29.

THOMPSON, M. (1992) Do 27 competences make a teacher?, *Education Review*, Vol. 6, no. 2, pp. 4–7.

TIGHT, M. (ed.) (1988) *Academic Freedom and Responsibility*, SHRE and Open University Press, Milton Keynes.

THE TIMES EDUCATIONAL SUPPLEMENT (1993) Training fails articled staff, *In Brief*, 29 January, p. 2.

THE TIMES EDUCATIONAL SUPPLEMENT (1994a) Harrow hasn't the time for trainees, 11 January, p. 3.

THE TIMES EDUCATIONAL SUPPLEMENT (1994b) Heads set to abandon training, 4 March, p. 5.

WALLACE, M.J. (1991) *Training Foreign Language Teachers: A Reflective Approach*, Cambridge University Press.

WARNOCK, M. (1987) Teacher power, *New Society*, 2 October.

WATERHOUSE, A. (1993) Mirror mirror on the wall what is the fairest scheme of all? Reflections on the induction needs of newly qualified teachers, *British Journal of In-Service Education*, Vol. 19, no. 1, pp. 16–22.

WATKINS, C. and WHALLEY, C. (1993) Mentoring beginner teachers – issues for schools to anticipate and manage, *School Organization*, Vol. 13, no. 2, pp. 129–38.

WILIAM, D. (1993) Costing activities at the Centre for Educational Studies. Unpublished departmental working paper, King's College London Centre for Educational Studies.

WILKIN, M. (1990) The development of partnership in the United Kingdom, in M. Booth, J. Furlong and M. Wilkin (eds), *op. cit.*

WILKIN, M. (1992a) *Mentoring in Schools*, Kogan Page, London.

WILKIN, M. (1992b) On the cusp: from supervision to mentoring in initial teacher training, *Cambridge Journal of Education*, Vol. 22, no. 1, pp. 79–90.

WILLIAMS, A. (1993) Teacher perception of their needs as mentors in the context of developing school-based initial teacher education, *British Educational Research Journal*, Vol. 19, no. 4, pp. 407–20.

WILLIAMS, E.A., BUTT, G.W. and SOARES, A. (1992) Novice teacher perceptions of a secondary postgraduate certificate in education course.

WITTROCK, M.C. (ed.) (1986) *Handbook of Research on Teaching* (3rd edn), Macmillan, New York.

WRIGHT, N. (1993a) Partnership for initial teacher training: retrospect and prospect, in B.V. Spence (ed.), *op. cit.*

WRIGHT, N. (1993b) Counting the cost of students in the classroom, *Education*, Vol. 182, no. 9, p. 156.

WRIGHT, N. (1993c) What teachers need to learn, *Education*, Vol. 182, no. 10, p. 174.

WUBBELS, T. (1993) Taking account of student teachers' preconceptions, *Teaching and Teacher Education*, Vol. 8, pp. 137–49.

YOUNG, M.F.D. (ed.) (1972) *Knowledge and Control: New Directions for the Sociology of Education*, Collier-Macmillan, London.

ZEICHNER, K.M. (1983) Alternative paradigms of teacher education, *Journal of Teacher Education*, Vol. 34, no. 3.

ZEICHNER, K. and LISTON, D. (1987) Teaching student teachers to reflect, *Harvard Educational Review*, Vol. 57, no. 1, pp. 23–48.

ZIMPHER, N.L., DEVOSS, G.G. and NOTT, D.L. (1980) A closer look at novice teacher supervision, *Journal of Teacher Education*, Vol. 21, no. 4, pp. 11–15.

Index